Buddha
The Compassionate Teacher

His Teachings
and Practice

A Bodhi Tree on the Nerajana River

Buddha
The Compassionate Teacher
His Teachings
and Practice

by
K.M.M.Swe

Published by

May-Su-Thin-Nu & Brothers Maw

BUDDHA,

THE COMPASSIONATE TEACHER

His Teachings and Practice

Copyright 2002, by K.M.M. Swe

Text and illustrations by K.M.M. Swe

Published by May-Su-Thin-Nu and Brothers Maw

4528 Corliss Avenue North, Seattle, Washington 98103

206.547.4487

Library of Congress Control Number: 2002114308

ISBN: 0-9726009-0-6

First Edition

Book designed by Lari T. Power of Mercer Island, Washington, USA. The typestyle used is Adobe Caslon and Times CSX Plus (Pāli).

Printing by Larry Jablon of Mercer Island, Washington, USA

A Buddha is not easily found;

He is not born everywhere.

When such a sage is born,

The World prospers!

A leaf of the *Bodhi* tree symbolizes the Buddha.

Out of deep reverence for the Buddha, no pictures of Him have been included (to avoid disrespectful handling of the book, should a picture of the Buddha be included).

Also by K. M. M. Swe

The Teaching of the Buddha

TABLE OF CONTENTS

PREFACE   a

ACKNOWLEDGEMENTS   e

INTRODUCTION   i

The Life of Buddha   iv
  • The Four Great Sights
  • The Great Departure in Search of Truth
  • Taking the Middle Path
  • Success
His Noble Teaching and Practice   xii
  • Buddha's Message
  • Good Habits
  • How to Gain Happiness

THE VIRTUES AND ATTRIBUTES OF THE BUDDHA

Praising the Buddha   1
  • His Virtues and Attributes
A Brief Flashback: the Start of His Enlightenment   4
The Ten Perfections   8
  • Classification of Perfections
  • Requirements
A Classic Example of Aspirant Sacrifice   15
What is *Sabbaññuta Nana* (Omniscient Knowledge)?   19
What is *Dhātu*?   23
The Venerable *Sāriputta's* Survey   25
What is a *Tathāgata*?   27
THE ORDER OF MONKS   33

The First Discourse and the First Order   34
The Second Discourse: *Anatta Lakhana Sutta*   37
More Joined the Order   39

The First Refugee of the Triple Gem 41
Yasa's Friends Join the Order 42
Buddha Sends out "Messengers of Truth" 44
The Lord Buddha Exhorted the *Sangha*s 46
The Wonder Response 47
Buddha Delegates the Authority of Ordination 49
• Requirements for the Second Form
• The Third Form of Ordination
The *Vinaya* Rules 50
• The Ten Aims of *Vinaya* Rules
• The Ten *Sīla* or *Dasa Sīla*
Why and When Buddha Formed the Order 53
A Little Suggestion 54

HIS TEACHINGS

The Spread of Buddhism 57
• His Teachings Spread Far and Wide
• What Emperor Asoka Did
How His Teachings Are Preserved and Perpetuated 61
• The Six Great Councils
• Theravāda Buddhism and Burma (Myanmar)
The Four Noble Truths and the Eightfold Path 68
• The Four Noble Truths
• The Noble Eightfold Path
Sīla (Morality) 74
• The Five Basic Precepts
• Higher Moral Principles
• Moral Codes for Different Classes
• To Promote or Develop *Sīla* (Morality)
• *Hiri Ottappa* or *Lokapala Dhamma*
• What Are the Benefits of *Sīla*?
• What Are the Disadvantages?
Samādhi (Mental Development) 88

• Right Effort
• Right Mindfulness
• Right Concentration
Paññā (Wisdom)   92
  • Right Understanding
  • Right Thought
Role of the *Sanghas* and His Teachings   94
  • The Six Attributes of the *Dhamma*
  • *Ariyas'* Realization and Experience

THE LATER YEARS OF BUDDHA'S LIFE   97

His Daily Routine   99
  • Before-Breakfast Habits
  • After-Breakfast Habits
  • First Watch of the Night (6:00 PM to 10:00 PM)
  • Second Watch of the Night (10:00 PM to 2:00 AM)
  • The Last Watch of the Night
    (2:00 AM to 6:00 AM)
His Perfect Wisdom and Skills   105
  • His Wisdom and Skills As a Teacher
  • His Management Skills
  • The Story of the Mustard Seed
Buddha's *Parinibbāna* and Farewell Address   122
  • His Desire
  • A Thought Came to Him
  • He Addresses Ānanda
  • Māra Urges Passage into *Parinibbāna*
    and Buddha Limits His Lifespan
  • Ānanda's Earnest Request
  • Buddha Announces His *Parinibbāna*
  • Further Instructions Given
  • His last Invitation to *Swun*
  • The Show of His Wondrous Power

- The Offering of Robes of Gold
- Defending Cunda
- Under the Twin Sala-Tree
- The Buddha Tells of the Vivid Scene
- Ānanda Asks Further Instructions
- The Last Pupil
- The Last Words of the Buddha
- The Buddha Attains *Parinibbāna*
- Buddha's Final Farewell Speech

DID YOU KNOW?

The Body 149
- What Is the Body Made of?

Taking Refuge in the "Triple Gem" ... 152

Social Principles (Obligations and Duties) 155
- The Six Quarters
- Respect for the Five

Destinations 162
- The Nether Planes
- The *Brahmā* Planes
- The *Deva* Abode, or Six Heavens
- The Human World

THE JUNIOR CORNER

The Prince and the Swan 177

The Story of Kisagotami 178

Angulimala, the Robber 180

Vessantara 182

Why the Hare Is on the Moon 186

Khantivadi-Jataka 193

The Divine Messengers 198

How to Be Happy and Successful 203

Conclusion 212

A Look Into the *Abhidhamma Pitaka*   215

  What is *Abhidhamma*?   218
  The Mind (*Nāma*)   219
    • The Working of the Mind
    • Developing the Mind
  The Body (*Rūpa*)   233
    • Realities
  Philosophy of Change   240
    • How Rebirth Takes Place
    • The Right View of a Buddhist
    • The Wheel of Life, *Paṭicca Samuppāda*
    • *Paṭicca Samuppāda* and the Four Noble Truths
    • *Paṭicca Samuppāda* and Insight Meditation
    • Growth of Wisdom, *Paññā*
    • Reference to the Wheel of Life Terms
    • Death and Rebirth as a Buddhist

Taking the Path with Understanding,
Enthusiasm and Diligence

  Understanding in Depth   255
  Manifold Destinies of Men in the World   256
  What is *Kamma*, the Law of Cause and Effect?   257
    • The Knowledge of Decease and Rebirth
    • The Law of Cosmic Order
    • Taking Care of *Kamma*
    • Good *Kamma* (to practice):
    • Bad *Kamma* (to avoid):
    • The Benefit of Understanding *Kamma*...
  How to Take the Path   269
    • Practice *Sīla* and *Samādhi*
    • Practice *Mettā Bhāvanā*
    • Mental Cultivation for Concentration
    • Practical Methods to Develop *Paññā*

Meditation 275

What is *Nirvāna/Nibbāna?* 284

A Profound Tribute To Ven. Mahasi Sayādaw 285

Benefits Gained 288

Hierarchy of *Ariyas* (Noble Ones) 289

Names of the Buddhas 292

A CORNER FOR LOVERS OF POEMS AND SAYINGS

The *Dhammapada* 295

Poems by K.M.M. Swe 300

CONCLUSION

The Essence of His Teachings 307
- Causes for the Origin of *Kamma*
- The Need for Extinction of *Kamma*
- How to Have Success in Living
- *Mettā* (Loving-kindness)
- *Karunā* (Compassion)
- *Muditā* (Sympathetic Joy)
- *Upekkhā* (Right Discernment)

Buddha on Truth (*Dhamma*) and Teaching 315

As Regards Practice, the Setting of Example 316

His Teaching (*Dhamma*) as a Religion 317

His Teaching and World Peace 319

FACTS AT A GLANCE

The Teachings of the Buddha 323
- *Dhamma*
- The Four Noble Truths
- *Dukkha*
- The Five Aggregates
- The Path of Purification
- The *Paññā* Group: Wisdom
- The *Sīla* Group: Morality

• The *Samādhi* Group:

• *Kamma*

Vipassanā Bhāvanā (Insight Meditation)   329

Saṁsāra: Wheel of Life, Round of Rebirth...   331

   • The Law of Causation of Dependent Arising

The Path to *Nibbāna*   333

GLOSSARY OF *PĀḶI* WORDS   335

REFERENCES   345

ILLUSTRATIONS

The Place Where the Buddha Gained His
Enlightenment – K.M.M. Swe   Frontispiece

Leaf – K.M.M. Swe

Map Showing the Spread of Buddhism   59
– K.M.M. Swe

The Swan and the Lake   176
– Kaythy Win

The Hare on the Moon   191
– Kaythy Win

The Tree of Greed, Hatred and Delusion   229
– K.M.M. Swe

Wheel of Life – K.M.M. Swe   332

Buddha
The Compassionate
Teacher

His Teachings
and Practice

PREFACE

The actual and exact teachings of the Buddha are called "*Theravāda* Buddhism." Very few books and literature on this are to be found in shops and libraries. As His teachings are essentially based on moral conduct and the right way of living, this book will be helpful to anyone anxious to build up a successful, healthy and happy life.

The aim and object of writing *Buddha The Compassionate Teacher, His Teachings and Practice:*

1. To give a clear, correct account of His Teaching for those who have little or no knowledge of it. Leaving out *Pāḷi* and Sanskrit words where practicable, reading will be made easy and comprehensible.
2. To help those who may think they have understood His Teaching, but still need to have a thorough knowledge of the *Dhamma* in order to appreciate and practice.
3. To encourage those who understand His Teaching to have confidence and to practice steadfastly, till they reach the goal of self-realization.

I am one of those in the second group of people ("may think, but actually do not"). This realization has made me carry out a good, thorough research of His teachings.

Another reason for writing this book is to satisfy my great desire to dedicate this work to my parents and grandparents, under whose guidance I have acquired the right and proper way of living. Although they have passed away and will have no knowledge of the result of their successful guidance, I would still have immense satisfaction from expressing my thanks to them in this manner. This may seem unusual to some, but I would say, "It's better late, than never." It is right and proper to express one's gratitude, even behind the back of one's benefactor.

Should anyone still ask, "Why has it to be so important, only now?" the answer to this question can be obtained by reading the following very small passage of His Teaching:

Buddha addresses the monks:
"Monks, one can never repay two persons,
I declare.
"What two? Mother and father.
"Even if one should carry about his mother on one shoulder and his father on the other, and while doing so should live a hundred years, and if he should attend to them by massaging, bathing and rubbing their limbs, and they should even void

their excrements there: even by this, he would not repay them.

"Even if he were to establish his parents as the supreme lords and rulers over this earth so rich in the seven treasures, he would not do enough for them.

"What is the cause of that? Parents do much for their children, O, Monks! They bring them up, feed them, and guide them through this world.

"But, O, Monks! He who encourages his unbelieving parents to settle and establish in the Teaching ... Encourages his immoral parents to settle and establish in morality and liberality (i.e., uphold morality, "*Sīla*" and perform acts of charity and generosity) ... Encourages his ignorant parents to settle and establish in wisdom ... Such a person, O, Monks, does enough for his parents: He repays, and more than repays them for what they have done."

(Refer to *Anguttara Nikāya, The Discourse Collection, an Anthology, Part 1* (ii. IV, 2))

Understanding His Teaching that "gratitude must be shown where gratitude is due," I dedicate this work of research and writing on *Buddha, The Compassionate Teacher, His Teachings and Practice* to my grandparents and my parents.

I hope everyone will enjoy reading it and at the same time learn something about the Great Compassionate Teacher with a unique personality.

K.M.M. Swe
Seattle
February 2003

ACKNOWLEDGEMENTS

I take this opportunity to make known my deep reverence and profound gratitude to the following *Sayādaws*:

❋ First and foremost, I would like to express my sincere reverence and profound gratitude to Aggamahapandita Ovadacariya, Sayādaw U. Pandita Bhivamssa of the Hse Mine-gone Forest Meditation Center and the Panditarama, Mahāsi Shwedaung-gone Meditation Center, Rangoon, Burma for the interest shown and encouragement given to my writing on Buddhism, not to mention the patience, time and trouble that he has taken to go through my prepared manuscripts of *Buddha, The Compassionate Teacher, His Teachings and Practice.*

Being a very experienced and reputable teacher of *Vipassanā* meditation, and with his many meditation centers established in many countries, the responsibility he has taken upon himself leaves him little or no time for himself. For that one reason alone, I consider myself as having had a stroke of good luck the moment he said, 'Oh, what a lot you have written; leave it and I will read it,' when I visited him at his forest meditating center to show him my final scripts and ask for his blessings.

At the time of my visit, Sayādaw was very busy. The forest center was giving a long *Vipassanā* meditation course (a 60 day retreat) attended by over 100 *Yogis*, all from foreign lands – many from the USA, Canada, many European countries, and some from the countries of Asia, Sri Lanka, India, China, Korea, Taiwan and Japan (as noted from the register the receptionist showed me). I was kept waiting till the ambassador from Sri Lanka left his presence. Having seen how busy the Sayādaw was, I felt a little reluctant and ill at ease; but I had come all the way to get his blessings, so I waited until he could see me.

My meeting with him was brief, but the visit to the forest meditation center was very rewarding. Not only did I get his encouragement, but I also had the chance to see the entire estate, soak in the peaceful and tranquil atmosphere, and witness the efficient operating and management of the center – perfect in every way. It is indeed "a unique meditating center."

Once again, let me say, "I am most grateful to you, Sayādaw."

❋ Next, I would like to thank the Sagaing Shw-Hin-Tha Sayādaw Gyi, "Ovadacariya Abi-da-za Mahā-ratha-guru, Abi-da-za Agga-Mahā-tha-dhamma, Zaw-ti-ka," and his incumbent Agga-mahā-pandita Ovadacariya Sayādaw U Thanwarar Bhivamssa for their teaching and inspiration given me to practice as well as to write on *Dhamma*.

❋ There are also many *Sayādaws* to whom I would like to say, "Thank you!" for their encouraging words after reading my first book, *The Teaching of the Buddha:*

Abbot Ven. Ashin Pynner Htoe of the Burmese Temple, Sydney, Australia

Abbot Ven. U Vampasala of Tisarana Vihara, Perth, Australia

Abbot Ven. U Pannathami of Panditarama Meditating Center, Sydney, Australia

Ven. U Panobhatha of Vancouver BC, Canada

Ven. U Lokanatha of Dhammadipa Vihara, Jamaica

Ven. U Khemissara of Dhammodaya Myanmar Vihara, South Gate, PMB, South Africa

Ven. U Lokanatha of Alohtaw Pyaie Dhamma Yeiktha, El Sodrante, CA, USA

Ven. Asin Kaythawa of Buddhist Monastery, Elmhurst, IL, USA

Ven. U Asara of Dhammaramsi Meditation Center, Echo Park, CA, USA

Ven. Ashin Gunissara, Dhammajoti Meditation Center Inc., Baldwin Park, CA, USA

Ven. U Kitsayana, Myanma Buddhist Meditation Center, Baltimore, MD, USA

Ven. Ashin Dhammakpiya, Mettananda Vihara, Fremont, CA, USA

Ven. U Panyeinda, Bodhi Vepullakari Vihara, Pomona, CA, USA

Ven. A. M. Pandita of Sitagu Buddhist Vihara, Austin, TX, USA

Ven. U Nanujjota of Mahāsi-Dhamma Fellowship, who has always encouraged me to continue writing since I published my first book.

There are many others *Sayādaws* I have not mentioned by name to whom I would like to say, "Thank you very much for your encouragement!"

To my friends and acquaintances in India, Sri Lanka, France, Switzerland, Australia, America and Burma, allow me to say, once again, "Thank you very much for your appreciation and encouragement!"

To my friend, Ms. Kari Blom of Seattle, Washington, USA, I am very grateful for her kind assistance in preparing the manuscript and getting it printed.

I also wish to express my gratitude to Ms. Lari Tiller Power of Island Graphic Services Ltd. and Mr. Larry Jablon of Five Star Reproduction, both of Mercer Island, Washington, for their interest taken and effort given to produce the book that now stands before you — attractive, positive and most inviting!

Lastly:

❉   I wish to express my gratitude to my brothers and sisters, for "The Strength of Eight makes everything great!" I could not have succeeded without their help in every way. Their interest, encouragement and assistance given every step of the way to the successful completion and printing of this book are greatly appreciated and acknowledged with, "I am most grateful to you all!"

❉   My thanks to every member of the family, especially to the grandchildren: Thank you so much for your interest in the book and effort made to create a corner for children in my book. The inclusion of this corner makes the book unique: both young and old alike can enjoy reading it.

I would also like to express my gratitude to the printers and publishers of the book. For it takes the effort and interest of each and everyone concerned working on any single project to make it a great success.

Thank you everyone!

I would like everyone to share the merit I gained by the performance of this meritorious deed, for "merit shared is merit multiplied."

May all readers experience delight in reading the book and benefit from the merit, too!

"A gift of *Dhamma* excels all other gifts!"

K.M.M. Swe
Seattle
February 2003

INTRODUCTION

The Teaching founded by the Buddha is known in English as "Buddhism."

Many have defined Buddhism in various ways, and various points of view have been given in comparison with other religion. The right definition for it is as stated below:

> "Buddhism is a system which knows no God in the Western sense, which denies a soul to man, which counts the belief in immortality a blunder, which refuses any efficacy to prayers and sacrifice, which bids men look to nothing but their own efforts for salvation, which in its original purity knew nothing of vows of obedience and never sought the aid of the secular arm, yet spread over a considerable society of the world with marvelous rapidity – and is still the dominant creed of the large fraction of mankind."

Why? Because:

- It is a course that guides a person through pure living and pure thinking to gain supreme wisdom and deliverance from all evil.
- His Teaching is about the Law of Righteousness that exists in a man's heart and mind, as well as in the universe. Therefore Buddhism demands

understanding. The keynote of it is *rational understanding*.

- It teaches that man can gain salvation by self-exertion without depending on God or mediating priests. It expounds no dogmas that one must believe. There are no creeds that one must accept, no faith without reasoning, no superstitious rites of ceremonies to be performed, and no meaningless sacrifices or penances for one's purification. It is a doctrine of actuality.

- It is not a system of faith or worship and does not demand that anyone believe in the Teaching. The Buddha was, no doubt, highly venerated in His own time, but He never claimed divinity for Himself. What He expects from His disciples is the actual and sincere observance of His Teaching.

This is what He said: "He honors me best, who practices my Teaching best." That is His everyday admonition. Great emphasis is laid on high moral principles and meditation that tends to self-discipline, self-control, purification and enlightenment. He is respected as a great teacher.

To seekers of truth, Buddha says, "Do not believe in anything on mere hearsay, or because it is the tradition and custom handed down through generations; do not believe in rumors or written testimony of some ancient sage or anything on the mere authority of thy teachers or priests; but believe in whatever agrees with thy reason and is conducive to thy own wellbeing and to that of all other living beings."

Buddhism is concerned with facts and has nothing to do with theories and philosophies. Buddha did not try to make any new material sciences, but explained to us things related to the truth and facts about life and all that is connected with our emancipation. He laid out the path of deliverance, which is the way to the highest happiness, *Nirvāna* or *Nibbāna*.

Buddhism contains not just an excellent code of morals, but the highest standard of morality. It is much more than ordinary morality, as explained clearly in His teachings.

Buddhism is neither a philosophy, nor a religion, nor an ordinary ethical code. It is a doctrine of actuality, a means of deliverance from the heavy burden of birth, old age, suffering, disease and death, or the cycle, or rounds of existences.

Buddhism is not merely to be preserved in books, nor is it a subject to be studied only from a historical or literary point of view; on the contrary, it is to be learned and put into practice in the course of one's daily life. No one can appreciate the truth without actual practice. Based on logic, Buddhism is rational and practical and, therefore, devoid of esoteric doctrines (those intended only for people with special knowledge or interest), coercion (compulsion or threats), persecution and fanaticism.

The Life of Buddha

A Buddha is one who has attained *Bodhi*, an ideal state of intellectual and ethical perfection that can be attained only by man and by purely human means.

About 623 years before the Christian era (623 BCE), a Sakyan Prince was born in the Lumbinī Park in the neighborhood of Kapilavattu, now known as Padaria, in the district of modern Nepal. He was none other than Prince Siddhattha Gautama, who was destined to be the greatest teacher of the world.

His parents were King Suddhodana and Queen Mahā Māyā of Kapilavattu. As the Queen died when He was seven days old, His aunt, the Queen's younger sister, took care of him.

He had a very luxurious, happy life. At the age of sixteen, He was married to Princess Yasodhara. But His contemplative nature and boundless compassion did not encourage Him to enjoy the pleasures of the royal household.

It was written in His stars that He would one day seek the life of an ascetic and become a Buddha. Naturally, the king did everything in his power to prevent Him from seeing the woeful state of life, pain, sickness, old age infirmity, and death, and tried to keep Him happy. He was very anxious to have his son to take his place and rule the country.

The Four Great Sights

Prince Siddhattha knew no woe, but He felt deep pity for sorrowing humanity. Amidst comfort and prosperity, He realized "the universality of sorrow." He was destined to become a Buddha, and in spite of all the efforts to keep Him happy, when the time came for Him to leave His wonderful worldly way of life, there was nothing to stop him.

This great event, this sudden turning point in His life, came when He saw the "Four Great Sights" – an old man, a sick man, a dead man and an ascetic – all on separate occasions, on His way to the Royal Leisure Park. On each occasion His charioteer explained to Him that everyone has to become sick, old, decay and die, and that there was nothing in the world to prevent such universal sufferings.

The Prince said to himself, "Must I leave my loved ones behind sooner or later, and like others, I cannot avoid death? How terrible and frightening that must be!" He wondered whether there was no way out of this morass of suffering. From that day, He was restless and very unhappy.

However, the sight of the ascetic, who looked calm and aloof, as though the sorrows and joys of this world did not touch him, brought Him some consolation. He thought about the homeless life, the satisfaction of one frugal meal a day, and the life of discipline and simplicity of the ascetic. The contented and carefree way of life of an ascetic gave Him some encouragement and made Him think, "Surely there must be a way to happiness, for this holy person seems to be enjoying happiness in a way." He then decided to go in search of that "great happiness."

By then, He was twenty-nine, married to a beautiful princess and the father of a lovely son, Rāhula. Anyone in His place would have been contented and happy. But He was restless and unhappy, and nothing could divert His sudden melancholy mood, which grew more persistent day by day.

He thought of universal suffering and wished to find a way out of it. So, one night, determined to go in search of a way out of suffering, He took silent leave of His wife and son, and left the palace.

The Great Departure in Search of Truth

He renounced all worldly pleasures and, wearing the simple yellow garb of an ascetic, wandered forth in search of the truth and peace that could liberate one from universal suffering, or *Dukkha*.

First, He sought the advice of Ālāra and Uddaka, two renowned Brahman spiritual teachers. Their teaching did not satisfy him. He could not believe in the existence of a soul or its transmigration. This, He viewed, would get one back again to the cycle of birth, old age, suffering and death.

Next, He went to the priests officiating in temples to find if He could get any information on how to escape from suffering and sorrow. However, the unnecessarily cruel sacrifices performed on the altars of the gods horrified and disgusted him. He was so shocked and terrified that He had to take immediate action then and there. He instantly preached to them the futility of atoning for evil deeds by the destruction of life and of the cruel way of practicing religion by the neglect of moral life. He felt thoroughly disgusted, left the place at once and wandered on.

He continued to visit many distinguished teachers of the day. Nobody proved competent to give Him any ideas on what He wanted to know. So, He wandered on through Magadha, until He came to the settlement of the five pupils of Uddaka in the jungles near Uruvelā in Magadha. He saw the five keeping their senses in check, subduing their passions and practicing austere penance. He admired their zeal and earnestness. In those days, it was believed no salvation could be gained unless one led a life of strict asceticism, so He subjected himself to all forms of practicable austerities.

Adding vigil to vigil and penance to penance, He made a superhuman effort for six long years until He grew withered and weak. The more He tortured His body, the farther away He was from His goal. He realized that this strenuous endeavor was leading Him nowhere. He had learned the utter futility of self-mortification and started making reasonable adjustments. He took an independent course, avoiding the two extremes of self-indulgence and self-mortification. The new path was the *Majjhima Paṭipadā*, "The Middle Path," which later became one of the salient characteristics of His Teaching.

Taking the Middle Path

At that point, His disciples immediately deserted Him, saying that the great holy man had eaten like sinners did. Abandoned, He wandered on until He came to a spreading *Bodhi* tree. Here He sat down, determined to go no farther, until He found a solution to the problems He had set His heart to solve.

Just as He was about to act on His final determination, Sujata, the daughter of the village chief,
Senani, offered Him milk-rice. He accepted it and then
went to wash Himself in the River Nerajana before eating. After He had freshened up, He made the milk-rice
into 49 balls, each large enough for a mouthful. He then
partook of them.

With renewed energy, He was more determined
than before to sit as long as need be in order to accomplish His task. In deep meditation, He sat under the
Bodhi tree for hours. Māra the Evil, with his army and
followers, disturbed and distracted Him in various terrifying and wicked ways, but He overcame all on account
of the good deeds and perfections He had carried out
during His previous countless lives.

Success

Finally, He was left in peace to meditate. He
sat for hours in meditation until early one morning, on
the full-moon day of May, seated in deep meditation,
the consciousness of true insight possessed Him.
Illumination came as the light arose to reveal all things
in their true nature. In the first watch of that night, He
gained the knowledge of His previous existences; in the
middle watch of the night, with the help of His divine
eye, He could see everything – deaths and rebirths –
that was taking place on all the 31 planes of existence;

and in the last watch of night, He gained the bliss of complete emancipation.

Now, He realized suffering in its entirety: first the cause of suffering, then the cessation of suffering, and finally, the path leading to the cessation of suffering. He saw the mistaken ways that all various faiths maintained. He discerned the sources whence earthly suffering came and the way that leads to its annihilation, complete destruction. He saw that the cause of sufferings lay in the selfish attachment to life, and that the way to escape all sufferings was by treading the Eightfold Path.

On acquiring this knowledge and realization, His mind was free from the defilement of lust and ignorance and the desire for existence. He knew at once that He had gained complete emancipation, that this was His last birth – everything had been done; there was nothing He could wish for – and that full omniscience had been attained. Thus, without doubt, He was the Fully Self-Enlightened One.

He spent seven weeks (49 days) at the place where He gained enlightenment, enjoying the bliss of emancipation, reviewing all the newfound, extensive, exhaustive knowledge. He also showed His profound gratitude to the inanimate *Bodhi* tree that sheltered Him as He sat beneath it, determined in the attainment of enlightenment (a good example of a show of gratitude).

After a superhuman struggle of six strenuous years - unaided, unguided, and only by self-reliance, effort and wisdom - He came to realize things as they truly are. By His intuitive knowledge, He attained the supreme state of perfection and became a Buddha, "the Enlightened One," at the age of thirty-five.

Having attained Buddhahood, Buddha devoted 45 years of His life to serving humanity both by example and precept. Without any selfish motive, and only out of deep compassion for all who wish to free themselves from universal suffering (*Dukkha*), He taught enthusiastically, till He passed away at the age of eighty. He left no successors, but instructed His disciples to regard His doctrine and discipline as their teacher.

His iron will, profound wisdom, universal love, boundless compassion, selfless service, great renunciation, perfect purity, unique personal life, and the exemplifying methods employed to propagate His Teaching and His final success – all these factors have compelled mankind to acknowledge Buddha as the greatest teacher that ever lived. Buddha discarded the authority placed upon Him by His followers and stated clearly, "You, yourselves should make the exertion. Buddhas are only teachers." Thus, He is respected as "the Great Compassionate Teacher." Buddha was the one person in the world who was unique, without a peer, without a counterpart, incomparable, unequalled, unrivalled, and the best of humans.

His Noble Teaching and Practice

Buddha explained that the Natural Law of Cause and Effect governs everything in the universe. The cause always becomes the effect, and the effect becomes the cause; so also birth is followed by death, and death is followed by birth. Both birth and death are phases of the life process. This chain must be broken to free oneself from suffering. Buddha revealed to mankind that the only straight path that leads to everlasting peace and happiness is the Noble Eightfold Path.

Buddha explained how the Natural Law of Cause and Effect governs the life process of the universe, and how "the nature of cosmos" participates in bringing about the cause of it arising and passing away. He explained the real cause of suffering, together with the way in which it could be brought to an end. The nature of cosmos was neither heard nor dreamt of, neither was there an inkling, a hint, or a suspicion of any kind of this science at that time, 600 BCE.

Buddha explained that every action produces its effect. It is the action or cause that comes first, and the effect follows. He, therefore, spoke of *Kamma* as the "Universal Law of Cause and Effect."

Buddha stressed human dignity. He taught the worth of a human being, how precious the life of a human should be to everyone, and how difficult it was to attain life as a mortal or human being. As a Buddha-in-the-making, a *Bodhisatta*, He had gone through countless births, and suffered all, sacrificed all and fulfilled every perfection, so that He might achieve His unique goal: deliverance (freedom from birth, old age, disease and death – rounds of existence.)

He taught men:

1. To rely on themselves to achieve their own freedom from suffering and to not look to any external savior.
2. That to have a happy successful life, one must start from a strong foundation built on moral principles and the sense of fear and shame to do evil. He enunciated a great degree on moral code. It could, in fact, be said that His Teaching is founded on moral discipline, without which no happiness or success can be experienced.

Buddha's Message

Taking a general overview of the world today, there are so much turmoil, bloodshed and suffering in many parts of the world. Why is this so? Because every citizen of the whole world is in dire need of moral awakening, ethical excellence, and philosophical understanding.

"High moral discipline" is the synonym for Buddha's Teaching. His message can be summed up in a verse:

To refrain from all evil.
To do what is good.
To purify the mind.

Added to morality and philosophical understanding comes loving-kindness, **Mettā**. *Mettā* goes hand in hand with helpfulness, and even the willingness to forgo self-interest in order to bring about the welfare and happiness of mankind. This perfection is one of the Ten Perfections Buddha had lived up to in all His lives while completing His rounds of existences before He attained self-enlightenment. When *Mettā* prevails in one's heart, acts of benevolence such as wishing to do good for others, being kind and helpful and charitable are readily and happily performed.

Every dignified human being is required to uphold the basic moral principles, the Five Precepts. This aspect of His Teaching is termed as *Sīla*, morality or moral discipline. Right Speech, Right Action and Right Livelihood of the Eightfold Path come under the broad heading of *Sīla*.

Next comes *Samādhi*. This means concentration, or Right Concentration, and requires one to control the mind in a proper and wholesome manner. To have mind fixed on a certain object, thought or mental concentration is called *Samādhi*, i.e., mental development.

The third aspect of His Teaching pertains to *Paññā*, or wisdom. According to the Noble Eightfold Path, Right View and Right Thought come under *Paññā*, or wisdom. It is the knowledge consisting of insight conjoined with meritorious thoughts. Only by the development of wisdom, insight is one able to completely dispel the first of the stages of defilement that are unaffected by morality or concentration. The three stages of defilement – the initial stage like the roots, the second stage like the trunk, and the third stage like the branches of a tree – will never arise again once one has *Paññā*, or wisdom.

Within the category of concentration, or *Samādhi*, are Right Effort, Right Mindfulness, and Right Concentration. These will help in the practice of meditation that brings awareness of the mind. With awareness, a person learns to control his thoughts, words and deeds, and to reason through every situation rather than react emotionally according to his likes and dislikes or to be influenced by prejudice, customs, and tradition. In this way, he thinks rationally, becomes aware of every happening or event, and gains the supreme ability to handle any situation. With continued practice, moral purity can be attained, which enables one to ignore ill will, anger, hate, delusion and greed, as well as other unpleasant, negative thoughts, words and deeds. *Samādhi* is nothing but the control and culture of the mind.

The three aspects, *Sīla*, *Samādhi*, and *Paññā* are interdependent and interrelated, and all of them should be practiced at the same time. In the same way that it is easier to have right concentration and right view by living a right life, a moral life, it is by practicing right concentration that one lives a right way of life and has the right view. It is not possible to have right view without the right way of living and right concentration. It is necessary to understand His Teaching, then practice and realize it. Understand, practice and realize; self-realization is the goal.

Good Habits

Any physical action, when repeated again and again, becomes a habit. Allowing thoughts to come up repeatedly gives rise to a tendency to reproduce that kind of thought and those thoughts, therefore, become a habit. Thus, it is essential to cultivate and maintain good and wholesome thoughts until they become good habits. Cultivate good habits of the mind, watch your thoughts and control them; be aware at all times. This is the initial stage from which to start one's development.

How to Gain Happiness

Buddha teaches us that misery and suffering are not the result of the wrath of a god or gods, but are the direct consequences of man's ignorance of his own nature, and of his surroundings. It is only by the desire of the human heart to uphold morality and avoid self-ishness and violence – which are the products of greed, anger, hatred and delusion – that we can hope to bring peace and happiness to this disorganized society of the world. *Lobha* means "greed," *Dosa* means "anger," and *Moha* means "delusion." The need here is to discipline the mind, cultivate it and make it wholesome and pure, free of all evil thoughts (*Lobha, Dosa* and *Moha*).

By means of awareness of self and surrounding, and meditation, one learns to realize the experience of life in an understanding way. With understanding, one is able to consider rationally all matters and problems of both fortunate and unfortunate nature. If such awareness can be exercised, every event in our life can be approached with understanding and tolerance. Were we to get to this point of understanding in the present day, the very common, mild mental illnesses known as "break-down" and "depression" would no longer be heard of.

It is up to each and every individual to perfect himself in every way. Buddha teaches that human per-fection can be won through unselfishness, discipline and wisdom. It would not be worthwhile to just know that a thing or an action is good, wholesome, and benevolent. We must act conscientiously upon that knowledge, if we wish to benefit. Everyone knows "actions speak louder than words." We must live in the right manner not only in our own interest, but also in that of others, all of whom desperately seek peace and happiness in this fast-moving, materialistic world where moral values are deplorably and acutely overlooked.

oooooo

The Virtues and Attributes of the Buddha

Praising the Buddha

It is a common sight to see someone with clasped hands raised and touching the forehead, bowing down in front of a person, a statue, or an image. Such an act does not always mean praying to a god asking for favors. In the case of a devotee of the Buddha, it is an act that shows deep respect and profound gratitude to the Buddha, because He is a Great Compassionate Teacher. It is also to acknowledge that one takes refuge in the Buddha.

The Buddha has repeatedly stated, "You yourself must work for your own good, and for the higher levels of moral and spiritual attainment and salvation. I am only a guide to instruct you in how to walk along the path, The Noble Eightfold Path, I have discovered. This path leads to a set destination, *Nibbāna*."

He did not profess to be a god or a savior, who could perform miracles or make anyone happy. His encouragement was, "Take refuge in yourself. Work for your own salvation, for man is the master of his own fate!" His Teaching is based on a systematic practical analysis of the problems of life by means of which we can find the way to solve them.

He was a thinker of unexcelled philosophical power, a giant intellect exhibiting unequalled and keen analytic understanding. Thus he gained an exhaustive knowledge of the world – the omniscient knowledge.

Not only was He a man with a unique personality, but He was also a man of rich and responsive sympathy, with a great deal of patience and goodwill. He was always ready to help anyone who might wish to learn about the truth of the world – the *Dhamma*.

How did this great being, the Compassionate Teacher, manage to achieve this unique position? How did He work to achieve it? What were His virtues and attributes? Would it not be worthwhile to consider?

Why His Virtues and Attributes Should Be Known (Refer to the *Brahmajala Sutta*)

On a certain occasion, a pupil of the Buddha was to have been praising the Buddha in all good faith. But the praise was incomplete and fell well short of what the Buddha possessed. Everyone knows that a Buddha appears in the world after an incalculable thousands of years (measured in world cycles) and that His appearance in the world is for the welfare of *Devas* (celestial beings) and men. If people were to take advantage of His presence, it would be necessary for them to know His virtues and His ability to help.

On many occasions, the Buddha stated that He was present for the welfare of all and wanted everyone to take advantage of this, and that to accomplish this purpose, the virtues and attributes of the Buddha must be known. It would, therefore, be necessary for everyone to know all about the Buddha and His Teaching, the *Dhamma*.

Buddha had boldly stated many times, "Don't take my Teaching as gospel truth or something that has been handed down to you; test it for yourself, and only when you feel that it is for your happiness and those of others, take it and live up to it." He did not convert anyone. He did not force His teachings upon anyone. He taught the *Dhamma* out of compassion to help others who would like to be helped.

In the *Brahmajala Sutta*, the Buddha repeated this declaration four times: "O, Monks, besides morality, there are other *Dhammas*, which are profound, hard to see, hard to comprehend, tranquil, noble, surpassing logic, difficult to detect and intelligible only to the *Ariyas* (people who have perceived *Nibbāna* by means of *Magga* and *Phala*)." So, anyone wishing to praise the Buddha should do so also in terms of His Teaching. This must be done with understanding and a firm conviction so that it will serve one's welfare and that of others.

One wishing to know the truth about the Buddha and His teachings (the *Dhamma*), should know the cardinal facts and figures that concern the Buddha and the *Dhamma*. In order to do so, we must return to the time when the Buddha, as the Buddha-to-be, or a *Bodhisatta*, began His steps towards His final goal, self-enlightenment, the gaining of *Subbaññuta Ñāṇa* (omniscient knowledge).

A Brief Flashback: the Starting Point of His March to Self-Enlightenment

Incalculable in world cycles, a very long, long time ago, during the time when the fourth Buddha, Dipankara, was present in the world, there lived in Amara, a *Brahman*. He was Sumedha, a very learned and wise man. He lived a luxurious and carefree life, for he rolled in wealth collected over many generations. He was orphaned at a very early age and had a treasurer to control, save and guard his treasures.

When Sumedha was old enough to manage his wealth, his treasurer handed it over to him. Bringing the account book, the treasurer opened all the rooms containing all the treasures: gold, silver, and other valuables. Pointing out the various possessions, the treasurer indicated, "One of these, young man, is your mother's; this is your father's, but this one is your grandfather's," and so on, going back seven generations. "Take good care of them!" So saying, the treasurer left.

Sumedha was delighted and lived very happily for some time until, one day, he had no desire for his possessions and worldly pleasures and decided to give away all that he owned. With due respect, he offered them to the King first. But the King said, "I have no need of your wealth; you may do as you please." So, Sumedha made a public announcement of his intended charity and gave away everything.

When the great giveaway was completed, he felt relieved and lighthearted – as if he had unloaded a heavy burden from his back – and without a moment's hesitation, Sumedha happily dressed in a garment made of tree bark and began life as a wandering ascetic.Taking the name of Sumedha the Hermit, he lived a homeless life and started to enjoy living under trees and eating fallen fruits for his meals.

Having given up the desire for worldly pleasures and being detached from all kinds of cravings, he was able to practice the three aspects of the Buddha's teachings – *Sīla*, *Samādhi*, and *Paññā* – easily and effectively. Because of his steadfastness, he gained the Eight Attainments[1] within a week. He could easily have worked towards higher attainments and consequently gained *Nibbāna*, which means the extinction of greed, hate and delusion, but he had another ambition.

This ambition suddenly overwhelmed him when he saw the Buddha Dipankara coming to visit the town: on seeing him, Sumedha strongly desired to be a Buddha one day. He thought, "Now is the time for me to make my resolution in the presence of the Buddha." Taking this very rare chance, Sumedha went to the path the Buddha was to walk along, took off his garment, and spread it over the mire. Next, he undid his matted hair and lay prostrate on the garment. As he lay there, he wished that the Buddha and his followers would pass over him, treading on him, just as one would over a bridge. He then made a resolution: "May I be a Buddha one day!"

The Lord Dipankara saw the hermit Sumedha lying down and perceived the reason for his doing so, and also his aspiration. He reflected, and perceiving into the future, as every Buddha is able to do, He then smiled.

"Do you see that hermit lying on the mire? Look, look!" exclaimed the Buddha.

"Yes, Reverend Sir!" replied the 400,000 monks.

"He is lying down after having made resolve to be a Buddha one day. He will certainly be one," declared the Blessed One.

He proclaimed further, "His greatest of all great ambitions will be fulfilled a hundred thousand æons[2] from now. He will be the Buddha named Gautama.

"His mother will be Queen Mahā Māyā, the father, King Suddhodana.

"His two disciples and attendant will be Upatissa, Kolita and Ānanda.

"His two women disciples will be Khema and Uppalavanna.

"When his knowledge is fully matured, he will depart on the Great Departure and strive the Great Striving. When this has been completed, he will accept a gift of milk-rice at the foot of a banyan tree.

"After partaking of this gift on the banks of the Nerajana River, he will sit on a dais of the *Bodhi* tree and gain self-enlightenment."

Now the great populace heard Lord Dipankara's declaration. They cheered and applauded: "The ascetic Sumedha is the sprout of the Buddha-seed!" Sumedha was very happy, for it was certain his aspiration would definitely succeed.

After the proclamation, Lord Dipankara and His order of monks walked on, passing on the right side of Sumedha, and proceeded to the town center, leaving the crowd still shouting, cheering, for they could hardly believe their own ears.

Sumedha stood in the crowd, trying to take everything in – his stroke of luck and the loud and clear proclamation of the Buddha. "It's too good to be true! But everyone present heard the Lord's words," he said, trying to convince himself. "For certain, I will be a Buddha!" said Sumedha to himself. "Indeed, the utterance of the Buddha is to be respected."

The Ten Perfections

Joyously, Sumedha began to reflect seriously on the things a Buddha-to-be would do. "Where are these things? What can they be? Where can I find them?" he asked himself again and again, as he sat still and contemplated.

Gradually, examining the entire ideational element *Dhammadhatu,*[3] He understood that former *Bodhisattas* (Buddhas-to-be) advised the perfection of giving. He said aloud, "Oh yes! Giving, *Dāna*, generosity," and then added, "Just like a jug full of water that has been overturned, discharged, taking nothing back, I must perform such acts. Thus, not even in consideration of saving anything, not caring for wealth, or fame, or wife and children, not even my life or limbs, I must give generously." He was absolutely determined on the first perfection: giving (*Dāna*).

On contemplating further, he saw the second perfection to be morality, or *Sīla*. He addressed himself thus, "Sumedha, you, from now on, should fulfill the second perfection: protect morality." He would not kill, steal, lie, or slander; he would avoid using harsh words and taking intoxicants – all these primary principles – for failing to do so would mean creating fresh troubles and obstacles on the road to enlightenment. Even if he were to lead a householder's life and even though his interests might be at stake, he would adhere to the five elementary principles of regulated behavior. He was firmly and resolutely determined on the second perfection: morality (*Sīla*).

The third perfection appeared to him to be renunciation, or *Nekkhama*, a perfection with which he was well acquainted since he had already been enjoying the good results of it. He had sat in the lap of luxury and worldly pleasures and had felt restricted and unhappy. Now, having forsaken all that he owned and feeling like a freed bird, he was happy. The third perfection of renunciation was nothing new to him. He was enjoying it at that very moment, and would always enjoy taking up this mode of life.

The fourth perfection, wisdom, or *Paññā*, means the right understanding of the real nature of the world, seeing things in their reality. Sumedha was determined to strive to acquire knowledge from every possible source: avoiding no one among the low, middle, or high; approaching wise man asking questions, unashamed to plead ignorance. This would be how he would seek knowledge and thus gain wisdom. Whatever he had learned and gained would be imparted to others without any reservation. He resolved to seek the fourth perfection: wisdom (*Paññā*).

It then occurred to him that there would be more to the list, and reflecting further, he saw energy, *Viriya* to be the fifth perfection. "How shall I carry this out?" He considered and considered, and finally he remembered the lion, the king of beasts, being firm in energy, not lacking in any behavior, and having all energy. This did not mean physical strength in the general sense, but mental vigor or strength of character: a relentless effort to work for others both in thought and deed. "So be it! I must endeavor and work towards this perfection – energy (*Viriya*)," he muttered to himself. Firmly established in this virtue, Sumedha would develop self-reliance, viewing failures as steps to success. Under oppression, he would step up his courage and strength. Thus would he fulfill this perfection – energy (*Viriya*) – he challenged himself.

Next, Sumedha discovered patience or forbearance, *Khanti*, to be the most-needed perfection. It calls for the highest form of endurance in the face of suffering that might be inflicted upon either oneself or others.

A *Bodhisatta*, or Buddha-to-be is indifferent to praise or blame. He will practice this perfection to such an extent that, even if his hands or feet were to be cut off, he would not be provoked.

Next came truth, *Sacca*. Keeping one's promise is another characteristics of all Buddhas-to-be. He holds truth as his guide and holds to it firmly. He considers well before making a promise and, once it is made, fulfills it at any cost. He has to be trustworthy, sincere and honest. He is required to act as he speaks, with perfect harmony among his thoughts, words and deeds. He would never descend to flattery to win the hearts of people. Neither would he exalt himself to win admiration. Sumedha then thought, "Wise Sumedha, from how on, you should fulfill the seventh perfection, that of truth-speaking." He urged himself to work on this virtue of truthfulness. Whatever the consequences, he would always be truthful.

"Determination," or *Adhiṭṭhanā*, means the will power or steadfastness required for one to succeed. A Buddha-to-be needs to have great determination to overcome all obstacles along the path he would have to tread. He also needs to be stable like a mountain that does not tremble or move when the wind strikes, but remains precisely in its own place. "I will never turn away my eyes from my goal, and with determination, I will walk towards it. Nothing shall stop me." Thus Sumedha made his *Adhiṭṭhanā* firm; his resolution was determinedly established.

He considered the ninth perfection to be very important. This is *Mettā*, loving-kindness. It is essential for everyone to have *Mettā*. *Mettā* seems to be lacking in the hearts of men, and as a result, not only unpleasantness, but also trouble and suffering exist in the world. Because of His excessive love and kindness for everyone in the world and the entire universe, a Buddha has made a vow to help everyone. To secure this position, He has had to go through endless trouble to perfect Himself; of that there is little doubt. Thus, a Buddha-to-be must cultivate this perfection, *Mettā*, or loving-kindness, for it is essential.

Loving-kindness is not a sensual, emotional, sentimental, or self-satisfying kind of love, but an active benevolence. When effectively administered, it brings about peace, harmony, and happiness that will put an end to much of the unnecessary trouble and suffering taking place in the world. It has a cool, soft touch and brings forth a calm, pleasant atmosphere.

"I will extend my *Mettā* to men, *Devas*, *Brahmās*, and even to the animals." Sumedha decided to carry out this perfection seriously and extensively, and immediately began to do so. "As my only wish is to help everyone, I must take this perfection seriously – cultivate it, practice it, in earnest and always. 'Make this practice as easy and natural as breathing, Sumedha!'" he told himself.

He perceived the next perfection to be equanimity, or *Upekkhā*. This means discerning rightly, viewing justly, or looking impartially without attachment or detachment, and without favor or disfavor. He cautioned himself: "Sumedha, you must be indifferent towards happiness and suffering, just as the earth is indifferent to anything that has been put upon it. I will be resolute on all matters concerning the effective maintenance of this excellent behavior."

Sumehda contemplated further, but he found no more perfections. "Are these all? Only ten! Where can these be found?" After a little thought, he answered his own question: "Why, they can be found nowhere but within one's own heart, so I must set my heart on them."

He sat still and reflected on the Ten Perfections again and again, thoroughly and exhaustively. Thus he contemplated: "These perfections are truly the sacrifice of external possession; higher perfections are truly a sacrifice of anyone's limbs; but the ultimate perfections are truly a sacrifice of one's own life." Sumedha reflected on the Ten Perfections – the basic perfections, and ten higher perfections, and ten ultimate perfections – again and again.

He made a firm resolution, determined to walk the path necessary for someone who wishes to attain Buddha-hood. "Now, I shall begin the journey along this path that will lead me to the attainment of Buddha status," declared Sumedha. No sooner had he said this than there was a loud cry of joy from the heavens of *Devas* and *Brahmās*. This was followed by a "Buddha-uproar," a loud outcry that can be heard when the celestial beings cry out joyously. In this way, the world welcomed and acknowledged the great news: "Friends, after the lapse of thousands and thousands of years, an omniscient Buddha is to arise in the world!"

Classification of Perfections:

The Ten Perfections can be classified by degree as "ordinary," "medium" or "superior" according to the extent of the serious nature of the sacrifice made.

Taking the first perfection, giving or *Dāna*, as an example:

- Sacrifice of wealth, wife or children, any three, or all, is an ordinary degree of sacrifice.
- Should one sacrifice one's eyes, limbs or both, this kind of sacrifice is considered medium.
- But, when one's own life is sacrificed, this is the highest, the superior kind of sacrifice.

Requirements:

An *Aggasāvaka* (a chief disciple) would be required to fulfill the Ten Perfections at the ordinary level.

A *Paccekabuddha* (a private Buddha who cannot disseminate the *Dhamma*) must fulfill both the ordinary and the medium kinds of perfections.

For anyone aspiring to be a Buddha, all three levels of perfections must be met during the course of his lives, one rebirth after another, until enlightenment is obtained. This would entail countless numbers of existences. Thus:

"A Buddha is not easily found;
He is not born everywhere.
When such a sage is born,
The race prospers!"

A Classic Example of a Sacrifice Made by One Aspiring to Be a Buddha

Once in the remote past, there lived a very rich king, Maharatha. He had three sons, Mahapranada, Maharadeva and Mahasattva.

One day, the king and his sons went to relax in a park. Enchanted by the beauty of the park, the princes were very excited and walked about until they came to a large, thick, bamboo forest. There they dismissed their servants and rested for a while.

When they were all alone, the eldest prince said, "I feel rather scared; there might be wild beasts about and we could be attacked."

The second, Prince Maharadeva, replied, "I feel a little ill at ease, too. But it is not my body I fear for; it is the separation from those I love that terrifies me."

The youngest, Prince Mahasattva, on hearing his brothers' remarks, said:

"No fear feel I, nor any sorrow either,
In this wide, lonesome wood, so dear to sages,
My heart is filled with bursting joy!
For soon, I'll win the highest boom!"

Silence fell, and the princes continued their stroll - rather timidly - and entered the thick and deeper parts of the grove. They stepped slowly and cautiously as they moved deeper and deeper into the thickest part of the grove.

Suddenly, all three stopped at once. There, in front of them, lay a tigress with her newly born cubs close by. They thought of running away, but gave a second look and found the animal to be too weak even to move.

Considering whether to turn back or not, the eldest of them remarked, "Tigers live on fresh meat and warm blood!"

The second prince said, "She is quite exhausted and in such a poor state; she wouldn't be able to catch any prey." Looking quite sorry for the animal, he added, "Who would sacrifice himself to save her life and those of her cubs?"

Nodding his head, the eldest remarked again, "Yes, but there has been no one who has ever made a self-sacrifice, as far as I know. Who would readily do that when life is so precious to everyone?"

All this time, the youngest prince stood in silence staring at the tigress and her cubs, deep in thought. Suddenly, he replied, "It is difficult for people like us, who are so fond of our lives and bodies and who have little intelligence. It is not difficult for those who are true men, intent on benefiting their fellow creatures and who desire to sacrifice themselves. Holy men are born of pity and compassion and regardless of whatever body they may get in heaven or earth, they would readily and happily give their body and life so that others might be saved."

There was silence as each stood absorbed in deep thought. They drew closer to have a good look. The tigress neither stirred nor blinked her eyes. It was certain she would die, leaving her cubs, too, to eventually die.

The youngest, Prince Mahasattva, thought to himself, "For a long time I have served this putrid body of mine – fed, clothed and cared for it. It is doomed to perish, fall, break away and be destroyed very soon. It would be wise to leave this body of one's own accord in good time. What attachment need I have for this body?"

His boundless compassion for the tigress and the cubs overwhelmed him. "What is this body and life to me, when I wish to win enlightenment? Now, I shall give away my body and life." Thinking thus, he asked his brothers to leave him alone.

Once he was left alone, he muttered, "For the weal of the world I wish to win enlightenment," and threw himself in front of the tigress. Still she did not move or open her eyes, and the prince did not know what he should do in order to attract the attention of the tigress. After a little hesitation, he came upon the idea to attract her attention by the smell of fresh warm blood. He had no sword on him, so he had to find a piece of sharp bamboo to cut his throat deep enough to get the blood pumping out. He found one, thrust it into his throat and made a deep wide cut. The great slit in the throat brought blood pouring forth, and soon the prince fainted and fell near the beast. He was soon covered with blood. The smell of the fresh warm blood caused the tigress to open her eyes, and seeing the blood-covered body of the prince, she immediately ate him up.

Buddha related this account and concluded by telling Ānanda, His attendant, "It was I who, at that time and on that occasion, was the individual, Prince Mahasattva."

What is *Sabbaññuta Ñāṇa* (Omniscient Knowledge)?
(With Reference to Brahmajala Sutta.*)*

Sabba means "all"; *nu* means "knows."
Sabbaññuta Ñāṇa means "supreme enlightenment," which enables the Buddha to know all the truth, (*Dhamma*), correctly, without any guidance or help from anyone. A Buddha is referred to and looked upon as a sage, a profoundly wise man having gained wisdom from His own experience. He is a compassionate teacher.

Buddha's Teaching is fundamentally based on the Four Noble Truths, inclusive of the Eightfold Path. Its aim is the extinction of suffering, *Dukkha*.

The truths, or *Dhammas* perceived, experienced, exercised and taught by Him are about:

1.	*Citta*	Mind
2.	*Cetasika*	Mental concomitants
3.	*Rūpa*	Matter
4.	*Nibbāna* and	Extinction of *Citta*, *Cetasika* *Rūpa*
5.	*Paññatti*	The conceptual objects, the language that will enable one to make everyone know his conception correctly, and many more *Paññattis*, such as: *Attha Paññatti, Satta Paññattis*, etc.

These five are known as the Five *Nēya Dhammas*. With the knowledge and mastery of the fifth, *Paññatti*, Buddha teaches the *Dhamma* precisely, making every relevant fact understandable. He uses similes and many examples to make it interesting.

A *Paccekabuddha*, like the Buddha, achieves *Magga* without guidance from anyone. But, unlike the Buddha, he does not attain *Subbaññuta Ñāna*, and therefore, is unable to proclaim and disseminate the *Dhamma* he has discovered.

Together with *Subbaññuta Ñāna*, the Buddha achieves ten other *Ñānas*, or powers:

1. *Thāna-thāna Kosalla Ñāna* This insight enables the Buddha to perfectly distinguish between right and wrong positions. (Literally, it means what is the cause and what is not the cause.)

2. *Kamma Vipāka Kosalla Ñāna* This is the insight that gives the Buddha a complete knowledge of *Kamma* and its good or bad consequences. *Kamma* means action or deed: any intentional action whether by body, speech, or thought. Thus, all moral and immoral volition is *Kamma*.

3. *Sabbattha Gāminī Patipadā Ñāna* This special insight enables the Buddha to have the knowledge of all the ways and means of reaching goals or destinations. Here goals or destinations means the four nether regions (hell, animal, *Athuyake* and *Pait-tar*), human world, *Deva* worlds, *Brahmā* worlds, and *Nibbāna*.

4. *Aneka Dhātu Nānā Dhātu Ñāna* This insight gives Buddha a complete knowledge of the basic as well as the subsidiary *Dhātus* (elements). There are six basic *Dhātus*, which will be explained later.

5. *Nānādhimuttikatā Ñāna* This *Ñāna* enables the Buddha to have a perfect knowledge of diversity of strongly ingrained dispositions. There are sixty-two kinds of *Ditthi*.

6. *Indriya Paropariyatta Ñāna* With this *Ñāna*, the Buddha enjoys the power to judge a person's

mental ability and keen interest in the *Dhamma*, whether one has a disposition to understand what is being taught, and which level of *Magga* and *Phala* is attainable for them. He is able to determine the mental ability of a person and starts His Teaching at a level suited to that person's mental capacity (put simply, the IQ of a person).

7. *Jhānasaṁkilesādi Ñāṇa* This insight gives Buddha the knowledge of the causes that spoil *Jhānas* (mental absorption) and of the causes that strengthen them. He can pre-determine the time before the achievement of the *Jhāna* and the end of that particular time.

8. *Pubbenivāsa Ñāṇa* This insight enables Buddha to recall the past. There is no time limit. This means He can go straight back to any event that took place in any existences, into unlimited world cycles. In the course of His Teaching, Buddha would often use this *Ñāṇa* and say, "At such a time, such an event took place," or "That happened during [his various and uncountable life cycles]." This is why we are able to enjoy reading His birth stories, known as *Jataka* Tales.

9. *Dibbacakkhu Ñāṇa* is often referred to as "the psychic eye" ("Buddha's vision," or "Buddha's eyes"). In the scripture, Buddha's eye is referred to as the Sixth Insight, through which He sees

the spiritual status of a person. He is able to see any form at any place. He is able to see beings on the verge of death and just after rebirth. This insight is also known as *Cutūpapāta Ñāṇa*.

10. *Āsavakkhaya Ñāṇa* This enables the Bodhisatta to uproot *Anusayas* (underlying latent dispositions or tendencies), which are the causes of false views (*Diṭṭhi*), attachment, lust of life, and ignorance of the Four Noble Truths.

What is *Dhātu*?

It is the force of nature that behaves in accordance with the laws of nature.

Dhātu is not *Satta*.
Satta means "creature" or "being."

Dhātu is not *Jīva*.
Jīva means "soul" or *Atta* (self).

According to Buddha's Teaching, *Dhātu* is neither soul nor *Atta* (self). It is a force of nature and manifests only in accordance with the laws of nature. It is absolutely free of the attributes, ways, and mode of a creature. It is also free of the functions, performances, and duties of a creature.

Dhātu means "elements." There are six basic *Dhatus* in the Universe:

1. *Pathavī Dhātu*
2. *Āpo Dhātu*
3. *Tejo Dhātu*
4. *Vāyo Dhātu*
5. *Ākāsa Dhātu*
6. *Viññāna Dhātu*

Pathavī Dhātu (Earth Element of Extension, characterized by hardness) is the force of nature that is endowed with the attribute of causing hardness.

Āpo Dhātu (Element of Cohesion) is so called because it is the force of nature endowed with the attribute of causing cohesion. It also has the attribute of causing liquidity.

Tejo Dhātu (Element of Heat) is the force of nature endowed with the attribute of causing heat and cold.

Vāyo Dhātu (Element of Motion) is the force of nature endowed with the attribute of causing impetus that prevents a thing from collapsing. It has the attribute of causing motion.

Ākāsa Dhātu (Space Element) is the force of nature endowed with the attribute of causing demarcation of *Kalapas*, the minutest particles of which matter is composed; these do not coalesce (combine and form a whole) with each other because of *Ākāsa Dhātu.*

Viññāna Dhātu (Consciousness) is so called because it is the force of nature endowed with the attribute of causing consciousness, hence the mind.

Matter is nothing but the composition of the first five kinds of *Dhātu* (elements). Mind, in turn, is nothing but the composition of *Viññāna Dhātu* and its concomitants, which arise and disintegrate simultaneously with *Viññāna Dhātu* whenever it comes into contact with one of the six objects – namely form, sound, smell, taste, tangible things, ideas – by means of appropriate senses. Thus, Buddha explained:

"Man is not created, but is the product of the six *Dhātus.*
There is no soul, no ego, no self, or no *Atta.*
Therefore, we say, *Anatta* (non-self). All conditioned things are subject to change, and are forever changing, and are never the same for any one second and thus, impermanent."

(Refer to *Brahmajala Sutta.*)

The Venerable Sāriputta's Survey of

Buddha's Virtues and Attributes.
(Refer to Sampasādanīya Sutta*)*

After his customary retreat for insight meditation, Sāriputta, Buddha's chief disciple, emerged from *Phalasamāpatti* [4] as usual. He enjoyed the mastery and analytic insight. One day, after his usual seclusion for insight meditation, he decided to view his past existences.

He started from the time of Buddha Anomadassi (the tenth Buddha) — when he made a firm resolution to become a chief disciple of a Buddha – and continued to the present moment of entering into *Phalasamāpatti*. In his mind's eye, he could readily perceive all the virtues he possessed that had to do with *Sīla, Samādhi* and *Paññā*. He was unable, however, to see the full extent and depth of these virtues.

This caused him to wonder. After some consideration, he said to himself, "Why don't I try viewing our Great Teacher's virtues?" The surge of inquisitiveness possessed him, and he tried to survey the extent and depth of the *Sīla, Samādhi* and *Paññā* of the Lord. He went over them in groups of two, three, four, etc., until he got to *Mahāvajiri Ñāna* and could go no further.

The *Mahāvajiri Ñāna* is the most powerful insight and can only be developed between sessions of *Phalasamāpatti*. Only the Buddha, the Enlightened, the Awakened One, enjoys this. It is known as the

Thunderbolt or Diamond Insight. This insight, which is the Buddha's alone, was used to discover the Law of Dependent Origination, the twelve links in the chain of *Paṭicca Samuppāda* (the Wheel of Life).

Now the highest-ranking disciple of the Buddha, Sāriputta, was fully convinced that the Buddha is the one and only individual in possession of omniscient knowledge, unsurpassed knowledge, and the only one with the ability to teach the profound *Dhamma*. With great admiration for the Buddha's virtues and attributes, he remarked, "I am, indeed, very fortunate to be his chief disciple!"

With a strong conviction, Sāriputta's faith in the Buddha's Teaching grew absolutely firm, and his respect and devotion for this Genius, this Great Being, became dramatically so profound, that he uttered spontaneously, "Right now, I must go to the *Tathāgata* to declare my devotional faith and confidence in Him!" And off he went with great urgency.

What is a *Tathāgata*?

By way of explanation, the Buddha said,

"Monks, the world is fully understood by a *Tathāgata*;
And from the world[5] a *Tathāgata* is released.

The origin of the world is fully understood by a *Tathāgata*. The origin of the world is abandoned by a *Tathāgata*. The cessation of the world is fully understood by a *Tathāgata*. The Path to the cessation of the world is completely realized by a *Tathāgata*. The Path to the cessation of the world is fully understood by a *Tathāgata*. The Path to the cessation of the world has been developed (made to become or cultivated) by a *Tathāgata*.

Whatsoever in the whole world with its *Devas*, *Māras, Brahmā* gods and its hosts of recluses and humans, is seen, heard, sensed, cognized, attained, searched into, pondered over in mind – all that is fully understood by a *Tathāgata*. That is why he is called a *Tathāgata*.

O, Monks moreover, whatever a *Tathāgata* speaks, utters, and proclaims from the day of His full enlightenment up to the day when He utterly passes away into the *Nibbāna*-element, which is without a residue of groups[6] – all that is just so and not otherwise. Therefore, He is called a *Tathāgata*.

Monks, as a *Tathāgata* speaks, so He acts; as He acts so He speaks.

Therefore He is a *Tathāgata*. He is a
Conqueror, unconquered,
And is 'one who sees all at will,' 'a wielder of
power!'
A unique being, an extraordinary man arises
in this world for the benefit of the many,
For the happiness of the many, out of com-
passion for the world,
For the good, benefit and happiness of
Devas and human beings.
Who is this unique being?
It is the *Tathāgata*, the exalted, fully enlight-
ened one."

(Anguttara Nikāya, 1.22)

(Further reading: *Anguttara Nikāya*, An Anthology (Bk
iv, 23, 33), translated by Nyanaponika Thera)

Summary

Ten factors comprise the ten powers of a
Buddha (*Tathāgata-batani*), which differentiate Him
from other beings and even from His own enlightened
disciples. He knows, according to actuality:

- Causes and conditions and their results.
- Past, present, future deeds and their results.
- The practices leading to good and bad destinies
  of beings after death.

- The world (of aggregates, etc.) in all its diversity.
- The various bad and good dispositions of beings.
- The state of faculties (*Indriya*, of faith, energy, etc.).
- The attainments of meditation.
- His many former births, and remembers the various experiences He had in them.
- He sees beings arising and passing away according to their deeds.
- Through the destruction of taints (*Āsava*), he dwells in freedom of mind (*Ceta-vimutti*) and freedom through wisdom (*Paññā-vimutti*).

(All are enumerated fully in *Majjhima Nikāya, Sutta* 12.)

The Five Eyes of the Buddha

Dibba-cakkhu	the psychic eye
Paññā-cakkhu	the knowledge connected with *Arahatta-Magga*
Dhamma-cakkhu	the knowledge connected with the three lower *Maggas*
Buddha-cakkhu	the knowledge through which the Buddha sees one's spiritual status
Samanta-cakkhu	the Omniscience

oooooo

Footnotes

1   The Eight Attainments mean that the Mind is composed, quite purified, without blemish and defilement, that it has grown soft, workable, fixed, and has gained the power of super-knowing, on the basis of eightfold "*Jhānas.*"

2   Early assumption of two kinds of time: historical time measured in years and centuries; cosmic time measured in æons.

3   *Dhamma* means phenomenon or mental object; *Dhātu* means element.

4   *Phalasamāpatti* is the fruition of *Magga Ñāna*. It can be enjoyed by one who has already gained one of the other four *Maggas* and *Phalas*, as a climax of *Vipassanā Bhāvanā, Vipassanā* meditation.

5   "World" means "suffering."

6   "Groups" means the five groups of aggregates of clinging and attachment.

THE ORDER OF MONKS

Buddha's only aim was to liberate all beings from the trap of *Tanhā* (craving), also known as *Kilesa* (defilement). *Devas* or celestial beings and human beings make their sensual pleasures their main base from which craving and attachment for things originate. This leads to *Dukkha* (suffering).

Buddha himself had experienced all the pleasures of the world, and had enjoyed the most luxurious way of life. But, after witnessing the Four Great Sights on His way to the leisure park, He came to know about suffering for the first time. He was alarmed and unhappy. He decided to find a way out of universal suffering, namely, unhappiness, illness, separation from loved ones, old age infirmity, death, decay, and the vicious cycle of birth and death. His logic, endeavor, and unyielding human effort were the tools He used for six long years, until He succeeded. This was when He gained omniscient knowledge.

He was a very compassionate teacher and wished to help everyone. Buddha set himself the responsibility to teach and guide all beings to uphold human dignity, to have self-esteem and self-reliance, and to seek no gods or savior for one's own salvation. He has realized the path known as the Eightfold Path and would be happy to guide anyone serious and diligent enough to take it. This path leads to a set destination, *Nibbāna*. It was a task He set himself to perform.

Buddha needed assistance to carry out His self-imposed noble work, so He needed to establish a ministry, or an order of monks. He could then delegate the monks to carry on His noble work. This was why it was necessary to form the Ministry of *Sanghas*.

The First Discourse and the First Monk of the Order

Soon after Buddha's enlightenment and at the request of Brahmā Sahampati (a sublime being), the Great Wheel of *Dhamma* was set in motion in the Deer Park of Isipatana in Benares. Lord Buddha gave His first sermon to the five monks who had attended Him while He went in search of truth. This first sermon or discourse, known as the *Dhammacakka Sutta*, contains the essence, the core of Buddha's teachings. He explained what universal sufferings are, what causes them, and the way to end them by taking a path He had discovered and established. This path is known as the Middle Way, or the Eightfold Path. It produces vision and knowledge of the Four Noble Truths, and thus leads to higher knowledge, enlightenment, and *Nibbāna*.

Out of the five monks who received Buddha's first sermon, Kondañña gained insight, a complete knowledge of the Four Noble Truths. His mind was free from lust (*Rāga*), free from defilement or wrong views (*Diṭṭhi*), and free from doubts (*Vicikacchā*). His eyes opened to wisdom and He gained the state of a stream winner, the first level of realization.

At the End of the First Sermon

Buddha ended His first discourse saying, "Monks, when I obtained a clear and right vision of he Four Noble Truths with their turns, consisting of twelve folds, I professed to the entire world – men, gods, *Brahmās* (sublime beings), leaving no one out – that I had realized full and supreme enlightenment. The knowledge of insight rose in me that emancipation had been achieved and that this was my last birth; henceforth, there is no rebirth for me!"

As soon as He uttered the last word, there was a confirmation of this momentous event by the terrestrial gods. Loud and clear was their applause: "The Blessed One has set the Wheel of *Dhamma* in motion here in the Deer Park of Isipatana in Banares! This Supreme Wheel of Doctrine cannot be set back by any ascetic or *Brahman* or god or *Māra* (obstructive, evil beings) or *Brahmā* (a sublime being) in the world!"

There were shouts of joy and applause in the seven heavens. The *Brahmā* world above and the thousand universes quaked, shuddered and trembled, and an infinite and lofty light flashed through the worlds, surpassing the glamour of gods. A deafening proclamation could be heard: "The Buddha has, indeed, attained the highest of all perfections and He is the fully Self Enlightened One!"

Amidst those shouts of jubilation, there was a shout of utter joy from the Blessed One – "Kondañña has, indeed, mastered the Truth!" – for He knew that this monk, out of the five, had gained a crystal clear perception of His Teaching.

Kondañña was very happy and at once requested, "O, Venerable Sir! May I be a monk under you and receive higher ordination?"

In answer to that request, Buddha raised His right hand and replied:

Etha Bhikkhu, come *Bhikkhu*, well taught in the *Dhamma*. Come and practice the holy life for the complete ending of suffering."
(*Vinaya Piṭaka* 1.13)

That was how Venerable Kondañña became the first monk in the Buddha's order. He was received and ordained at the same time.

Later, when the remaining four monks – Bhaddiya, Vippa, Mahānāma and Assaji – achieved complete knowledge of the Four Noble Truths, they were accepted into the Order at their request. By that time, then, there were five monks in the Order.

Everyday, the Buddha gave the monks guidance and instruction on the practice of the *Dhamma*. On the sixth day of their meeting, the Blessed One assembled the five monks and gave the second discourse, the *Anatta Lahkana Sutta*, which concerns the truth of impermanence, or soul-less-ness.

The Second Discourse: *Anatta Lakhana Sutta* (Soul-less-ness)

The Buddha started His discourse saying,

"O, Monks, the body is not a soul. If it were,
this body would not be subject to afflictions
(pain, distress and misery).
If the body were a soul, one would be able to
say, 'Let my body be like this or let my body
be not like this.'
It's because the body is not the soul that it is
subject to affliction. That is why we cannot
get the body to be one way or the other.
Similarly, feeling is not the soul. Perception
is not the soul. Activities are not the soul.
Consciousness is not the soul."

"O, Monks, what do you think? Is the body permanent or impermanent?" asked the Blessed One.

"It is impermanent, Reverend Sir."

"If it is impermanent, is it attended with suffering or happiness?" inquired Buddha.

"It is attended with suffering, Reverend Sir," was the monks' unanimous reply.

"Then, if something is impermanent and attended with suffering, is in the nature of changing, would it be proper to treat it as 'It is I,' 'It is myself,' 'It is my soul'?" Buddha questioned the monks.

"Not at all, Sir," replied the five monks.

The same questions were posed about feeling, perception, activities and consciousness, and the answers were as expected.

Lord Buddha explained:

"Therefore, Monks, whatever the body may be – whether of the past, the present or the future, internal or external, rough or tender, base or pleasant, far away or close by – it must be treated with wisdom, right and proper, as: 'It is not I,' 'It is not myself,' and 'It is not my soul.' So is feeling. So is perception. So are activities and consciousness. A noble disciple, who sees thus, will not be attached to body, feeling, perception, activities and consciousness, etc. By not being attached, he will be detached. Through detachment, he will be emancipated. He will have the knowledge that he is emancipated, and that he has done what would have been done and that there is nothing to be wished for."

At the end of the sermon, the five monks rejoiced, for they fully understood the absence of "ego," attained emancipation from all fetters, and achieved the final stage of realization and became *Arahats* (perfect ones who have eliminated all passions).

Buddha was the only teacher to realize that there is no ego (soul or self) to be found anywhere in the universe. Others take it for granted that a permanent entity exists and transmigrates when the being dies to be born again elsewhere, and that it will continue to exist forever. According to these people, there is a knowing mind or nature and it is permanently in existence.[1]

More Joined the Order

Next to join the Order was Yasa, the son of a millionaire. He lived a luxurious life in great pleasure. However, one day, suddenly and to his great surprise, he felt the danger of living in such a manner. It came as a kind of sudden, unfamiliar uneasiness.

This strange uneasy feeling tormented him, so one day, he left home unnoticed. To find some comfort and relief, he walked towards Migadaya Forest, where Buddha was living. When Yasa approached the Deer Park, Buddha perceived him by means of His divine eyes, and also perceived the previous lives of Yasa, the various meritorious deeds he had done and his reason for this great uneasiness.

Buddha was pacing up and down the yard, and as Yasa came nearer, He came down the yard and sat on His seat.

On seeing Buddha, Yasa cried out, "I am in danger. I am afflicted!"

"Yasa, there is no danger or affliction here. Come, I will preach the doctrine and all will be well," exclaimed Buddha.

Relieved of his fear, and having been invited, Yasa removed his footwear, paid his respect and sat down at Buddha's side. Once Yasa appeared to have regained his composure, Buddha began His teaching.

He began His teaching on the merits of charity *Dāna*, morality *Sīla*, and then about the evils of sensual pleasures and the blessing of renunciation. Because of his good deeds or the good *Kamma* of his previous existences, Yasa was receptive of the *Dhamma* and showed his interest and impatience to learn more. So, the

Buddha continued to preach the Four Noble Truths, a self-realized doctrine of all Buddhas. Yasa gained the first stage of realization as soon as the teaching ended.

The First Refugee of the Triple Gem

Meanwhile, Yasa's father was seen approaching the Deer Park. With His psychic powers, the Buddha willed that the father should not be able to see his son.

When he saw the Buddha, Yasa's father inquired, "Reverend Sir, did you see here a nobleman, Yasa?"

The Buddha replied, "Sit down here. While being seated, you will be able to see the nobleman, Yasa, who is seated here."

Overjoyed at the prospect of seeing his son, the millionaire sat down and paid his respect to the Buddha. The Buddha gave a talk on the *Dhamma* as He would usually do.

When the discourse ended, the millionaire expressed his appreciation and exclaimed: "Excellent Sir, Excellent Sir! Now I have a complete understanding of the *Dhamma*! May I take refuge in the Buddha, His Teaching, the *Dhamma*, and the Order of the *Sanghas* (monks)?" On this request, he became the first refugee to "the Buddha, the *Dhamma*, and the *Sanghas*," commonly known as the "Triple Gem," or "Three Jewels."

Yasa, still unseen by his father, also heard the discourse given to his father and attained the final stage of realization and became an *Arahat*.

Now the Blessed Lord willed for Yasa to be seen by the father. Very much surprised and happy, the father entreated his son to return home to please his mother.

But Yasa wished to remain with the Buddha and requested an ordination; he promised to visit home soon. Thus, the father was obliged to return home alone.

Before he left, Yasa's father paid his respect to the Buddha and invited Him and the Order to his house for lunch on the following day. He then returned home happy and contented.

Yasa's entire family took refuge in the Triple Gem. They spent the rest of their lives doing good deeds – especially giving charity – and providing for the needs of the Order, giving the monks the essentials of food, clothing, medicine, and land and buildings for dwellings.

Yasa's Friends Join the Order

There were now six monks in the Order. Yasa's four very intimate friends came to pay homage. Yasa welcomed them, took them to the Lord, and asked if they might be admonished.

On seeing the four anxious to hear the *Dhamma*, the Buddha wasted no time and began His sermon. Starting with morality, loving-kindness, charity, He continued with the Four Noble Truths. At the end of His teaching, they expressed their desire to join the Order and so were ordained. This brought the total number of monks in the Order to ten.

Similarly, 50 more of Yasa's friends came to see Yasa, and after hearing the discourses, joined the Order. Now there were 60 monks in the order, and Buddha had to set His program in such a way as to have time for Himself and to teach and admonish the *Sanghas* (monks).

As the number of monks in the Order increased, *Vinaya* or monastic discipline, had to be introduced both for the smooth running of the Order and for the wellbeing of the *Sanghas*. It was also considered to ensure the long-term effective functioning of the Order so that Buddha's Teaching, the *Dhamma*, would be practiced, kept alive and active even after His death, or *Parinibbāna* (a Buddha's death).

Every day, Buddha would assemble the monks and instruct them on the practice of the *Dhamma*. However, on one special day, He addressed them thus:

"In life, O, Monks, there are two kinds of happiness,

Happiness of a life of a householder and
that of a life of a monk:
But the happiness of a life of a monk is the
higher of the two.
The happiness of senses and the happiness
of renunciation:
The happiness of renunciation is the higher
of the two.
Tainted happiness and untainted happiness:
Untainted happiness is the higher of the two."

In the same manner, He gave examples for carnal happiness and non-carnal happiness, noble happiness and ignoble happiness, bodily happiness and mental happiness, and so on. He was interested in the happiness of the *Sanghas* and taught them all that was relevant for the purpose of their salvation and freedom from suffering. The account of His daily habit will show His earnestness.

Buddha Sends out Messengers of Truth

Buddha and the 60 monks resided in Deer Park for the three months of the rainy season, beginning about mid-July and ending about mid-October. This period was their *Vassa* (the time during which the monks reside at a certain place paying all attention to the practice of the *Dhamma*). Buddha would regulate His time in such a way as to have ample time to teach, preach, and admonish the *Sanghas*, as well as to carry out His daily routine, until the day He passed away.

As soon as the *Vassa* was over, Lord Buddha called the assembly of all 60 monks and addressed them:

"Monks, I have liberated Myself from the traps of *Tanhās* (*Kilesa*). You all have liberated yourselves, too. Now, you are all free from all *Kilesa*, both divine and human.

Go forth, from place to place, and preach for the welfare of the many, and for their happiness. Have compassion for the world.

Go we must, for the benefit and welfare and happiness of *Devas* (celestial beings) and men! Preach the *Dhamma* – sound in the beginning, sound in the middle, and sound in the end – which is replete with the quality of goodness and with nothing deficient or superfluous.

O, Monks, proclaim the holy life in all its fullness and purity! I, Myself, will be going to Uruvelā Forest to preach the *Dhamma* to a thousand hermits led by the three hermit brothers."

So saying, He sent the 60 monks in all directions with a note of caution: "Go – no two of you together –

and preach, 'Avoid evil, and do what is virtuous!' Go out and liberate everyone!"

After giving those instructions, He set out for the forest of Uruvelā.

This, then, was when the Order of Monks was actually formed.

The Lord Buddha Exhorted the *Sanghas*...

"O, Monks! One can abandon evil, O, Monks! If it were impossible to abandon evil, I would not ask you to do so. But, it can be done. 'Abandon evil!'
If this abandoning evil would bring harm and suffering, I would not ask you to abandon it. But, as the abandoning of evil brings weal and happiness, therefore I say, 'Abandon evil!'
O, Monks! Cultivate the good! One can cultivate what is good; if it were impossible to cultivate good, I would not ask you to do so. But, it can be done; therefore, I say, 'Cultivate good!'
"If cultivation of the good would bring harm and suffering, I would not ask you to do so.

But as the cultivation of good brings weal and happiness, therefore I say, 'Cultivate the good.' Make unremitting effort!

There are two things I came to know so well: not to be content with a good state of mind so far achieved, and to be unremitting in the struggle (for the goal). Unremittingly, indeed, did I struggle (and I resolved).

Let skin, sinews and bones remain; let flesh and blood in the body dry up; yet there shall be no ceasing of energy till what has been sought for has been gained. It can be won only by manly strength, manly energy, and manly effort!

Through heedful effort have I won enlightenment, through effort have I won the unsurpassable security from *Saṁsāric* toll (the vicious cycle of death and rebirth attended with suffering).

Therefore, O, Monks, you should train yourselves thus: 'Unremittingly we struggle! And resolve.' Thus, you should train yourselves!"

The Wonder Response

Very soon the Buddha's message of freedom from *Dukkha* (universal suffering) had spread far and wide. More and more joined the Order, including kings and queens, ministers and their wives, wealthy people, learned men and even ordinary laborers. Many – by the thousands and thousands – came to take refuge in the Triple Gem.

The monks taught the main divisions of the *Dhamma* – *Sīla, Samādhi,* and *Paññā*:

- *Sīla* requires one to take vows to refrain from doing or speaking what is not right. This is done by means of keeping the Five Precepts, or codes of morality.
- *Samādhi* requires one to practice meditation to acquire mental concentration.
- *Paññā* requires one to practice the four methods of *Satipaṭṭhāna* in order to perceive the *Anicca* (impermanent), *Dukkha* (universal suffering), and *Anatta* (non-self) nature of mind and body.

The beauty of the *Dhamma* is that everyone can test it: only if one feels that it brings him happiness and serves his wellbeing and that of others should he believe in it, accept it. Should anyone accept the *Dhamma*, Buddha's request is, " Try to live by it."

Those who wanted to join the Order had to be brought to the Blessed One for ordination. As more and more joined, it meant more work and increasing inconvenience for the Order of the Monks. So, the second form of ordination was introduced.

Buddha Delegates the Authority of Ordination to the Monks

Requirements for the Second Form of Ordination:

- One must shave his head, moustache and beard.
- He then must wear robes that have been dyed.
- After being robed neatly, he must approach the monk who is to ordain him,
- Showing his respect by having the palm of the two hands touching each other and raised to his forehead, and bending down at his feet, he then makes the request.
- He then declares that he takes refuge in the Triple Gem by repeating these lines:

> *Buddhaṁ Saranaṁ Gacchāmi:* I take refuge in the Buddha.
>
> *Dhammaṁ Saranaṁ Gacchāmi:* I take refuge in the *Dhamma*.
>
> *Sanghaṁ Saranaṁ Gacchāmi:* I take refuge in the *Sanghas*.

This verse of pledges is repeated three times, adding *Dutiyampi* to each line on the second round, and *Tatiyampi* to each line on the third and final round.

The Third Form of Ordination

The second form of ordination was again changed to a third form. This was a combination of the second form and a third set of new rules created to meet requirements for the perfect and harmonious operation of the Order of Monks.

The *Vinaya* Rules

As the Order of the Monks grew larger and larger, appropriate changes to the *Vinaya* Rules were made for various reasons, but the main aim always was to preserve the purity of the Order, which forms the mainstream of the Buddha's *Sāsana*.

The Doctrine is conveniently divided into three, or placed in three baskets or *Tipiṭaka*:

- The Basket of Discipline (*Vinaya*), or "the *Vinaya Piṭaka* consists of five books expounding on the rules of monastic life. These contain 227 *Vinayas* or rules.
- The Basket of Discourses (*Suttas*), or the *Sutta Piṭaka*, is a collection of discussions, stories, poems, and proverbs imparting all the precepts of practical Buddhism, and is very interesting.
- The third Basket of Ultimate things, the *Abhidhamma Piṭaka*, covers everything on epis-

temological, metaphysical and psychological matters. It is the most important and interesting part of His doctrine, because it elaborates on the four ultimate things: consciousness (*Citta*), mental properties (mental concomitants, *Cetasika*), matter (material qualities, *Rūpa*), and *Nibbāna*.

The Ten Aims of Vinaya *Rules*

1. To serve as rules for the good conduct of the monks.
2. To promote the wellbeing of the monks.
3. To suppress the defaulting monks.
4. To protect the good monks.
5. To keep the monks clear of offences.
6. To save the monks from rebirths in any of the four nether worlds, or *Bhumis*.
7. To enable the monks to receive the respect of those who have no faith in the monks.
8. To enable the monks to receive increased respect and reverence from those who have faith in the monks and thereby perpetuate the three aspects: teaching, practicing, and achieving (of *Magga* and *Phala*, the steps towards realization).
9. To give due place to the *Vinaya* Rules, for the maintenance of discipline.
10. To help the monks to perpetuate three *Sāsanas*:
    · The teaching of the Buddha.

- The practice of meditation for the achievement of *Maggas* (path, path insight) and *Phalas* (fruition, result attained by work, i.e., by insight meditation).
- The achievement of *Maggas* and *Phalas*.

(Refer to *Dīgha Nikāya, Sāmaññaphala Sutta)*

The Ten Sīla *or* Dasa Sīla (Sīla *Observed by the Novices and Monks)*

- Not to kill
- Not to steal
- To be celibate
- Not to lie
- Not to take intoxicants and drugs
- Not to eat after midday or before dawn of the next day
- Not to dance and sing or play music
- Not to put on cosmetics to cause sensual excitement
- Not to use luxurious chairs and beds, indulging in luxury
- Not to handle silver, gold, and all kinds of currency

In addition to observing the *Vinaya* Rules, the *Sanghas* keep the following four kinds of *Sīlas*, or codes of morality:

Pātimokkha Saṁvara Sīla
Ājīva Pārisuddhi Sīla
Indriya Saṁvara Sīla
Paccaya Sannissita Sīla [2]

Why and When the Buddha Formed the Order of Monks

The order of Monks was formed to preserve His Teaching (the Monks are the custodians of the *Dhamma*). The Monks were to study the 37 *Bodhie Pakkhiya Dhammas*, commit them to memory and practice *Vipassanā Bhāvanā* in accordance with these *Dhammas*, based on the Noble Eightfold Path. (The abridged 37 *Dhammas* become the three *Sikkhas*, namely *Sīla, Samādhi and Paññā.*)

Buddha's aim and object were to enhance His *Sāsana* (i.e., His Teaching) so it would still be possible to help human beings and *Devas* to achieve freedom from suffering.

The *Sanghas* are qualified to undertake this colossal, serious and prestigious responsibility entrusted to them by Lord Buddha. They have complete knowledge of the *Dhamma* and practice, since the Great Master had seen to every detailed requirement that would be needed for them to carry it out competently and effectively, with no kind of disturbance or hindrance from either within or outside the Order.

When laymen take refuge in the Triple Gem, even though they have their various occupations and family obligations, they help with the promotion and preservation of His teachings by supplying the Order of Monks with the four necessities of life – food, dwelling, medication and clothing robes. This helps the monks to carry out the responsibilities entrusted to them.

A Little Suggestion

We have seen good deeds of this nature being carried out earnestly by the lay society during the lifetime of the Lord Buddha. It is necessary that we continue to do so in our time in order to help the *Sanghas* enhance the *Sāsana*, the Teaching of Buddha, which is fundamentally based on the Four Noble Truths.

For.....   "Not gold, or silver, and, jewels....be
            Not one....dear and loved, you see,
            Nor all the possessions bound and bind,
            Can follow him who leaves this life;
            As all things must be left behind."

But...   "But every deed a man performs,
            With body, or with voice, or mind,
            'Tis this that he can call all the time.
            Like a shadow, never to depart,
            This is what follows close and fast.
            Sure, he soon will find."

So...   "Let all then, noble deeds perform,
A treasure-store for future weal (welfare),
For merit gained this life within,
Will yield a blessing in the next."

oooooo

Footnotes

1   For further reading there are writings on "The Absence of
Ego" and "All Signs of an Ego are Absent" in *Buddhism in
Translation* by Henry Clark Warren, 1963 by the Harvard
University Press.

2   *Pātimokkha Saṁvara Sīla:*   Self-control to refrain from
breaking any of the Vinaya Rules established by the
Buddha.

Ājīva Pārisuddhi Sīla: Self control from adopting the
wrong mode of gaining a living

Indriya Saṁvara Sīla: Self control to restrain or subju-
gate the senses arising in the sense-organs, namely, eyes,
ears, nose, tongue, body, mind.

Paccaya Sannissita Sīla: Self control to have appropriate
contemplations when any of the four necessaries, clothing,
alms-food, dwelling place, and medicine are taken or
received. (Example: when adorning the robe, he would consider that it has been done to protect himself from heat and
cold and for modesty; when alms-food is taken, he would
consider that he has taken to sustain lie and not otherwise.

Such contemplations will bring about awareness of all actions and prevent unwholesome thoughts and desires arising from these acts.)

His Teachings

The Spread of Buddhism

Buddha's Teaching is based on the right way of living. With the understanding of the conditions of life, one can live in harmony with other people and in harmony with the Laws of Righteousness, the Universal Law and the Law of Cause and Effect (*Dhamma Niyāma*). His teachings are about facts and truths of life and the nature of the universe.

He did not preach all that He knew, only what was required. On one occasion, while passing through a forest, the Buddha took a handful of leaves and said to some *Bhikkhus* (monks), "O, *Bhikkhus*, what I've taught is comparable to the amount of leaves in my hand, and what I've not taught is comparable to the amount of leaves in the forest." He has taught us only what was required for our emancipation. (Incidentally, He made some statements that are accepted as scientific truths today.)

His Teachings Spread Far and Wide Across the World

Some would wonder how the Teaching of the Buddha had been perpetuated, since it was accepted and practiced as early as 600 BCE throughout India and had also spread to Nepal and beyond to Afghanistan. At the time when Alexander the Great invaded Afghanistan in 329 BCE, it still flourished side by side with Greek culture and continued to do so until the invasion of the Arabs in the seventh century.

With a unique, vigorous, and radiant personality, Buddha was a great competent teacher with His well-founded system of teaching. Together with His well-disciplined Order of *Bhikkhus* (monks) and *Bhikkhunis* (nuns), He set good examples for people of every walk of life. For many centuries, His doctrine – based on logic and demanding no rites and rituals – not only spread very quickly, but also commanded deep respect, great devotion and encouragement from many kings and emperors, both during and after the Buddha's life. Events that took place during the Emperor Asoka's reign illustrate this astonishing development quite well.

What Did the Emperor Asoka Do Out of Respect and Devotion for the Buddha and His Teachings?

The Buddha passed away in 543 BCE. Two-hundred-and-twenty years after His passing, in the year 323 BCE, Emperor Asoka of India, the defender of Buddha's Teaching, gave his deep respect and royal protection to the Order of *Sanghas* (Monks).

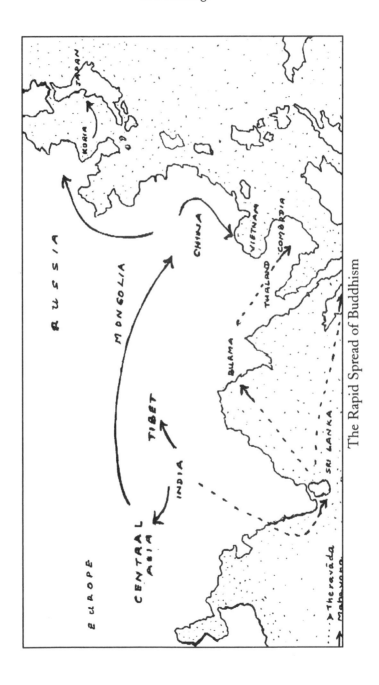

The Rapid Spread of Buddhism

Emperor Asoka was an ardent believer in Buddha's teachings and sent his son, Mahindā, and daughter, Saṅghamittā, to Ceylon (now known as Sri Lanka) to introduce the Buddha's teachings. Monks were dispatched to introduce Buddhism to fourteen Indian nations surrounding Asoka's country, and it soon spread over almost the whole of India and beyond.

Furthermore, Asoka made treaties with five Greek kings, his allies, to admit his religious preachers into their country to introduce the teachings of the Buddha. The names of the five kings – mentioned in the edicts of the Emperor Asoka and inscribed by him on stone pillars – are Antiochus of Syria, Ptolemy of Egypt, Antigonus of Macedon or Macedonia, Magas of Cyrene (a Greek State in North Africa) and Alexander of Epirus. Asoka's stone pillars still stand as concrete testimony to those treaties.

In the third century BCE, Asoka sent five monks to the five provinces of China, and from there, Buddhism reached Korea in 372 AD and Japan in 552 AD. It also spread to Cochin, China, Mongolia and other Asiatic countries during that time.

Sona and Uttara, two of Asoka's monks, introduced Buddhism into Burma, and from there it quickly spread to Cambodia, Thailand, and Laos. It became the state religion of Thailand and Sri Lanka. The Buddha's exact teachings, called *Theravāda*

Buddhism, are followed, practiced and respected in all five of these countries.

How His Teachings Are Preserved and Perpetuated

His teachings, the doctrine or the scripture is preserved in the *Tipiṭaka*, meaning "the Three Baskets." The *Tipiṭaka* contains the words of the Buddha and comprises 84,000 discourses. It is estimated to be about eleven times the size of the Christian Bible. Professor Rhys Davids estimated the total number of words of the text of the *Tipiṭaka* to be 1,752,800.

As the word itself implies, the *Tipiṭaka* consists of three baskets, namely, the Basket of Discipline (*Vinaya Piṭaka*), the Basket of Discourses (*Sutta Piṭaka*), and the Basket of Ultimate Things (*Abhidhamma Piṭaka*).

The *Vinaya Piṭaka* is divided into five books, and deals with the rules and regulations of the order of *Bhikkhus* and *Bhikkhunis* (monks and nuns). The detailed account of the life and ministry of the Buddha can be found in this *Piṭaka*.

The *Sutta Piṭaka* is divided into 26 books, and consists of discourses preached by the Buddha and a few discourses given by His disciples. Each sermon was propounded to suit the occasion and temperaments of the individuals He was teaching.

The *Abhidhamma Piṭaka* is the most important, the most interesting part of His doctrine, for it is here that the four ultimate things – consciousness (*Citta*), mental properties, mental concomitants (*Cetasika*), matter, material qualities (*Rūpa*), and *Nibbāna* – are all clearly explained.

In the year 543 BCE, Buddha passed away at the age of eighty. He left no successors. He left the *Vinaya* Rules (the rules and regulations for the *Bhikkhus* and *Bhikkhunis*) and His teachings to take His place. It, therefore, became necessary to preserve and perpetuate them as soon as the Buddha passed on. Immediate action had to be taken.

The First Great Council at Rajagahā in 543 BCE

On the seventh day after Buddha's death, under the patronage of King Ajātasattu and supervised by Mahā Kassapa, Chief of the Order of *Sanghas*, the first council was held in *Rājagaha*. This was done to establish as well as preserve the authoritative teaching of the Buddha.

At the time, there were 700,000 monks in the Order. The convocation was convened by 500 principal *Theras*, great celebrities who had overcome the dominion of passions and were perfect in every religious attribute, well versed in the doctrine and all the discourses given by Buddha during His 45 years of teaching. All His teachings were collected, classified, arranged and chanted. This council took seven months to complete its task.

The Second Great Council at Vesali in 443 BCE

Again, to secure the permanency of the doctrine, another council met during the reign of King Kālāsoka, in Vesāli. It was conducted in precisely the same manner as the first. Seven hundred leading *Arahats* formed the Council, with Arahat Revata serving as chief. They worked diligently for eight months.

The Third Great Council at Patana in 308 BCE

King Asoka was a devoted Buddhist and, having great influence, did much to help the Order. His interest, power, and sway brought the quick and extensive spread of Buddhism to more countries around the world. The third council was carried out under his patronage.

This council was comprised of 1,000 monks of sanctified character, perfect in religious knowledge and versed in the *Tipiṭaka*. Chief among them was

Moggaliputta Tissa. The council concluded its work after nine months.

King Asoka sent messengers of the *Dhamma*, the Teaching of Buddha, to various foreign countries known at that time. Through his influence, Buddhism not only spread to large areas of India, but also to Ceylon and other neighboring regions. For a millennium, it served as a force in molding the religious, moral, artistic, educational and social life of India.

The Fourth Great Council in Ceylon

Supported by King Vaṭṭhagāminī Abhaya and headed by Mahā Agga, the fourth council convened in Ceylon, or Sri Lanka, in about 80 BCE. Here the doctrine was not only chanted, but also put into writing for the first time. The *Tipiṭaka*, transmitted from memory in Pāḷi, was written down on palm leaves.

The Fifth Great Council at Mandalay in 1871

The fifth council was held in Mandalay, Burma in the year 1871 (twenty-fifth century according to the Buddhist era), under the backing of King Mindon. Jāgara Thera presided over the council. This time, the entire *Tipiṭaka* was chanted and inscribed on 729 marble slabs, which were placed at the foot of Mandalay Hill, where they still remain for all to see. The Burmese monarchs encouraged the teaching and practicing of Buddhism, and their influence, like Emperor Asoka's, had great and lasting effects.

The Sixth Great Council at Rangoon in the Years 1954–1956

Preparations for this great and elaborate council took three years. The editing of the text and the building – of an assembly hall, an ordination hall, a library, a few blocks of hostels and dormitories, a large dining hall for the monks and lay people, a sanatorium and smaller buildings for meditation, lecture theaters, staff-residential flats and quarters and offices, roads, avenues, every little structure that was befitting for this great council – were finally completed just in time for the auspicious first day. In the presence of dignified guests and learned monks from Cambodia, Ceylon, India, Laos, Nepal, Pakistan and Thailand and a group of 500 learned Burmese monks (all well-versed in the doctrine and practice of the teachings), the council was declared open, with great pomp and ceremony, on the full-moon day of May 1954. This occasion also marked the Vesakha Festival (the day to celebrate Buddha's birthday, the day of His enlightenment, and the day of His passing away).

The truly arduous task began the day following the opening ceremonies, and was completed two years later on the full-moon day of May 1956. At the sixth council, the *Tipiṭaka* was recited in Pāli, and steps were taken towards translating it into other languages. This council had a wider significance than previous ones, as learned monks from the invited countries also participated in this great work of preserving and perpetuating the *Dhamma*, the exact and actual teachings of the Buddha. The 500 Burmese monks, who took sole responsibility for the meeting, were selected *Sayādaws*, (reverend, learned monks) well versed in the study and practice of the teachings of the Buddha. Most of them were elderly, very experienced and highly revered for their authority on the doctrine. A large group of lay scholars edited the draft of the Pāli text and translated it into Burmese for submission to the monks for translation into many foreign languages.

Theravada Buddhism and Burma (Myanmar)

Buddha's teachings have been seriously practiced and taught in all monasteries and colleges in Mandalay, Burma since 323 BCE. Today, monks and nuns take monastic examinations leading to *Pathama-kyaw* and *Pathama-gyi*, the standard basic qualification required for monks and nuns. A candidate must memorize a total of 15 volumes from the *Tipiṭaka* to gain entry to the oral section of the examination alone. The study of Pāli and of the *Abhidhamma Piṭaka* has been offered at

Rangoon University since the 1930s. Initially, when construction began for the Sixth Great Council, authorities planned to use the entire block as a new University for Buddhist Learning, Culture and Civilization after the convocation. It was to serve as a kind of spiritual center for South East Asia.

As a result of the periodic councils held following the Buddha's passing away or *Parinibbāna*, the doctrine has been well preserved and perpetuated. It has now reached all corners of the world. Many associations and universities offer studies on Buddhism, especially the *Abhidhamma Piṭaka* (the psycho-ethical analysis of things in their ultimate sense as opposed to their conceptual form). The Association for Asian Studies at the University of Michigan, USA is one of the many places where Buddhism can be studied.

Another school of Buddhism slowly developed after the Second Great Council and came to be known as "*Mahāyanā*". *Mahāyanā* Buddhism taught the doctrines of the Buddha and some new metaphysical theories. It is practiced in China, Japan, Tibet, and Korea.

To clarify, however, we need to mention again that the actual, exact Teaching of the Buddha is called *Theravāda* Buddhism as it is practiced in Burma, Cambodia, Ceylon, Laos, and Thailand. "*Theravāda*" means "the way of the elders."

The Four Noble Truths and the Eightfold Path

The Four Noble Truths are the starting and focal point of Buddha's Teaching. By understanding the Four Noble Truths and walking along "the Great Superhighway," the Eightfold Path, practicing *Sīla*, *Samādhi* and *Paññā*, one would be free from suffering and ultimately reach the goal of *Nibbāna*.

The Four Noble Truths

Buddha gave His first sermon, on the Four Noble Truths, to a group of five monks in the Deer Park of Isipatana. Buddha said,

"O, Monks, the Four Noble Truths must be understood and fully realized.

"What are they?

1. "The **truth of suffering or *Dukkha***. Birth itself is suffering, old age is suffering, and sickness is suffering. Death is suffering, and is followed by sorrow, lamentation, dejection and despair. Association with the unpleasant is suffering, separation from loved ones is suffering, and non-acquisition of desired things is suffering. This must be understood.

2. "The **cause of suffering** is craving that brings rebirths. Craving, when attended with enjoyment, is the main cause of sufferings: Craving for sensual desires (*Kamma-tanhā*) and for existence (*Bhava-tanhā*).

    "The desire to possess, to preserve, to accumulate worldly material and pleasures is man's greatest enemy. Sense of desire destroys the sense of value, for selfish desires place worldly possessions above wisdom and personalities above principles. This must be given up. This has been given up by Me.

3. "The **cessation of suffering** is quite simple: make a complete avoidance, abandonment, release of and detachment from all cravings, and all sufferings will cease. We may live in this world quite happily if we are not attached to it, at least not to the extent to let it cause worry, trouble and sorrow. Be in it, but we must not be of it. If we take this life with philosophy, we shall find that, for us, sorrow almost entirely ceases. We must develop this understanding.

4. "The **Path that leads to the cessation of suffering** is the Eightfold Path. It has been developed by Me.

"O, Monks, when I gained a clear and proper vision of the knowledge of the Four Noble Truths, with their three turns consisting of twelve folds, I professed to the entire world that I had realized full, supreme enlightenment."

Thus, the Buddha declared, as He set the Wheel of *Dhamma* in motion in Isipatana in Benares.

The Noble Eightfold Path

Understanding of the Eightfold Path:

1. **Right Understanding, or the Right View:** This is the understanding of the Four Noble Truths: (a) what suffering, or *Dukkha* is; (b) what causes it; (c) what the cessation of suffering is; and (d) that there is a path leading to the cessation of suffering. One must understand this fully; only then may one wish to cease suffering by giving up craving and eradicating the false "ego," greed, hatred and delusion. Understanding alone is not good enough: it must be put into practice.

2. **Right Thought:** Thoughts can be dangerous, for no one can see them. Thoughts can be evil, brimmed with hatred, envy, greed and wickedness. Thoughts should be neutral, if not kind and benevolent. We should cultivate good and

wholesome thoughts. The practice of giving loving-kindness should keep bad thoughts away and cause good thoughts to stay.

Guard against these thoughts: anger, anxiety, bitterness, despair, fear, hatred, impatience, jealousy, spite, and worries. Treat them like poisons, for in excess, they can cause trouble to the heart, brain, and blood vessels. For the ultimate result of these thoughts is the show of folly, misery and weakness, and could even bring about untimely death.

On the other hand, positive and constructive thoughts – such as appreciation for good acts received (thoughts of gratitude), goodwill to others, kindness, pity, sympathy, and thoughts full of altruistic motives – are to be welcomed and cultivated.

Give loving-kindness to all beings and animal. This is a good benevolent thought and is also one of the perfections that Buddhas have practiced throughout their uncountable rounds of existences.

3. **Right Speech:** It is important to speak with regard to others, as we would wish others to speak of us. Telling lies and tale-telling are not only not right, but they are also degrading to the speaker. One should uphold the basic moral precept, "Abstain from lying!"

Something said to hurt others' feelings and saying things to show off how smart one is are not considered right speech. Such speech may not seem important to the speaker, but at least a show of consideration for others should be discreetly maintained. Moreover, one should not forget the saying, "Wounds caused by words are hard to heal."

Right Speech comes under morality, where one's thoughts, speech, and actions should not be the product of one's likes and dislikes, but of what is right and proper.

4. **Right Action**: Right Thought, Right Speech, and Right Action are not merely qualities a person possesses, but powers one can use. All are meant for the service of good purposes. As rational beings, and with great responsibility, we should take care of our thought, speech and actions and uphold human dignity.

5. **Right Livelihood**: Right livelihood means the kind that harms no one in any way. The right kind of livelihood as advised by Buddha: "Refrain from trading in these – human beings, animals for sale to be slaughtered, selling arms, intoxicants, drugs, and poison." Dishonest ways of trading, cheating in any form, and misleading ways cannot be termed Right Livelihood.

6. **Right Effort or Endeavor:** Right Effort means to cultivate the mind in order to purify it. Effort must be made to do what is good and proper and to avoid evil to purify one's mind. Evil thoughts must be prevented from arising, and at the same time, one must try to develop good, pleasant thoughts and maintain those that have already arisen.

   Evil thoughts are thoughts of attachment, delusion, conceit, aversion, envy, stinginess, and selfishness.

   Good thoughts are thoughts of moral shame, confidence, mindfulness, amity and composure.

7. **Right Mindfulness:** Right mindfulness is constant mindfulness with regard to:
   a) Body (whatever bodily action is doing)
   b) Feelings (whatever sensation; whether pleasant, unpleasant, or neutral)
   c) Thoughts (whatever mental actions)
   d) General Objects (seeing, hearing, etc.)

   We must be conscious of our movements, both physical and mental; nothing should go unnoticed. The practice of attention is a means of learning to know oneself, to know the world we live in, and consequently to acquire right understanding.

8. **Right Concentration:** Right concentration is needed to develop *Samādhi*. This helps one to see things in their true nature and to attain insight. No wisdom can be gained without right concentration. Meditation can be practiced only with concentration. By meditation, we increase and expand our knowledge of wisdom.

All eight of these conditions come under one of the headings of *Sīla* (morality), *Samādhi* (development of the mind, or concentration), or *Paññā* (wisdom). By understanding and practicing, walking diligently along the Eightfold Path, anyone can acquire his goal of self-realization.

Sila (Morality)

From the listing in the Eightfold Path, Right Speech, Right Action and Right Livelihood all come under the heading of *Sīla* (morality). This feature of Buddha's teaching must be understood first.

What is meant by "morality"? Morality means moral principles or rules. What is moral? It is that which concerns itself with the goodness and badness of human character or with the principles of what is right and wrong in conduct. It is based on a person's sense of what is right or just. If a person wishes to be dignified and happy, he must live by upholding moral principles.

A man is judged by his perfect and sound morality, not by the amount of wealth he possesses or the position he holds. A man may be poor, but if he has good moral principles, he would earn the respect of his family, friends and society. Only then could he be a part of a happy, prosperous society. No man is an island, and he thus must learn to live amicably with others. Buddha teaches us that morality should be understood, valued, and practiced because it is necessary to help one lead a good, and happy life. He has set down some basic moral principles.

One might want to know why morality is the bedrock of His teaching, and why *Akālika* is one of the six attributes of the *Dhamma*. *Akālika* means that good results can be enjoyed as soon as the *Dhamma* is practiced, immediately. (This refers directly to the four *Maggas*, which are immediately followed by their respective results, the four *Phalas*.) Can this be true? How? Take the simple example of a mother shouting out to her child, "Child, be good!" The result of being good is happiness. She wants her child to be happy, so she has asked her child to be good. Happiness is enjoyed immediately. (This might be considered a childish example, but it is certainly a simple and straightforward one.)

Taking this as an example, we can be sure that by observing moral principles and being good, we will be happy. That is why the Buddha, the Compassionate

Teacher, has taught us the right way of living: to observe *Sīla*, or morality, so as to be happy. His Teaching is "avoid evil and do what is good and proper!" The moment one is good, one can be happy. It is true. *Akālika* means that, without delay, one can enjoy the benefit of being good. Moral forces govern human behavior, so morality has to be the base from which to begin one's moral and mental development.

Sound moral principles must be observed by anyone who wishes to make a worthwhile, happy and socially acceptable way of life. According to His Teaching, there are Five Basic Precepts to be seriously observed on a daily basis. The higher moral principles are the Eight Precepts, the Nine Precepts and the Ten Precepts. The basic, the most important set of moral principles will be mentioned first.

The Five Basic Precepts:

1. Abstain from Killing:

Life is the most precious, invaluable and priceless thing to every living being. The greatest and most indescribable fear is felt when a living being's life is endangered.

Killing means the destruction of any living being, including animals. To commit violation of this precept, there must be the intention to kill, followed by the effort and action, with the consequence of death. Killing by accident does not infringe on this moral conduct. However, wisdom must be exercised: get the best solution to get rid of insects and pests without killing them.

Hunting or killing for sport or sacrifice is a show of cold indifference to other beings' welfare. It is cruel, inconsiderate and very selfish. Killing and trapping animals to earn a livelihood is inexcusable for there are many ways and means of earning a living.

Causing or recommending euthanasia and abortion must be avoided.

2. Abstain from Stealing:

Anything belonging to someone – money and things, valuable or not – should not be taken without the owner's knowledge or permission, for this amounts to stealing. Shoplifting is stealing, and will always, eventually, be found out. It causes uneasiness and shame, and discredits the doer.

Even if something belonging to somebody is found, it is proper to find the rightful owner and return it.

3. Abstain from Adultery or Sexual Misconduct:

Engaging in sex out of wedlock harms others and creates strong guilt feelings. Adultery often results in quarrels and damaged relationships between husband and wife, often leading to divorce. The breaking up of homes, followed by destabilization of the children's life by playing on the emotion of the children and damaging their sense of security, would be the end result.

Such actions must be deplored and prevented. Children's welfare should be of paramount importance to any parent. All-out effort should be made to set good examples for children.

4. Abstain from Lying:

A man is always judged by his words and deeds. Often one lie leads to another and then another to cover up the first, making one very uncomfortable. Lies can be very damaging to both parties. A little twist in words can sometimes cause great harm and misery. It could even turn out to be a matter of life and death. One should be ashamed to do this evil deed, for fear of the consequences. No lie detector need be used, for lying is always found out, sooner or later. The good reputation as an honest, trustworthy, and respectable person is lost. No man is an island and he needs to live amicably and harmoniously with his family, friends, neighbors and the entire society.

. The conditions necessary to commit this offence are: untruth, the intention to deceive, effort made, and the communication of the matter (falsehood) to the other.

The teaching of the Buddha, "Do no evil!" not only prohibits lying, but it also urges us to not use harsh, course speech, malicious tale-telling (causing disharmony), or even frivolous talk and abusive language. It is good practice to be refined in our thoughts, words, and deeds. This helps to raise one's moral standard.

5. Abstain from Taking Intoxicants and Drugs:

When taken, liquor (strong or weak) and drugs dull one's faculties, resulting in lapse of memory and inactivity. Drinking in excess causes diminished responsibility, resulting in annoyance, quarrels and fights. Fatal accidents are often experienced as the result of excessive drinking. "Don't drink, if you drive!" is the caution given, but little or no attention is paid to it. Drugs users become addicted and, for want of resources by which to get supplies for themselves, they will most likely commit theft, robbery and other serious crimes.

When one is not sober, one is apt to commit any kind of crime, so we must refrain from taking these substances.

The Advantage of Upholding These Five Basic Precepts

By upholding these Five Basic Precepts, one earns a good reputation as a man of high morals. A sense of self-esteem is enjoyed. High regard and respect from society are gained.

At the same time, wealth is conserved since nothing would be unwisely spent. A man of such moral discipline would enjoy a serene conscience and be able to hold his head high in public and command respect.

These conditions are the prerequisites of a happy, healthy, long life. These advantages, which one enjoys by upholding just the Five Basic Moral Precepts, are immediate. (*Akālika*, the results of the *Dhamma* are not delayed.)

Higher Moral Principles

The above mentioned Five Basic Precepts are a set of nominal moral standards that everyone must uphold each day of his life in order to acquire human dignity.

If, however, one wishes to maintain the highest moral standards and gain spiritual development, one should start observing the highest standards without a moment's hesitation. They are the Eight Precepts, The Nine Precepts and the Ten Precepts. The last must be observed strictly by monks and nuns.

The Eight Precepts (*Aṭṭhaṅga Uposatha Sīla*)

1. Not to kill
2. Not to steal
3. To be celibate
4. Not to lie (to not state anything that is untrue)
5. Not to take intoxicants and drugs
6. Not to eat after midday and before dawn of the next day
7. Not to dance, sing, enjoy music, and put on cosmetics
8. Not to use luxurious seats and beds

The Nine Precepts

In the *Dīgha Nikāya*, it is said that almost every virtue (such as unselfishness, loving sympathy and loving-kindness) is included in *Mettā*. Giving out *Mettā* is a virtuous act. Adding this (the practice of giving loving-kindness) to the Eight Precepts makes up the Nine Precepts.

These sets of moral principles are for the lay to observe. The sets of Eight and Nine Precepts are observed on all days of the Buddhist Lent, and on other important days, such as to celebrate the day of the Buddha's birth, His day of enlightenment, and the day of His death, or *Parinibbāna*, at the age of eighty. These three days are observed on the full-moon day of the Indian month of Vesakha, the Vesakha Festival Day.

Ajivaṭṭhamaka Sīla

Even finer points are to be added to the Five Basic Precepts. To "to not tell lies," we should add abstain from tale-bearing, using harsh language, abusive words, and engaging in frivolous talk and nonbeneficial talk. The right way of living also requires one to refrain from earning a wrongful livelihood.

When the Five Precepts are topped off with these finer aspects of morality, we call them the eight vows for *Ajivaṭṭhamaka Sīla*, or the Right Way of Living. (Refer to *Dīgha Nikāya*, the *Cakkavitti Sutta*.)

Moral Codes Appropriate for Different Classes of People

Buddha has given different kinds of *Sīla* (moral codes) appropriate for different class of people. These are:

- *Catupārisuddhi Sīla* to be observed by *Bikkhus* or monks of the Order

- The Ten Precepts (*Sīla*) to be observed by *Sāmaneras* (novices) and some lay people (outlined in chapter, "The Order of Monks")

- The Nine Precepts (*Sīla*) to be observed by lay people, including universal monarchs

- The Eight Precepts to be observed by ordinary lay people on any convenient day (*Aṭṭhaṅga Uposotha Sīla*)

- The Five Precepts are to be observed by all people every-day, to live the *Ajivaṭṭhamaka Sīla* right way of life

How to Promote or Develop Sīla (Morality)

a. *By association with good and wise people.* We must be mindful of this fact ourselves and teach our children to do the same. Remember, parents are their first teachers.

b. *By listening to discourses on* Dhamma.

c. *By believing in* Kamma. This means to understand that good results come from good actions or *Kamma*, and bad results from bad actions and *Kamma*. One's condition in the present existence is the result of the habitual practice of *Sīla* in former existences, and one must firmly believe that if one does only good *Kamma* now, one can hope to benefit from it in the next rebirth.

Hiri Ottappa *or* Lokapāla Dhamma

This is the moral force that governs human behavior.

Hiri means the sense of shame of doing evil deeds, both in thought, word and deed. Everyone is endowed with this sense, but it often goes unrecognized and unused. When a person has this sense, he is disgusted by evil – avoids it, fears it and shuns it – in consideration of his self-respect, his age, his status of learning, heritage, etc. By doing so, for whatever reason, he is trying to maintain his self-respect.

Ottappa, in turn, means the fear of doing evil, and dread of the consequences of that wrong deed. These could entail the dread of self-reproach (very seldom seen or heard), or the censure of others, or penal punishment that may follow. One's knowledge of the prospect of a bad destination in the four nether worlds after death could also be a factor in here.

I have heard elderly people say, *"Hiri Ottappa ta yar ma she-bu!"* to some good-for-nothing people, but did not understand exactly what was meant. (*Hiri Ottappa* means the sense of shame and fear of doing evil; *ta yar* means *Dhamma*; *ma she-bu* means "have not got" in Burmese.) Now, after an extensive reading of His Teaching, I am able to explain that *Hiri Ottappa* means the sense of shame and fear of doing evil deeds and saying evil things, which are the products of evil thoughts.

What Are the Benefits of Observing Sīla (Moral Principles)?

When the sense of shame and fear of doing evil deeds and practicing anti-social behavior is in constant check upon him, a man will be at peace with himself.

Immediate Benefits: Having peace of mind, complete self-satisfaction will be enjoyed. The feeling of happiness and peace of mind will reflect on the face, showing tranquility, serenity and gentleness. There will be a vast improvement in one's physical appearance.

Benefits to Follow: As the result of having peace of mind and happiness, a man can enjoy good health, and long life. Self-esteem is enjoyed, as greater respect has been gained because of his high moral standards. He will be trusted and honored wherever he goes. He will, indeed, be a very affluent and influential man.

He can expect to have a good rebirth; either being reborn in the human world or in the higher abode as a *Deva*. This would be the result of his good habitual *Kamma*, which would pave the way for a good death proximate *Kamma* (*Asanna*), which, in turn, is important at the moment of one's passing away. Moreover, because of his *Sīla* and the good deeds (good *Kamma*) he has accumulated, he would feel safe and happy even at his dying moment.

Illustration

Even kings and universal monarchs on observing the Nine Precepts and practicing *Dhamma* enjoy pleasing results. There are peace, prosperity and happiness in the country when its king observes *Sīla*, fulfilling the duties of a ruler: being just, protecting and safeguarding his subjects, and allowing everyone to depend upon him. They enjoy prosperity, dignity and power, as well as happiness. The life of Emperor Asoka the Great provides a good example: due to his *Sīla*, the Nine Precepts and his reverence and devotion to the Buddha, the *Dhamma* and the Order, he enjoyed fame, power, and fortune. (Read *The Life of the Emperor Asoka the Great and His Entrance into the Doctrine*, or *The History of Buddhism*.)

What Are the Disadvantages of Not Observing Sīla *(Moral Principles)?*

Immediate Disadvantages: Without the sense of shame and fear (*Hiri Ottappa*) and by not upholding the basic moral principles, a man is bound to be in trouble sooner or later. If the offence is serious enough, he will receive capital punishment. "No skeleton can be hidden in a closet;" sooner or later the crime committed will be uncovered. He would have no peace of mind for fear of being found out. Eventually, when the evil deed is discovered, he will experience shame and disgrace for himself, his family, and friends.

Disadvantages to Follow: Should one commit a serious crime, the end result of his behavior would be financial loss and possibly the loss of life and liberty. Such offence takes place when a man is not governed by the moral force of sense of shame and fear of committing evil deeds. By not upholding moral principles, and by living in a manner directed by his likes and dislikes, one invites every possibility of committing evil deeds. When not observing moral principles, one is unaware of his thoughts, actions and words – is unable to control them – and would often be in trouble.

No one can atone for others' sins; logically, "one reaps as one sows." This is true of the Law of Cause and Effect, the Law of *Kamma*. On account of bad actions or *Kamma*, one cannot hope to have a good rebirth and is likely to be reborn in the four nether worlds (in hell, reborn as an animal, etc.) More horrifying and unpleasant consequences need not be elaborated on, for everyone knows that any bad action brings an equally bad, if not worse result.

Summary

- To uphold *Sīla*, or morality, we have to observe Right Speech, Right Action and Right Livelihood.
- We need to discipline ourselves and control our thoughts, words, and deeds so as to avoid evil and do what is good and proper. Moral culture and development are required.
- Be aware of the moral force *Hiri Ottappa* (sense of shame and fear of doing evil). Unlike animals, every human being is endowed with this moral force. Recognize and exercise it.
- Counteract evil thoughts, words and deeds by upholding the basic moral principles, the Five Basic Precepts and the *Ajivaṭṭhamaka Sīla*.
- Practice the good habit of giving out loving-kindness to all beings and animals.
- Always be considerate, kind and understanding.

Samādhi (Mental Development)

When the mind has been disciplined and morality developed by means of upholding *Sīla*, one is refined in his thoughts, words and deeds. He is now well prepared to proceed to the second aspect of Buddha's teachings, *Samādhi*, or mental development.

Right Effort (or Endeavor), Right Mindfulness and Right Concentration come under the heading of *Samādhi*, or mental development.

Right Effort

One needs to control one's mind to avoid evil and unwholesome thoughts not yet arisen, and to overcome those that have arisen, by means of Right Effort, or Right Endeavor.

Try to maintain wholesome thoughts already experienced; work on good thoughts so that they reach a state of perfection. One must make every effort to upgrade his *Samādhi*, and to work diligently and seriously to achieve the stage of perfection.

Wholesome acts such as generosity or charity (*Dāna*), morality (*Sīla*), meditation (*Bhāvanā*), loving-kindness (*Mettā*), and compassion (*Karunā*) should be practiced.

Right Mindfulness

Right Mindfulness means mindfulness of the body, of the feelings, of the mind, and of general objects. With mindfulness, one dwells in the body, contemplating the body's material qualities, mindful of all feelings as they arise, and having clear comprehension of all mental objects. This is Right Mindfulness.

By being conscious of our movements and actions (both physical and mental), nothing goes unnoticed. Any feeling that arises is recognized and dealt with appropriately. By practicing Right Mindfulness, one would have the power to enhance good thoughts and dispel bad ones, and to prevent unwholesome thoughts from rising. In this way, one could powerfully influence his mind and minimize selfish moral values. This practice of perfect attention is a means of learning to know oneself, to know the world in which one lives, and consequently to acquire right understanding.

The purpose of mindfulness:

- To purify beings of mental defilement
- To overcome sorrow and lamentation
- To do away with pain and distress
- To gain insight knowledge
- To realize *Nibbāna*

Right Concentration

Right Concentration means concentration of thought upon a single object. Meditation is to be practiced only after concentration. In concentration, one starts with simple objects, and in meditation one carries the clear conception of that simple object to the higher mental and intellectual level. Concentration steadies our consciousness; in meditation, however, we observe an object clearly and understand its function in conjunction with other things. This increases our knowledge and wisdom.

By meditating, one's thoughts and consciousness are freed of selfish desires, hatred and delusion, and when the mind is thus purified, one will see things as they truly are and wisdom is gained. Meditation is the truly constructive practice of thinking.

Once our meditation is fully developed, it opens the way for intuition and many supernormal powers, which some people call occult powers. We can call them occult, because they are hidden from those who have not developed their mind in this way. These powers may be obtained even before one reaches the state of *Nibbāna*.

In the same way, by practicing meditation sincerely and strenuously, we extend the mental powers we use every day of our life, so we can develop our consciousness, thoughts, words and deeds to a state of purity. Even before attaining the level of perfection in meditation, one can experience peace of mind and happiness. This happens because one has learned to control his mind and use it for the good purpose for which it is intended.

Meditating is like polishing our mind as if it were a mirror that reflects everything that appears before it. Polishing the mirror, developing it by means of meditation, our consciousness and thoughts become clear of selfish desire, hatred and delusion (*Lobha, Dosa* and *Moha*). Everything can then be viewed in its true nature. Thus, when Right Thought is coupled with Right Understanding, *Paññā*, (wisdom), is finally acquired.

Paññā (Wisdom)

Right Understanding

Right Understanding involves a clear understanding of the Four Noble Truths: the first noble truth of *Suffering*, the second noble truth of the *Cause of Suffering*, the third noble truth of the *Cessation of Suffering*, and the fourth noble truth of the *Path Leading to the Cessation of Suffering*.

When Right Understanding presides, one would seek ways and means to free himself from suffering, and begin to think and acquire Right Thought. So, then, what do we mean by Right Thought?

Right Thought

"What, O, *Bhikkhu*, is Right Thought?
Thoughts free from sensuous desire,
Thoughts free from ill will, and
Thoughts free from cruelty.
This is called Right Thought."
(From *Dīgha Nikāya* 1.387)

All thoughts of good deeds are considered factors of renunciation (*Nekkhama-saṅkappa*). These include the practice of generosity, and the renunciation of selfish attachments (such as leaving home into homelessness). Listening to discourses, practicing righteousness, and engaging in *Vipassanā* meditation are all aimed at eliminating attachments and cravings, or sensuous desires.

Thoughts of non-killing, wishing others happiness, and developing loving-kindness, consideration and compassion towards other beings are right thoughts free of ill will and cruelty.

Summing up:

Right Thought: We must think about right things and view people without prejudice. Right Thought must never contain the slightest touch of evil or ill will. Whenever unwholesome thoughts arise, they must be destroyed and shut out forever. We must be sure our thoughts are only kind and good.

Vipassanā meditation directs the mind toward recognizing the reality of mental and material states in their true nature of arising and dissolving. The truth concerning their impermanence, suffering, and insubstantiality or soul-less-ness (*Anicca*, *Dukkha*, and *Anatta*) is ultimately realized.

Role of the *Sanghas* and His Teachings

The Buddha's way of life is a system for cultivating a good, righteous and happy life. Men must develop themselves and work for their own salvation by cultivating good habits of mind and body. Buddha has established a system, developed the path along which He Himself has not only traveled, but has also guided all those choosing to follow the path.

Out of boundless compassion for everyone, He delegated His Order of *Sanghas* to carry on His Teaching. This in itself is a demanding task requiring great responsibility on the part of the *Sanghas*, who, in addition, have to live by the *Vinaya* Rules. As the result of His foresight and perfect administrative skill and planning, Buddha's Order of *Sanghas* has been able to carry out His wishes very effectively, bringing goodwill and peace wherever they go. Although it is now well over

2,500 years since the death of the Buddha, the *Sanghas* carry out their responsibilities with amazing ease, confidence and enthusiasm, in precisely the same manner originally taught by the Buddha. His teachings have reached every corner of the world. Many have come to understand His Teaching and practice *Vipassanā* meditation to relax and enjoy peace of mind

It must be noted that His teachings are all about the right way of living. Only by living in the right manner can one enjoy peace of mind and happiness, and they can do so immediately, in this very life.

The Six Attributes of the Dhamma *(from the* Dhajagga Sutta*)*

1. *Svākkhāta:* The *Dhamma* taught by the Buddha is well expounded. It is the exposition of the Four Noble Truths, for the realization of *Nibbāna.*

2. *Sandgiṭṭhika:* The truths of the *Dhamma* can be actually expe.   ced and comprehended by anyone through adequate practice of insight development.

3. *Akālika:* The result from the practice of *Dhamma* is immediate; without delay, one can benefit, achieving *Magga* and *Phala.*

4. *Ehipassika:* The truth can be tested. It can withstand any investigation. Come and see for yourself.

5. *Opaneyyika*: The *Dhamma* is worthy of being perpetually borne in mind. It is meant for achieving freedom from endless rebirths and their concomitants, such as old age, disease, death, and separation.

6. *Paccattaṁ Veditabba Viññūhi*: The truths of the *Dhamma* can be realized and experienced by the *Ariyas* individually, by their own effort and practice.

Ariyas' *Realization and Experience*

Those who accept the invitation of the Buddha and take up *Vipassanā Bhāvanā*:

- Can perceive by means of *Vipassanā* insights the true nature of mind and body.
- Can perceive the cessation of *Nāma-rūpa* by means of *Magga* and *Phala*.
- Can experience absolute tranquility due to the absence of *Kilesas* (defilements that will be uprooted by having attained the four *Maggas*).

oooooo

THE LATER YEARS OF BUDDHA'S LIFE

Buddha spent all His life expounding the *Dhamma*, organizing the Order of *Bhikkhus* (monks), and giving discourses to and teaching the community of monks, His disciples, and laymen from all walks of life, without reservation and discrimination. He would take any and every opportunity to help anyone who might come His way and ask for help. Every discourse given would be made interesting with similes and examples appropriate to the occasion and to the temperament of the person He was teaching.

All His activities in the early part of His life can be read in the "Canon and Commentaries," up to the point when the essentials of *Dhamma* had been formulated and expounded completely, and the Order of the *Bhikkhus* definitively organized and well established. There is only a narrative of Buddha's last journey in the *Mahāparinibbāna Sutta*. It would be interesting to know about His *Parinibbāna* (death of a Buddha) and how zealously He had worked throughout His life, teaching for over 40 long years.

The Buddha lived with His Order of Monks in several monasteries throughout His life of 45 years of teaching. His concern and constant care were for the welfare of the monks, and He worked enthusiastically.

Good habits were retained and practiced after His enlightenment and continued throughout His long life.

The most compassionate teacher, the Lord Buddha, taught up to the last moment of His life. His last pupil was the wandering ascetic, Subhadda, who came for help at an inappropriate moment when Buddha was giving His final farewell speech to Ānanda.

He taught not only men, but also the deities throughout the entire system of 10,000 worlds. On the first watch of every night, the celestial beings or gods usually took their opportunity to draw near The Blessed One and ask questions on matters unclear to them. He taught the celestial beings and the gods of the seven heavens for 45 years, until He passed away into *Nibbāna* at the age of eighty.

He left behind His doctrine and discipline to take His place. Before He passed away, He declared, "Ānanda, this doctrine and discipline I have taught – and which has been enjoined upon you – shall be your teacher."

"When I am gone, all monks shall not address each other by the title of 'brother.'
A senior priest is to address a junior priest either by his given name or by the title of 'brother.' A junior priest is to address a senior priest with the title of 'Reverend Sir' or 'Venerable.'"[1]

His Daily Routine

After His attainment of enlightenment, His good and profitable habits remained with the Buddha. These were five-fold: His before-breakfast habits, after-breakfast habits, habits of the first watch of the night, habits of the second watch of the night, and habits of the last watch of the night. This is a brief account of the daily duties carried out by the Lord Buddha to the end of his life.

Before-Breakfast Habits

Buddha would rise early in the morning and, out of kindness to His body-servant and for the sake of bodily comfort, rinse His mouth, cleanse His body. He then would sit retired until it was time to go for alms round.

When the time came, He would put on His tunic, girdle, and robes, and taking His bowl, He would enter the village or town for alms. He would either be surrounded by an order of monks or be accompanied by many protégés.

As the Lord of the World entered the village or town, the atmosphere changed: the gentle wind cleared the ground for Him; the clouds not only let fall drops of water to lay the dust on His pathway, but also served as a canopy over Him; other winds brought flowers and scattered them in His path; uneven grounds would be smoothened –

depressions elevated themselves, elevated grounds depressed themselves to make themselves even and pleasant to walk upon; lotus flowers received His treads.

As soon as He set His foot within the city gates, a ray of six different colors – which issued from His body – raced here and there over palaces and pagodas, and decked them, as it were, with a yellow sheen of gold. The sound of music filled the air, accompanied by the songs of birds. By these tokens, the people would know, "The Blessed One has entered the town for alms."

People would come out into the streets, carrying flowers and food to make their offerings. Some would take the monks they had already invited into their house and offer *Swun* (a meal offered to monks). Others would line up the street and wait their turns to make their offerings. The majority of the devotees, however, would ask anxiously, "Reverend Sir, I would like to have ten monks for *Swun* on the next day," or "Could I invite twenty monks for *Swun* next week?" These would be the typical sights and sounds one would see and hear on any day the Buddha went out on His alms collection.

When a fortunate devotee managed to get possession of Buddha's bowl, he invited Him to take a specially prepared seat, showed Him reverence, respectfully and generously placed food in it, and performed the meritorious act of charity. On such a rare occasion, the devotee would feel very happy, contented and proud.

On every occasion after having His meal, with due consideration, the Blessed One would teach the *Dhamma* at the level best suited to those present. The taking of the precepts, either the Five Precepts or the Eight Precepts, would then follow.

The event of offering *Swun* always ended with a merit-sharing ceremony. In this way, the Buddha showed His compassion and kindness to the multitude and also encouraged them to "do good, avoid evil deeds and purify the mind." The Buddha would then rise and return to the monastery.

After-Breakfast Habits

Having completed His before-breakfast duties, Buddha would sit in the perfume chamber until His body-servant informed Him of the presence of the congregation of monks waiting to see Him. He would then rise, take a stand on the landing of the jewel staircase that led to the perfumed room and address the monks:

"Monks, work diligently and persistently to work out your salvation: you are fortunate to be here, and at the most appropriate time. A Buddha appears in the world once after a long, long time, i.e. thousands and thousands of world and life cycles. So take this rare

opportunity to hear the true doctrine and
the advantage of being born a human being."

After His words of encouragement, He would
give them exercises on meditation suited to their many
characters. At the end of these sessions, the monks
would show their obeisance to the Buddha and go to the
places they usually spent the night or the day – some to
the forests, some to the foot of trees, some to the hills,
and some to the Heavens of the Four Kings, to
Vasavatti's heaven.

When everyone has left, Buddha would return
to the perfumed chamber and, if He wished, lie down,
mindful and conscious, on the right side after the manner of a lion. After He had relaxed, He would rise and
gaze over the world. Then, the people of the village or
town near which He might be dwelling would assemble
at the monastery after breakfast, bringing with them
perfumes, flowers and other offerings.

Once the audience had filled the lecture hall,
Buddha would be informed. He would then approach the
hall, take His specially prepared seat, and start teaching
the doctrine appropriate to the time and occasion. When
He perceived the time proper and right, He would dis-
miss the audience. At the end of these sessions, the audience would make obeisance to the Buddha and depart.

These were the after-breakfast duties Buddha would carry out without fail.

First Watch of the Night
(6:00 PM to 10:00 PM)

On the completion of His second round of duties, the Lord Buddha would enter the bathroom and cool Himself with the water made ready by His body-servant, while the servant fetched the Buddha-seat and spread it in the perfume chamber. After He had put on His robes, He would sit for a while, remaining solitary, and meditate.

Soon after His meditation, the monks who had come to see Him for various reasons would be invited in. Some would come to pay homage to the Lord Buddha and wait upon Him, some for sermons, but most of them would bring questions on His Teachings and exercises for meditation. Buddha would grant their desires. In this manner, He would complete the habits for the first watch of the night.

Second Watch of the Night
(10:00 PM to 2:00 AM)

Now, after the Lord Buddha had finished His duties of the first watch of the night and the priests had shown their obeisance and departed, the deities throughout the entire system of 10,000 worlds would seize the opportunity to draw near the Lord and ask Him any questions they might have. The Blessed One would complete the middle, or second watch of the night by answering their questions.

The Last Watch of the Night (2:00 AM to 6:00 AM)

The Buddha had only the last watch of the night to Himself, and this was divided into three parts. In the first, because He would be tired from so much sitting since morning, He would pace up and down in order to free Himelf from discomfort. Then, for the second part, He would enter the perfumed chamber and lie down, as always, on His right side, after the manner of a lion. In the third part, He would rise and gaze over the world with the eye of a Buddha, in order to discover any individual who, under some former Buddha, was keeping precepts or performing other meritorious deeds and might have made an earnest wish.

This was what He always would do on the last watch of the night.

As a Teacher He Shows Perfect Wisdom and Skills

The Buddha taught high spiritual goals for practice by recluses who had taken up homeless lives, and for the *Bhikkhus* and *Bhikkhunis* to practice full-time, leading a life of retirement. He taught them to *Devas* and men with the goal of emancipation. But His aim was one and the same for all: their welfare and happiness, and attainment of liberation from the rounds of rebirth. He would always teach what was appropriate for the occasion and adjust His teaching level to the intelligence level of His students.

In the *Siṅgāla Sutta*, we learn that, to beings of superior and penetrating intellect – such as *Devas* of the *Tavatimsa* realm, or His chief disciples – Buddha would expound on the *Abhidhamma*, the Higher Teachings, which deal with ultimate realities and the analysis of mind and matter into their absolute components, explaining the system of their casual relationships. For guidance and exhortation given to a *Samanera* (a novice monk), the level of the *Dhamma* would be just the basics. He set the level of *Dhamma* to the needs and intellectual capacity of His listeners.

When He was teaching His son, Rāhula, at the age of seven (a novice), He exhorted him on truthfulness and mindfulness, the foundation for building character, and for the development of the faculties of the mind. He gave simple examples and similes in His discourse to impress the young mind of Rāhula. But when Rāhula turned eighteen, Buddha's instructions were on meditation – starting on mindfulness of respiration – leading to insight meditation. He was taught the instability of the five groups of grasping and the importance of maintaining equanimity on all occasions. On the third teaching, as Rāhula had turned twenty-one and completed a year of practice as a *Bhikkhu*, he was given the *Cula Rāhulovada Sutta* and *Majjhima Nikāya* discourse that dealt with the three characteristics of all conditioned existence (impermanence, unsatisfactoriness, insubstantiality). By contemplating these characteristics, Rāhula attained *Arahattaphala*, the highest level of a recluse's life.

Illustration of His Perfect Wisdom and Skills As a Teacher

Although Buddha's effort was directed towards the same ultimate goal, in the discourse, *Siṅgāla Sutta*, *Dīgha Nikāya*, His approach and method of teaching were different.

Once, a wealthy family of Rājagaha had an only son by the name of Siṅgāla. Although his parents were devoted to The Lord Buddha and well established in the Path, he remained completely indifferent to the Teaching and the way of life his parents lead.

Singāla was interested only in the pursuit of wealth, and always believed that the act of charity, caring and sharing was something one should not do after working so hard. He would only see to the increase of his wealth. Thus, he worked hard and saved with never a thought of giving anything away. He thought that taking refuge in the Triple Gem, as his parents had done, served no purpose, and that it was only a drain on the family's wealth.

His parents would explain to him the benefits of listening to the *Dhamma* but Singāla had no interest in such matters and firmly believed that, by associating with the Buddha and the *Sanghas*, he would suffer material loss. He could never agree with his parents on this point, and this made them unhappy. As a dutiful parent, however, wishing the best for his only son, the father never gave up trying to persuade him to hear the *Dhamma* and to perform charitable deeds. Patiently, he kept trying till the last moments of his life.

One day, on his death bed, Singāla's father called Singāla and said to him, "Son, the moment has come, and soon I shall have to leave you and everything behind. You have never made me happy all my life, and this is my last request: at least worship the directions when I am gone." So saying, he passed away.

In that grief-stricken moment, Singāla made up his mind to fulfill his father's dying wish. Early each morning, he would rise, facing first to the East, and with clasped hands would worship in turn in each of the directions: in the East, in the Southeast, in the South, in the Southwest, in the West, in the Northwest, in the North and in the Northeast. He did this round of worshipping regularly, and soon it became a ritual for him.

The father had never given up his persuasion, and had hoped that by asking his son to worship the eight directions, there would be an occasion for either the Lord Buddha or his disciples to see him in the act. As the result of this fortunate event, his son would receive an appropriate explanation for this act – a suitable discourse that would benefit him in some way.

Fortunately, it happened just as Siṅgāla's father had wished, for one day, Siṅgāla was seen performing his peculiar act of worship by the Buddha, who took the opportunity to explain to him the actual meaning of "Worship the eight directions!"

Lord Buddha knew that He would have to give the young householder, Siṅgāla, a discourse on direct practical application, capable of immediate and fruitful use. He stressed social obligations, family responsibilities, and adequate discharge of duty to society founded on individual good conduct and moral purity. Siṅgāla understood Buddha's explanation, as well as the talk on *Dhamma* that Buddha gave later. Buddha stated the social obligation and responsibilities in relationship between parents and children, teacher and pupil, husband and wife, among friends, relatives, and neighbors, and between employers and employees.

He explained that everyone has duties and responsibilities to perform in whichever sector of the society one might live. He explained how the laity should look after the essential needs of the *Bhikkhus* of the Order with loving-kindness and respect, and how the *Bhikkhus*, in turn, should fulfill the spiritual needs of those who are less advanced intellectually and spiritually by teaching the *Dhamma*, leading them away from evil, and helping them along the right path.

Food for Thought

The right way of life as seen, visualized by Buddha and outlined in this *Sutta* for the young householder, Siṅgāla, is as applicable to the way of life we live today as it was during the time of Buddha.

The advice given covers all aspects of human relationship based on loving-kindness, charity, sympathetic understanding and tolerance and should be made a code of conduct for laymen, just as the *Vinaya* Rules are for the *Sanghas*. For whoever practiced these sound moral principles would be at peace not only with himself, but also with everyone else. Goodwill, peace and harmony would prevail in his family, in the society in which he lived and, consequently, in the world at large.

Could such a situation be possible presently? Would it be too difficult to try? What are these social obligations and responsibilities? They will be mentioned in the chapter, "Did You Know?"

Illustration of His Management Skills: How Buddha Managed a Schism Among His Disciples (Refer to the Maha-Vagga*)*

As the number of monks grew in number, little disputes arose in the Order now and again. The new *Vinaya* Rules had to be enforced from time to time to prevent such unhappy situations from repeating. Sometimes, the Buddha would leave them to deal with their own unhappy situation, warning them of the danger of division with the hope they would find a way to end the discord on their own. This did not happen as expected, for quarrels soon lead to hostile words and blows. Buddha had to take immediate action. So, one day, He assembled the monks and related a story. It was about Prince Dirghayu.

The Story of Dirghayu

In former times, there was a powerful king, Brahmadatta of Kasi, who lived at Banares. He went to war against the king of a small kingdom, knowing that he would certainly be victorious. The king of the small kingdom, Dirghati of Kosala, was unable to resist Brahmadatta's huge and strong army, and fled, leaving his kingdom in the hands of his enemy.

Dirghati ran for his life, wandering from place to place. He finally settled down with his queen outside the town of Benares, and there they lived under disguise in a potter's dwelling.

Not long after they had settled, the queen bore him a son whom they called Dirghayu. His father gave Dirghayu a good education. Dirghayu was very intelligent and worked hard, acquiring all the arts required of a prince. He grew up to be a handsome, skillful and wise young man. His parents were quite happy and contented. Although they were happy, there were times when they felt insecure, fearing that King Brahmadatta, would discover their place of hiding and kill all of them. So King Dirghati sent his son away.

Now, it so happened that the barber of King Dirghati lived at Benares, saw Dirghati, and at once recognized him as his former master. Being a greedy and heartless man, he betrayed him to King Brahmadatta. King Brahmadatta ordered that the fugitive king and queen be taken from their place of hiding, bound and executed. The sheriff who took the orders captured them and led them to the palace for execution.

While the captive King Dirghati and Queen were led through the streets, they saw their son return to visit them. Careful not to betray his son, yet anxious to communicate his last advice, King Dirghati cried out, "O, Dirghayu, my son! Don't look long; don't look short. For not by hatred is hatred appeased; hatred is appeased by not-hatred only."

The king and the queen were cruelly executed. Dirghayu wanted to take revenge, but controlled himself. He bought some wine and gave it to the guards to drink. While they were drunk, he took the opportunity to give his parents a proper funeral service. They were laid upon a funeral pyre and burnt with all honors and religious rites. When his duty to his parents was completed, Dirghayu went to the forest and wept to his heart's content.

When King Brahmadatta learned of this, he was terrified, for he thought, "Given the chance, Dirghayu, the son of Dirghati, will take revenge for the death of his parents." Yet he had no idea who Dirghayu was.

Dirghayu cried loud and long, and every time he set his mind to take revenge, the words of his father stopped him. He wiped his tears and went to Benares. Hearing that the royal elephant stable required assistants, he offered his service. Being the best candidate, he was chosen for the position by the master of the stable.

He settled down in his job and tried to be happy. To drown his sorrow, he would sing and play the flute.

One day, the King happened to hear Dirghayu's singing and felt light at heart. So, he inquired who the singer was and ordered the young man before him. On seeing Dirghayu, he was so impressed that he employed him at the royal palace. Not long after, he was given a position of trust, for Dirghayu proved to be responsible, wise, diligent and modest.

One day, it came to pass that the King was out hunting and got separated from the rest of his retinue. Dirghayu, his driver, was the only one with him. The King, completely worn out after the hunt, laid his head on Dirghayu's lap and slept. Now, Dirghayu had the chance for revenge. He thought about it and muttered, "I must act immediately. He has done great injustice. He robbed us of our kingdom and cruelly slew my father and mother. Now he is in my hands." He unsheathed his sword at once.

He was about to strike the sleeping King when his father's last words blasted out in his ears: "Do not look long; do not look short. For not by hatred is hatred appeased; hatred is appeased by not-hatred alone." His trembling hands brought the sword down from mid-air and quickly thrust it into the sheath.

Just then the King became restless and woke up with a fright. Dirghayu asked, "Why do you look frightened, O, King?"

The King replied, "My sleep is always restless because I often dream that young Dirghayu comes upon me with his sword. I had that dream again and woke up in alarm."

Dirghayu took hold of the King's head with one hand and took out his sword with the other and shouted, "I am Dirghayu, the son of King Dirghati, whom you have robbed of his kingdom and slain together with his queen, my mother. Now it is time for my revenge."

The King seeing himself at the mercy of Dirghayu, begged for mercy. In a shrill, shaky voice, he cried, "Grant me my life; grant me my life!"

Dirghayu returned calmly, "How can I grant you your life, O, King, since my life is endangered by you? It is you, O, King, who must grant me my life."

Then the King said, "Well, dear Dirghayu, then, grant me my life, and I grant you, your life."

Thus, King Brahmadatta of Kashi and young Dirghayu granted each other's life and shook hands and swore not to harm each other. The King asked Dirghayu what his father meant by his last words, "Do not look long; do not look short. For not by hatred is hatred appeased; hatred is appeased by not-hatred alone."

Dirghayu said, "O, King, when my father said, 'Do not look long,' he meant, 'Do not let your hatred last long.' By 'Do not look short,' he meant, 'Do not be hasty to fall out with your friends.' By 'For not by hatred is hatred appeased,' he meant, O, King, that you have killed my father and mother, and if I should deprive you of your life, your partisans again would deprive me of my life, and my partisans would deprive them of their lives. Thus, by hatred, hatred would not be appeased.' Now, O, King, you have granted me my life and I have granted you your life. Thus, 'By not-hatred is hatred appeased.'"

The King had to acknowledge Dirghayu's wisdom, for he understood the meaning of his father's words spoken so concisely. He happily kept his word. As soon as he returned from hunting, not only did he return Dirghayu his kingdom, but he also gave his daughter in marriage.

Having recounted this story, the Lord Buddha exclaimed, "O, *Bhikkhus*, if such can be the forbearance and mildness of kings who wield the scepter and bear the sword, so much more, O, *Bhikkhus*, must you so let your light shine before the world, such that you, having embraced the religious life according to so well-taught a doctrine and discipline, are seen to be forbearing and mild. Enough, O, *Bhikkhus!* No altercations, no contentions, no disunion, no quarrels!"

By relating this story, the Buddha clarified the futility and grief-producing character of hatred, and contrasted it with the hopeful promise of renouncing hatred. "Hatred can only be appeased by non-hatred." He also elicited that preferring to end hatred by loving understanding brought about the happy ending for both parties. Try to remember this:

> Hatred does not cease by hatred at any time.
> Hatred ceases by love....'Tis is an eternal law.

> He abused me, he kicked, he defeated me, and he robbed me.
> In those who do not harbor such thoughts, hatred ceases; you'll see.

> The world does not know that, here - we must all come to an end;
> But those who know it, their quarrels, at once - end!

(from the Dhammapada)

Another Story That Reveals an Essential Point in His Teachings: The Story of the Mustard Seed

There was a young lady, Kisa Gotami, reborn into a poverty-stricken home at Savatthi in India. She married and went to live in her husband's house, for that was the custom in those days.

Being from a poor family, she was treated with contempt and so was very unhappy. However, as time went by, she gave birth to a baby boy, and there came a sudden change in her life: she was honored and respected being the mother of a son. Life became bearable for her. She began to get used to the pleasant atmosphere at home, but that was not to last for long.

When the boy got to toddler-age, sorrow struck Kisa Gotami once again: her son died. As all mothers' affection for their children is so great and unfathomable, she kept her son on her hip. She had not the heart to discard him and feared others would cast him away. Taking her son with her, she went from house to house, begging, "Give me medicine for my son! Give me some cure for my son!"

Everyone she encountered, much surprised and amused, replied, "Whoever heard of a cure for the dead?" Some showed her a little sympathy, while others heartlessly clapped their hands and laughed. (Few can identify in feeling with the experience of others who suffer.) She paid no attention and went from door to door, until a certain wise person, in consideration, realized she really needed help, and suggested, "Woman, as for medicine for your son, there is no one who would know, except for that particular Professor, the foremost individual in the world of men and the worlds of gods. Go and ask him. He lives in the neighboring monastery."

Taking this good man's suggestion, she ran as fast as her legs could carry her. When she reached the monastery, she ran straight up, stepped into the outer circle of the congregation, most pathetically sobbing again, and asked, "O, Reverend Lord, give me medicine for my son."

The Buddha saw that she was ready to hear the *Dhamma* and benefit from it and calmed down the sorrowing woman, saying, "You did the right thing to come to me, Gotami. Go and make a round of the whole city, visit every house and bring back some mustard seed from the house in which no one has died!"

Delighted, Gotami quickly muttered, "Very well, O, Lord," and off she went.

She entered the first house and said, "I've been asked by the Professor of men and gods to fetch tiny grains of mustard for medicine for my son."

The householder willingly brought some mustard seed, and Gotami said, "If these are from a house where someone has died, I cannot take them."

"What did you say, Gotami?" The householder looked puzzled. "It's impossible to count the dead!"

"Very well, then I cannot take this particular seed. The Professor said I was to get some mustard seed from a house where no one has ever died. Enough, I'll not take it," said Gotami. And off she went to the next house.

In the same way, she went to the second, third, fourth, and so on, getting nothing but the same answer. Then the thought dawned on her: "In the city, this must be the way! The Buddha must have seen this and had great compassion for the welfare of mankind."

By then, she was quite exhausted, and having come to her senses, she went outside the town to lay her son to rest. Still overcome with emotion, she said, "My dear little son, I thought that you alone were to be overcome with what is called death. But you are not the only one. This has happened to many, countless! It is a law common to mankind." She then cast her son away in the burning-ground.

Still muttering to herself:

"No law of a single house is this–
No law of village, nor of market town.
Of all the worlds of men and gods,
This, only is the law,
That all things are impermanent."

Immediately, she returned to the teacher, and she was asked, "Gotami, did you get the mustard seed?"

She answered calmly, "Done, Reverend Sir, is the business of the mustard seed! I have no need for medicine. Only give me my refuge."

Buddha knew (because of His omniscient knowledge) that, on account of her past accumulated meritorious deeds, Gotami had the spiritual capacity. He used the occasion of her overwhelming sorrow to guide her into an experience in which she would realize her power to identify in feeling with others who also bear sorrow.

This is Buddha's way of helping those who need help, and can be helped. Many such illustrations can be given from His teachings. This one is an appropriate one to show His superb and unmatched skills in the most effective way of teaching. It also reveals two important parts of His doctrine.

The First Part

1. Everything in the phenomenal existence is in change and transitory.
2. Whatever becomes has to pass away, i.e., whatever is born must die. (The only law of all the worlds of men and gods.)
3. Every living creature, like other things, is a compound of elements. Sooner or later, they must dissolve.
4. Thus, a realistic acceptance of death is an essential part of our adjustment to reality. Accept impermanence (*Anicca*)!

The Second Part

Buddha shows the essential connection in His experience and His Teaching between the true acceptance of death and the realization of an outgoing compassion toward all living beings, who (like ourselves) are subject to such ills. We must learn to adjust our feeling and identify with the experience of others.

Result

When one becomes well aware of impermanence, more or less the nature of "I," "my" and "mine" is being put in check. There will be less reserve of pride or conceit in one's heart.

Of all the defilements, pride (*Māna*) is the hardest to uproot. *Sīla* and *Samādhi* alone will not accomplish the work of eradication, the complete and successful uprooting of *Māna*. *Paññā* (wisdom) must be called on. So, work to gain wisdom, or *Paññā*!

(Refer to the *Mahāparinibbāna Sutta*.)

Buddha's *Parinibbāna* and Farewell Address
(Refer to the *Mahāparinibbāna Sutta*)

By the time the Lord Buddha had reached the age of eighty, He felt certain that He had accomplished all He had set out to do, helping both men and gods. He had absolute confidence in His Order of *Sanghas* to continue working to have the *Dhamma* understood, appreciated, practiced and enjoyed – in other words, to have the Light of *Dhamma* shine and flood every dark corner of the universe.

His Desire

As an extraordinary being, a Buddha could extend His life to any length of time He so wished to. As a mortal, however, He is also subject to disease, decay and death. The Lord considered eighty years to be a ripe old age and suddenly desired His *Parinibbāna*.

With that thought in mind, when the Buddha had remained as long as He wished at Ambapali's grove, He went to Beluva, near Vaishali. He requested His brethren to take up abode in the neighborhood of Vaishali, as He intended to enter upon the rainy season in Beluva.

A Thought Came to Him

He was conscious that He would pass away in His eightieth year. Being modest, He decided to take His last breath not in a renowned city like Sāvatthi or Rājagaha – where His activities were centered – but in a distant, unknown hamlet, like Kusinārā. Thus He contemplated the time and place when and whence He desired to take His last breath.

He considered, "It would not be right to pass away without taking leave of the Order of monks, who are My disciples." Then He went out from the monastery and sat down on a seat in the open air. (By that time, His two chief disciples, Venerable Moggallānā and Venerable Sāriputta, had already preceded Him to *Nibbāna*.)

He Addresses Ānanda

"Ānanda, what does the Order expect of me? I have preached the truth without making any distinction between exoteric or esoteric doctrines in respect of truth." ("Exoteric" means shared with all; "esoteric" means taught only to a few.)

"Ānanda, I will lead the brotherhood as the Order is dependent on me. I should then leave instructions.

"I am now grown old, O, Ānanda, and so much advanced in age. My journey is drawing to its close. I have reached the sum of my days: I am turning eighty years of age."

At that moment, Ānanda was either too shocked for words or possessed by the evil one, Māra, and said nothing. Or could it be that, although the suggestion made by the Lord was evident and so clear, Ānanda was incapable of comprehending? He ought to have invited the Buddha to remain for a *Kappa* (the normal life span of 100 years) for the good and happiness of many, and out of compassion for the worlds of deities and men. (*Tathāgatas* have the power to live on to the end of the aeon.)

For the second and third time, Buddha made the same statement. Still Ānanda was silent, so the Buddha went and sat at the foot of a tree not very far away.

Māra Urges the Buddha to Pass into Parinibbāna *and Buddha Limits His Lifespan*

As the Buddha sat alone under a tree, the evil one, Māra approached Him, reminding Him of the time he had spoken to Him on the bank of the Nerajana River immediately after His enlightenment. "I said to you, 'O, Sage, you have done what there was to be done. Now, enter the final *Nibbāna!*' But you replied, 'I shall not enter the final *Nibbāna* until I've given security to the afflicted and made them get rid of their defilements.'" He continued saying, "Now many have been saved and others desire to be saved, and others again will be saved. It is right therefore that you now should enter the final *Nibbāna*."

This time the Buddha replied, "Trouble not, Evil One. In no long time, the *Tathāgata* will attain *Nibbāna*. The *Tathāgata* will attain *Nibbāna* three months from now." This promise convinced Māra that his heart's desire would soon be fulfilled. Happy and contented, he disappeared immediately.

Tathāgatas have the power to live on to the end of the aeon, but the Buddha then entered into a trance with such a force of Yoga, that He gave up the physical life that was still due Him. After that, He continued to live on for a while in a unique way by the might of His miraculous psychic power. He limited His life span.

Just as He limited His life span, there shook a mighty earthquake, and the thunders of heavens burst forth, and in all directions, great fireballs fell from the sky. Thunderbolts flashed unceasingly on all sides, pregnant with fire and accompanied by lightening. There arose the terrible sound of the heavenly drums thundering in the sky.

Ānanda's Earnest Request

When Venerable Ānanda saw the commotion in the world, his hair stood on end and he wondered what it might be. Trembling and losing his habitual serenity, Ānanda rushed to the place where the Buddha remained seated, and asked what the cause of the great earthquake could be. The Buddha replied that the earthquake could be due to one of the Eight Factors; in this case, it was the announcement of the Buddha's passing away. Buddha related how Māra had tempted Him so many times, and repeated the conversation that had just taken place.

Ānanda then seemed to come to his senses and, realizing the seriousness of the event, with tear-filmed-eyes, begged the Buddha to live through the *Kappa*. "O, Exalted One, for the good and happiness of deities and men, out of compassion, vouchsafe, remain during the *Kappa*!

The Buddha's reply was, "Enough, Ānanda, beg not the *Tathāgata*! The time for making such a request is past."

Ānanda besought the Buddha for a second and third time, and each time, he received the same answer.

The Buddha Announces the Date for His Parinibbāna

"The earthquake indicates that I have given up the remaining years of my life due to me. For three months only, reckon from today, will I sustain my life," announced the Lord. There was dead silence as all present hung down their heads in stunned sorrow.

The Buddha then spoke on the fleeting nature of life, and went with Venerable Ānanda to Kutagara Hall at Mahavana where all the *Bhikkhus* in the neighborhood of Vesali were requested to assemble. He then spoke to the assembly, "O, Monks, Let me address you: conditioned things are subject to decay. I exhort you to practice the doctrine I have taught you. Work hard for your own salvation as well as for the good and welfare of deities and men. Have compassion on them! Not long after the *Tathāgata* will attain *Nibbāna*. The *Tathāgata* will attain *Nibbāna* in three months."

Buddha calmly continued to avail Himself of every opportunity to instruct the *Bhikkhus* and to go regularly on His alms rounds when there were no private invitations.

Further Instructions Given

He passed through several towns, and at Bhoganagara, He stayed at the Ānanda shrine and addressed the *Bhikkhus* on the Four Great Authorities (*Mahāpadesa*), the method of determining what is actually the doctrine. This method was a kind of test that should be drawn up by the Community in order to settle doubts about the authorized teaching before the Scriptures were committed to writing. It would show the arrangement of Buddha's teaching not only as *Dhamma* and *Vinaya*, but also as *Matika*, the lists forming the systematic treatment of *Dhamma* known as *Abhidhamma*.

The Buddha continued to instruct His disciples and strictly observed His daily routine until, one day, nearing the end of the three months of His announced *Parinibbāna* day, in the company of a large number of monks, He proceeded to the city of Pava. Here, they stayed at the mango grove of Cunda, a smith by family.

Buddha Accepts His last Invitation to Swun

When Cunda heard that the Buddha was dwelling at the mango grove, he visited Him and listened to a discourse. As was the custom, he invited the Buddha for lunch for the following day.

Early the next morning, the Buddha took His bowl and together with His monks went to Cunda's place. He sat on the prepared seat, and when He was seated, He addressed Cunda as follows, "Serve me, Cunda, with the *Sukaramaddava*[2] that you have prepared, and serve the Order with the other hard and soft food."

Cunda did as he was told. When the meal was over, the Buddha instructed Cunda to bury the remainder of that dish in the ground, as He saw no one, either in the world of *Devas*, *Māras* or *Brahmās* – or amongst other beings, deities or men – who could digest it, other than the *Tathāgata*. Cunda did accordingly, and the Buddha gave a discourse suitable for the occasion and left.

As the result of having eaten that specially prepared meal, the Buddha fell sick with sharp pain and stomach disorder. It was very severe, but the Exalted One, mindful and self-possessed, bore it without complaint, determined to set out to Kusinārā with Ānanda.

The Show of His Wondrous Power

On the way to Kusinārā, the Buddha desired to rest as His sickness worsened. Severe and sharp pain came upon him, even unto death. But mindful and self-possessed, Buddha bore it without complaint and continued on the last leg of His journey. On reaching a pleasant, shady nook, they stopped and rested and the Buddha asked Ānanda for a bowl of water from the stream nearby. Ānanda replied, "My Lord, wait till we get to the river Kakuttha where the water is clear, pleasant, cool and transparent. The water from this stream is muddy and unfit to drink, as many hundred carts pass over it daily."

The Buddha asked for water a second time, and Ānanda gave the same answer. However, when the Buddha asked for water the third time, Ānanda could not refuse. He took a bowl and went to the streamlet. When he reached the steam, to his utter disbelief, he found the water flowing clear, pure and fresh. He was taken completely by surprise and stood transfixed and gaped. "How could that muddy water change within a split second!" He could not help marveling at the wondrous power of the *Tathāgata*. However, he quickly filled the bowl with water and offered it to the Buddha.

This is not the first time the Buddha had shown His wondrous power. There were many astounding and incredible demonstrations on several occasions that have not been mentioned here in my book. But all these shows of miracle and His wondrous power were exhibited not out of pride or for personal gains. As a compassionate Teacher, He has to let others know of His virtues and attributes in order to convince them that He truly was The Awakened One, The Enlightened One, the teacher of men and gods, so that everyone could take advantage of meeting Him and hearing His Teaching, the *Dhamma.*

The Offering of Robes of Gold

On the way, He rested beneath a tree. Not far off was the Kakuttha River, and here He washed and freshened up.

While the Buddha was seated under the tree a young Mallian, named Pukkusa (a disciple of Ālara-Kalama) was passing along the high road from Kusinārā to Pava. He approached the Buddha and, admiring the serenity of the Buddha, made an offer of a pair of robes of gold. The Buddha gave a discourse and at the end of it, Pukkusa showed his obeisance, took leave, and left.

As soon as Pukkusa left, Ānanda placed the robe on the Exalted One, and as soon as it was placed on His body, it lost its splendor, and the color of the skin of the *Tathāgata* became clear and exceedingly bright. The Buddha then told Ānanda that on two occasions the color of the *Tathāgata* became exceeding clear and bright: on the night the *Tathāgata* attained enlightenment, and on the night He attains *Nibbāna.*

Defending Cunda

Even in the hours of great pain, the Buddha did not forget to speak defensively of Cunda. After He had taken His last bath in the river Kakuttha and crossed the river and entered the mango grove, He asked Venerable Cundaka to spread a robe fourfold for Him on which to lie down. He laid Himself down on His right side, with one foot resting on the other, intending to get up at the right time. He told Ānanda that Cunda, the smith might be blamed for the meal he had given. Cunda must have no remorse, for he is not to blame.

He added that there are two offerings that will receive a greater reward than any other offering. They are:

- The offering of food by means of which, once the *Tathāgata* has eaten it, He attains Supreme Enlightenment. That offering was made to Him by the lady Sujata.
- The other is the offering of food by means of which, once the *Tathāgata* has eaten it, He passes away into supreme *Nibbāna*. This offering has been made by Cunda.

Merits acquired by Sujata and Cunda are tendency to long life, to good birth, to happiness, to fame, to heaven, to lordship.

(From the translation *Mahā-Parinibbāna-Sutta,* v and vi of *Dīgha Nikāya*)

Then the Buddha addressed the venerable Ānanda: "Let us go hence, Ānanda, to the further bank of the Hirannavati River, and to the city of Kusinārā and the sala-tree grove of the Mallas."

Then the Blessed One, accompanied by a large congregation of *Bhikkhus,* drew near to the further bank of the Hirannavati River and to the city of Kusinārā and the sala-tree grove. By the time He reached there, He was exhausted and requested Ānanda to prepare a couch with its head to the north between the twin sala-trees, and then laid Himself down on His right side with one leg resting on the other, mindful and self-possessed.

A Spectacular Scene Under the Twin Sala-Tree

Now the twin sala-trees were in full bloom with flowers out of season, and the body of the Buddha was covered with flowers fallen out of reverence. The Divine Mandarava flowers, too, and the divine sandalwood powder came falling from the sky, and all these covered the Buddha's body out of reverence. Divine music and singing sounded through the air in His honor. But the Buddha said it was not merely thus that He was honored. "The monk, nun, layman or laywoman who continually fulfills all the greater and lesser duties, who is correct in life and acts according to the doctrines – it is he or she who rightly honors, respects, and reverences the *Tathāgata* most highly," stated the Buddha.

At that moment, Venerable Upavāna, the constant attendant of the Buddha, stood in front, fanning Him. Curtly, the Buddha asked him to step aside. This was a very unusual and uncalled for act of the Buddha, so Ānanda had to inquire what had displeased the Blessed One. The Buddha explained that the *Devas* had assembled in large numbers to see the *Tathāgata* and were displeased because Upavāna stood in front, obstructing their view.

The Buddha Gives Accounts of the Vivid Scene

"Ānanda, almost all the deities throughout ten worlds have come to behold the *Tathāgata*. Over the whole expanse of twelve leagues about the city Kusinārā and the sala-tree grove, Upavattana of the Mallas, there is not a spot left unfilled by powerful deities. They are angry, saying, 'From far we have come to behold the *Tathāgata*, for but seldom, and on rare occasions, does a *Tathāgata*, the Supreme Buddha, arise in the world, and now, tonight, in the last watch, the *Tathāgata* will pass into *Nibbāna*. But the powerful priest

stands in front of The Blessed One, conceal-
ing Him, and we have not the chance to see
Him.' Thus are they angered." (Buddha
often refers to Himself as "the *Tathāgata*.")

"What are the deities you have perceived doing,
Reverend Sir?" Ānanda inquired eagerly.

"Some of the deities are in the air with their
mind engrossed by earthly things, and they
let fly their hair, stretch out their arms, cry
aloud and fall headlong to the ground and
roll to and fro, saying, 'All too soon the
Blessed One passes into *Nibbāna*; all too
soon will the Light of the World vanish
from sight.'

"Some deities on the earth, engrossed in
earthly things, let fly their hair and in
anguish roll to and fro on the ground, crying
out, 'All too soon the Happy One passes into
Nibbāna; all too soon The Light of the
World will vanish.'

"But those deities who are mindful and conscious and free from passion bear it patiently, calmly, saying, 'Transitory are all things.
How is it possible for whatever has been
born, has come into being, and is organized
and perishable, to not perish?'"

Ānanda Asks Further Instructions

Ānanda then asked for instructions on several matters. As it was the custom for *Bhikkhus* to come see and attend the Buddha after the rainy retreats, he wanted to know what was to be done after the Blessed One's *Parinibbāna*.

The Buddha suggested the four places worthy to be seen by disciples and devotees:

- The place of birth of the Buddha (Lumbinī Park on the borders of India and Nepal)
- The place where He attained Enlightenment (Buddha Gayā)
- The place where He turned the Wheel of *Dhamma*, gave the first sermon (Deer Park in Isipatana near Benares, modern Saranath)
- The place where He attained *Nibbāna* (Kusinārā, modern Kasia)

Ānanda asked how the last rites were to be carried out, and the Buddha told him that the funeral rites for the Buddha should be the same as that of Universal Monarch. The body of a Universal Monarch should be wrapped up in corded cotton wool and finest cloth, 500 successive layers of both kinds. The body should then be placed in an oil vessel and covered and closed up with another oil vessel. A funeral pyre of all kinds of perfume should then be built, and the body burnt.

The Buddha also mentioned the four persons in whose memory a *Stupa* should be erected: the Buddha, a Pacceka Buddha, a disciple of the Buddha, and a Universal Monarch.

Suddenly, Ānanda was overcome by grief and instantly had to run into the monastery. Holding the lintel, he sobbed. "Alas, I am a learner with still much to do, and my teacher is on the point of gaining *Nibbāna*." The Buddha sent for him and consoled him by telling him how all things must change. He mentioned explicitly how he had attended to Him sincerely, single mindedly, with unbounded love in deed, word and thought. He exhorted him to strive earnestly. He also went on to point out, at great length, the four wonderful and marvelous qualities of Ānanda to the monks. Finally, He encouraged him, "Grieve not, Ānanda! You have acquired much merit. Exert yourself, and soon you will be free from all depravity!"

Thus consoled, Ānanda felt a little at ease and requested the Buddha not to pass into *Nibbāna* in this wattle-and-daub town, and suggested other great cities – Campā, Rājagaha, Savatthi, Kosambi and Benares – in which He might pass into *Nibbāna*. He pointed out that many wealthy men and devotees living in every one of those great cities would feel honored to perform the funeral rites for Him.

The Buddha replied,

"O, Ānanda, say not so! Say not so, that this town is a wattle-and daub town, a town of the jungle, a branch village. There once lived a king called Sudassana the Great, who was a Universal Monarch, a virtuous king of justice, a victorious ruler of four quarters of the earth, possessing a secure domain over his territory and owning the Seven Precious Gems (the wheel of empire, the elephant, the horse, the gem, the empress, the treasurer, and the Crown Prince). This city Kusinārā, Ānanda, was the capital of King Sudassana the Great, and had then the name of Kusāvatī. It was prosperous, and flourishing, populous and thronging with people, and well provided with food. The noise of the city included the noise of people crying, 'Eat, ye, and drink!' This showed how prosperous it was.

"Go, Ānanda, enter the city Kusinārā, and announce to the Kusinārā-*Mallas*: 'Tonight, O, ye *Vāseṭṭhas*, in the last watch, the *Tathāgata* will pass into *Nibbāna*. Suffer not afterwards to feel remorse, saying, 'The *Tathāgata* passed into *Nibbāna* while in our borders, but we did not avail ourselves of the opportunity of being present at the last moments of the *Tathāgata*.'"

"Yes, Reverend Sir," said Venerable Ānanda and he went to Kusinārā with another member of the Order.

It so happened that, at that precise time, the Kusinārā-*Mallas* were assembled together in the city hall on some matters of business. Venerable Ānanda drew near the city hall and made the announcement: "Tonight, O, ye *Vāseṭṭhas*, in the last watch, the *Tathāgata* will pass into *Nibbana*. Suffer not afterwards to feel remorse, saying, 'The *Tathāgata* passed into *Nibbāna* while in our borders, but we did not avail ourselves of the opportunity of being present at the last moments of the *Tathāgata*.'"

On hearing this announcement, everyone was overwhelmed by grief and sorrow. They stretched out their arms, let fly their hair, and cried loud and long, "All too soon will the Lord pass into *Nibbāna*. All too soon will the Light of the World vanish from sight." Instantly, everyone, with his entire family, headed straight for the sala-tree grove and to where Venerable Ānanda was. The Venerable Ānanda marshaled the *Mallas* by families, making them show their reverence to the Blessed One, and succeeded in giving turns to all the Kusinārā-*Mallas* to do obeisance before the first watch of the night.

The Last Pupil of the Compassionate Teacher

At that time of grief and sorrow, a wandering ascetic, Subhadda, was in the neighborhood and heard the news that the monk Gotama would attain *Parinibbāna* in the last watch of the night. He had some question that he intended to ask the Buddha, so he hastily drew near the sala-grove and went to where Venerable Ānanda was and made an earnest request.

"Venerable Ānanda, give me the opportunity to see the monk Gotama, for I have some doubts in my mind and I hope to be relieved of them if I can see Him," said Subhadda. "Seldom does a Supreme Buddha arise in the world, and this is His last night."

"Enough of that, Brother Subhadda. Don't trouble the Blessed One. He is weary," replied Ānanda.

But Subhadda continued to plead again and again, and the Blessed One overheard the conversation. Being a very compassionate teacher, not even considering His serious illness, and suffering, the Buddha called out feebly, " Ānanda, let Subhadda have the opportunity to behold the *Tathāgata*. What he shall ask of me will be for the sake of information and not for the sake of troubling me. And he will quickly understand my answers to his questions."

Ānanda was obliged to say, "You may come, Brother Subhadda; the Blessed One grants you an audience."

Then Subhadda, the wandering ascetic, drew near the Blessed One and exchanged greetings of friendship and civility, and sat down respectfully on one side. When he was seated, he spoke to the Buddha: "Gotama, all those monks and *Brahmans* who possess a large following and crowds of hearers and disciples, and who are distinguished, renowned leaders of sects, and highly esteemed by multitudes – to wit, Purana Kassapa, Makkhi Gosala, Ajita Kesakambali, Pakudha Kaccayana, etc. (all those who claim they have discovered the truth) – have they really discovered the truth as they have maintained, or have they not? Or have some of them done so, and others not?"

"Enough, O, Subhadda! Let us have the question: 'Have they all done as they maintained, discovered the truth, or have they not? Or have some of them done so and others not?' The doctrine will I teach you, Subhadda. Listen to me, and pay strict attention, and I will speak."

"Yes, Reverend Sir," said Subhadda, the wandering ascetic, in assent, and the Blessed One spoke as follows: "Subhadda, in whatever doctrine and discipline the Noble Eightfold Path is not found, no monk of the first degree, or monk of the second degree, or monk of the third degree, or monk of the fourth degree can be found.

And in whatever doctrine and discipline the Noble Eightfold Path is found, O, Subhadda, therein also are found the monk of the first degree, and the monk of the second degree, and the monk of the third degree, and the monk of fourth degree."

To cut short the Compassionate Teacher's method of teaching (step-by-step with similes), and to mention only the end result, the aged wandering ascetic, an adherent of another sect, fully understood and confirmed that he had no doubts, by uttering, "Oh, wonderful it is, Reverend Sir! As if one were to set up that which was overturned, or were to disclose that which was hidden, or were to point out the way to a lost traveler, the Blessed One has expounded the Doctrine, in so many different ways. Reverend Sir! may I be allowed to take refuge, and retire from the world under the Blessed One? May I receive ordination?"

At his request, even though there was a required probation period of four months before anyone can be received into the Order, the Lord gave Subhadda the privilege to be ordained right away and conferred on him the priestly ordination. Accordingly, Subhadda was admitted as the last disciple of the Buddha, and not long after, he became an *Arahat.*

This is the utterance of the Buddha...

"What time my age was twenty-nine,
Subhadda.
I left the world to seek the summum
bonum.
Now fifty years and more have passed,
Subhadda,
Since I renounced the world and
lived ascetic
Within the Doctrine's pale, that rule
of conduct
Outside of which no genuine
monks exist."

The Last Words of the Buddha

When the Buddha had completed His final and last session of teaching, He considered the time, and called the assembly of 500 monks and gave instructions on what was to be the relationship between the younger and elder monks. He also spoke on some *Vinaya* Rules.

Next, He declared that He has left no successor: "Ānanda, the Doctrine and Rules conjoined by you will be your teacher."

In His final address, Buddha said, "It may be, O, *Bhikkhus*, that some of you have a doubt or perplexity or confusion with regard to the respect of the Buddha, or the Doctrine, or the Order, or the Path, or the course of conduct. Ask any questions now, O, *Bhikkhus*, and suffer not that afterwards ye feel remorse, saying, 'Our teacher was present with us, but we failed to ask him all our questions.'"

The monks were silent. Buddha repeated His question the second time and the third time. "O, Monks, ask any questions, and don't regret later!"

"It may be, O, Monks, that it is out of respect to the Teacher that ye ask no questions. Then let each one speak to his friend."

When thus said, the monks were still silent.

Then the venerable Ānanda spoke to the Blessed One as follows: "It is wonderful, Reverend Sir. It is marvelous, Reverend Sir. I have faith to believe that in this congregation of monks not a single priest has a doubt or confusion respecting either the Buddha, or the Doctrine, or the Order, or the Path, or the course of conduct."

Then the Blessed One addressed the monks again. "And, now, O, Monks, I take leave of you. All the constituents of being are transitory. Work out your salvation with diligence, I exhort you. Strive with earnestness. '*Vayadhammā Saṁkhārā, Appamādena Sampādetha.*'" These were His last words.

The Buddha Attains Parinibbāna

Then the Buddha entered into the first Ecstasy (*Jhāna*), up to second, third, fourth, and into the five stages of attainments until He reached the stage of "cessation of Perceptions and Sensations" (*Sannavedayita-Nirodha*).

At that moment, Venerable Ānanda, who had yet not developed the Divine Eye, called out to Venerable Anuruddha, "O, Venerable Anuruddha, the Exalted One has passed away." Venerable Anuruddha replied, "Nay, Brother, the Blessed One has not passed into *Nibbāna*; He has arrived only to the cessation of Perceptions and Sensations."

Then the Buddha passed back through the stages of Ecstasy (*Jhāna*) to the first *Jhāna*, and back again, by stages, reaching to the highest, and from there, He attained *Nibbāna*.

At that moment, there arose a mighty earthquake and terrifying thunder. There was lamentation from those who were not free from passion. Venerable Anuruddha consoled them with the Buddha's teaching: "There are change and separation from all pleasant things, and everything having an origin must decay."

Buddha's Final Farewell Speech

"Everything comes to an end, though it may last for an aeon.
The hour of parting is bound to come in the end.

"Now, I've done what I could do for myself and for others.
To stay here would from now on be without purpose.

"I've disciplined, in heavens and on the earth,
All those whom I could discipline, and set them in stream.

"Hereafter, this My *Dhamma*, O, Monks, shall abide for generations and generations among living beings.

"Therefore recognize the True Nature of the Living World; and do not be anxious, for separation cannot possibly be avoided.

"Recognize that all that lives is subject to this law.
And STRIVE from today onwards that it shall be thus no more!

"When the light of gnosis has dispelled the darkness of ignorance,
When all existences have been seen as without substance,
Peace ensues when life draws to an end:
Which seems to cure a long sickness at last.

"Everything, whether stationary or movable, is bound to perish in the end.

Be ye, therefore, mindful and vigilant!

"The time for my entry into *Nibbāna* has now arrived!"

His last words were, "*Vayadhammā Saṁkhārā, Appamādena Sampādetha!*"

The Buddha, the Best of Sages, supreme in the mastery of trances, uttered His final farewell and entered into the four stages of ecstasy (*Jhāna*) and the last, from where He finally attained *Nibbāna*.

oooooo

Footnotes

1 From *Sumangala-Vilasini* (I-45) commentary on the *Dīgha Nikāya*.

2 According to the explanation given in the commentary, *Sukaramaddava* is a kind of meat dish prepared with the best ingredients of the best and greatest flavor obtained in the four great continents. The *Devas* imparted their richness to the dish about to be presented to the Buddha.

DID YOU KNOW?

The Body *(as Translated from* Visuddhi-Magga, *Chapter 1)*

"The body of a man of medium size:

It consists of an exceedingly fine and impalpable power of the earthly element.

This is prevented from dispersing and scattering around as it is held by the watery element.

It is preserved by the fiery element.

It is propped up by the windy element.

All these elements are masquerades in many different disguises, such as various members, organs of women and men.

The watery element is of juicy nature and serves to hold the body together.

It is prevented from trickling or flowing away as it rests on the earthly element.

It is preserved by the fiery element and propped up by the windy element –

Thus prevented from trickling over – and gives the body its plumpness and leanness.

The fiery element has heat as its characteristic and has a vapor nature, digests what is eaten or drunk. This fiery element rests on the earthly element, which is held together by the watery element and again propped up by the windy element, and cooks the body and gives it its beauty of complexion. And the body thus cooked is kept free from decay.

The windy element is characterized by its activity and its ability to prop up. Thus propped, the body can stand upright. And when impelled by the windy element, the body can perform its four functions – walking, standing, sitting or lying down – draw in and stretch its arms, or move its hands and its feet."

What Is the Body Made of? (as Translated from Visuddhi-Magga, Chapter 1)

"A body is a collection of 300 bones, framed into a whole by means of 180 joints held together by means of 900 tendons overlaid by 900 muscles, and it has an outside envelop of moist cuticle (skin at the base of a finger-nail or toe-nail) covered by an epidermis full of pores, through which there is an incessant oozing or trickling (as if from a kettle of fat).

Nine apertures are always discharging matter: the eyes, ears, nostrils and mouth, and the two lower orifices of the body.

From the mouth issue bile, phlegm and blood; from the two lower orifices – feces and urine.

From 99,000 pores of the skin, an unclean sweat exudes (to be thrust or squeezed out).

Well, that is what our body is made of!

When the body is impelled by the windy element, it performs the four functions – walking, standing, sitting or lying down – draws or stretches out its arms, or moves its hands and its feet.

The human body is like a machine made of the four elements, resembling a puppet. In actual sense, it deceives people with its femininity/masculinity, etc.

The four elements are:

Padawee – "earth," *Tay-zaw* – "fiery, heat," *Ar-baw* – "windy," *War-yaw* – "watery."

Do you still wonder when people say, "Beauty is only skin-deep"?

Taking Refuge in the "Triple Gem" or the "Three Jewels"

What do we mean by saying, "Taking Refuge in the Triple Gem, or Three Jewels"?

When one says, "I take my refuge in the Buddha; I take my refuge in the *Dhamma*; I take my refuge in the *Sanghas*," it is in context that one's dedication is to these three jewels. By "Triple Gem," or the "Three Jewels," one refers to the Buddha, His Doctrine and His Order of *Sanghas*.

Why the refuge in them?

"To the Buddha," who first achieved enlightenment and has shown the path to the peace and joy of *Nibbāna*, or *Nirvāna* – upon Him one looks gratefully as a beloved Master, a respected and trusted friend.

"To the *Dhamma*" means to the essential doctrine about suffering, or *Dukkha*, its cause and cure, as taught by the Master, which has been handed down for the disciples' guidance – at first by word of mouth – perpetuated and preserved. It now has been written down and is embodied in the canon of the "Three Baskets," which has been translated into many languages.

"To the *Sanghas*" denotes the community of monks established by the Buddha and given its regulation during His lifetime. It is now the representation on earth of His aggressive zeal in pursuit of the conditions of true wellbeing, and the custodian of His teachings, the *Dhamma*. The *Sanghas* are straight, upright and correct in their behavior, thus worthy of offerings, worthy of hospitality, worthy of gifts, worthy of respectful salutation, and they are looked upon as the world's peerless field of merit. This means that, because of these virtues of the *Sanghas*, they can be regarded as fields where seeds of merit can be sown and gained. It is a meritorious act to make offerings of the essentials to them. Even if one has no wish to embark on a homeless life, he will look to the monks as a spiritual guide since they embody more of the ideal of resolute self-purification. They are respected and trusted.

By taking refuge in the Three Jewels and aided by his good moral conduct with an accumulation of merit gained from charitable deeds, a person can hope to be reborn in a form less handicapped by torpor and worldliness than the form he is in at present (i.e., one will have a good rebirth.)

First and foremost, homage is paid to the Triple Gem by saying, "*Buddhaṁ Pujēmi, Dhammaṁ Pujēmi, Sanghaṁ Pujēmi.*"

The taking of refuge in the Triple Gem then follows:

Buddhaṁ Saranaṁ Gacchāmi
Dhammaṁ Saranaṁ Gacchāmi
Sanghaṁ Saranaṁ Gacchāmi

("I go to the Buddha, the Teaching, and the noble Order as my refuge.")

This little verse is repeated again, for the second time, adding, *Dutiyumpi*:

Dutiyumpi Buddhaṁ Saranaṁ Gacchāmi
Dutiyumpi Dhammaṁ Saranaṁ Gacchāmi
Dutiyumpi Sanghaṁ Saranaṁ Gacchāmi

("For the second time, I go to the Buddha, the Teaching and the noble Order as my refuge.")

For the third time, the verse is said in the above manner, this time with *Tatiyampi* ("thirdly") placing *Dutiyumpi*:

Tatiyampi Buddhaṁ Saranaṁ Gacchāmi
Tatiyampi Dhammaṁ Saranaṁ Gacchāmi
Tatiyampi Sanghaṁ Saranaṁ Gacchāmi

("For the third time, I go to the Buddha, the Teaching and the noble Order as my refuge.")

This is how respect is shown to the Buddha, His Teachings and His Order of Monks. He is deeply respected as The Great Compassionate Teacher.

Social Principles (Obligations and Duties)

In one of the discourses given by Buddha is the *Siṅgāla Sutta*. As always, Buddha adapted His Teaching in such a manner as to make the young householder, Siṅgāla, understand His discourse and apply it in the course of his daily life.

When Buddha was staying near *Rājagaha* in the Bamboo Wood at the Squirrels' Feeding Ground, He went out one morning on His usual rounds. As He entered the town, He saw Siṅgāla worshipping several quarters of earth and sky.

He inquired; "Why do you rise early and worship in this manner, young Siṅgāla?" Siṅgāla replied, "Sir, my father's dying wish was for me to worship the eight directions and this is what I do every morning."

Buddha told him that it was not in the religion of an *Ariya* (a noble one) to worship the directions in the way he understood and did. So Siṅgāla asked, "It would be an excellent thing, Sir, if the Exalted One were to instruct me on how to worship the directions according to the doctrine."

The Lord Buddha decided to take this chance to talk about the *Dhamma*, and said, "Young householder Siṅgāla, listen, I will speak."

Then He began His discussion.

He discussed matters such as how one should be on guard against various vices and temptations with which a young lay would certainly be overwhelmed. Siṅgāla took everything in and seemed very interested, so He continued to explain further: "Now, how does an *Ariyan* disciple serve the Six Quarters?"

The Six Quarters

"The following should be looked upon as the Six Quarters: parents as the **East**, teachers as the **South**, wife and children as the **West**, friends and companions as the **North**, servants and work people as *Nadir* (lowest point opposite to zenith), religious teachers and *Brahmins* as Zenith." (*Brahmins* were those at the top of the caste system in India in those days.)

East Quarter

"In five ways a child must attend to his parents. Once supported by them (parents), he will now be their support; he will perform his duties and obligations due to them in return for what they have done for him; he will keep up the lineage and tradition of the family and make himself worthy of his inheritance and heritage.

"In five ways the parents must minister to their children: "Show their love to them; encourage and teach them to be virtuous and restrain them from vice; train them to a profession, i.e., give them sound, good education; contract a suitable marriage for the child; and, in due time, give them their inheritance."

South Quarter

"In five ways should pupils attend to their teachers: respect them, and out of respect, rise from their seat in salutation as the teacher comes in; wait upon them by personal services; by eagerness to learn; by attention when receiving their lessons.

"In return, the teachers minister to their pupils' needs: love their pupils; train them in whatever they have been well trained in; instruct them in the tradition and knowledge of every art; speak well of them among their friends and companions; and provide for the pupils' safety from dangers that might come from any quarter."

West Quarter

"A husband will attend to his wife in this way: by respect; by courtesy; by faithfulness; by hand-ing over authority to her; and by providing her with ornaments (gold and jewelry).

"A wife must attend her husband in this way: love him by performing her duties, being hospitable to kin of both; by faithfulness; by watching over and keeping safe the goods he brings home, i.e., his earnings; and by being industrious and exercising her skills in the functioning of all her duties."

North Quarter

"The North quarter represents how the clansman associates with his friends, and he will do so in these five ways: by generosity, courtesy, and benevolence; by treating them as he treats himself; and by being as good as his words.

"In return, his friends and family associate with the clansman in five ways: they will love him; they will protect him when he is off guard, and on each and every occasion guard his property; they will be a refuge in danger; they will not forsake him in his troubles; and they will show consideration for his family."

Nadir Sector

"With regard to the nadir section, one can be protected and made safe and secure by the manner in which the master ministers to his servants and employees. This would be by assigning work according to their strength and ability; by supplying them with food and wages; by attending to them in sickness; by sharing with them delicacies; and by granting them leave at times." (Caring, sharing and being considerate.)

"In return, servants and employees will treat their masters or employers with love. They will rise early before their master, and go to bed after him; they are content with what is given to them; they are loyal to their master, conscientious and hard working, performing their duties well; and, at the same time, they carry about his praise and good fame." (Thus, by being sincere and thoughtful, understanding and respectful, there would be no backbiting or tale-bearing by the servants or employees.)

Zenith Sector

"Worshipping the zenith, the sky, means the way a clansman (layman) associates with recluses and *Brahmins*. This is done by show of affection in act and speech and mind, by keeping open house to them, and by supplying them with essential needs (food, medicine, clothing and dwelling).

"The recluses and *Brahmins* (*Bhikkhus* and spiritual teachers) will, in return, show their love for the clansman in six ways: they will restrain him from doing evil; they will exhort him to do what is good; they will have kind thoughts of him; they will teach him what he has not heard (the truth or *Dhamma*); they will correct or purify what he has heard; and they will reveal to him the way to *Nibbāna*, to peace and happiness.

"Thus by him the zenith is protected and made safe and secure." (Worshipping in the direction of the sky)

When the Buddha ended His explanation of what was meant by "worshipping the directions" as instructed by his father, Siṅgāla said, "The truth has been manifested by the Exalted One in many ways, and I, even I, go to Him, the *Dhamma* and the Order as my refuge. May the Blessed One receive me as His lay-disciple." (He emphasized "even I" because, however much his parents had wanted him to, he had never before had a belief in taking refuge in the Triple Gem.)

Finally, when Siṅgāla accepted Buddha's explanation with rapt attention and took refuge in the Triple Gem, his deceased father's life-long wish was fulfilled. This, of course showed how faithfully and persistently his father had carried out his parental duties (teach them to be virtuous, and restrain them from vices).

Respect for the Five

Buddha teaches us that human beings should be guided by both moral and social principles. Being a member of the human society, everyone has duties and obligations to perform. (Here again, Buddha explains the need for the right way of living.)

Another emphasis He placed was on respect, not just formal respect that should be shown for another human being, but deep profound respect for "the Five." Which Five? The Buddha, His Doctrine, His Order of monks, the parents and teachers: *Anan-daw Anan-da Nga Par* in Burmese. This is to be understood as having respect for the Triple Gem and having respect for the parents and teachers who would guide and teach, enabling one to live a purposeful life. Remember, parents are your first teachers.

In concluding this discussion of social principles, it would be proper to add that Buddha's Teaching had for a millennium been a powerful force in molding the religious, moral, artistic, educational, and social life of India. By the end of that period it had declined, and in another 500 years, it had practically disappeared from the land of its birth. But it continued to grow far and wide throughout northern and eastern Asia. In the west and northwest, it was checked by the surging tide of Islam. The culture, however – especially, that of social duties and responsibilities as explained to Siṅgāla by the Lord Buddha – is seen to be maintained by many in various parts of Asia where the Buddha's Teaching is still practiced to this day.

Destinations

The Lord Buddha explained that there are 31 planes, *Bhumis*, or abodes where one can go to on rebirth:

- The 20 abodes of *Brahmās* (sublime beings);
- The six abodes of the *Deva* or *Devatas* or celestial beings, referred to as "heavens";
- The human plane, or human world; and, right below this,
- The four nether planes for doers of evil deeds, and sinners.

The Nether Planes

The nether planes consist of hell, a realm for beings of the animal kingdom, a realm for ghosts, and another for miserable forms of existence that make their appearance through actions born of greed, hatred, and delusion.

Life in hell is a very unimaginably and indescribably painful, inexpressible state of woeful, suffering existence, but this does not imply eternal damnation. (The word "hell" itself should scare everyone.) Such a painful form of existence is the lawful result or consequence of evil deeds, and will come to an end when the causal forces conditioning it are exhausted. The more severe and serious an evil deed is, the longer is the time of stay in hell and, to be sure, the greater the degree and intensity of suffering.

Deeds such as suicide, patricide, matricide, genocide, harming of a Buddha and the Order are very serious, and the offender will definitely find his way to hell, for a long, long stay (sometimes throughout many world cycles). He will also still be accompanied by *Vipāka* in many existences following his release from hell. (*Vipāka* is the result of a bad *Kamma* that generally continues to take place even after several life cycles of committing that bad *Kamma*.) It must be a great relief, however, to know that anyone who is born into such woeful existences has good causes of the past and may gain a happier rebirth should those good causes have a chance to operate.

The Brahmā *Planes (the Abode of Sublime Beings)*

These realms are attainable by beings that have performed meritorious deeds and developed meditative absorption, or *Jhānas*.

As mentioned in Buddhist cosmology, *Brahmās* are the highest beings in order of beings. We call them sublime beings because they are the most exalted, noble and lofty of beings. They live happily and peacefully by upholding moral principles, performing good deeds, and practicing their four sublime virtues.

The *Brahmā* worlds consist of a total of 20 abodes. These sublime beings are not born but appear in these abodes by direct transformation into form and formless *Brahmās*. Their life span, which is very long, is reckoned in terms of world cycles and so, in terms of human years, is uncountable.

It was a *Brahmā* who appeared before the Buddha Gautama and requested and implored Him to preach His doctrine, for there were beings capable of receiving and benefiting from it.

The Four Sublime Virtues Always Maintained by *Brahmās* (Referred to as *Brahmā-vihara*)

- *Mettā*, loving-kindness (giving unconditional, unselfish love) to all beings. "May all living beings be well and happy!"
- *Karunā* (unconditional, unselfish compassion), sincere and deep compassion for all beings, wishing all woes be removed from all who suffer. "May all living beings be free from all kinds of sufferings!"
- *Mudita*, expressing and feeling pure, unselfish and boundless sympathetic joy when others succeed. The practice of cultivating *Mudita* destroys the green envy, jealousy that is latent in the nature of human beings, and it should be cultivated in earnest.
- *Upekkhā* is the most difficult and most essential sublime state of mind. It means "discerning rightly," "viewing justly," or "looking impartially," without attachment or aversion. It is the most essential and difficult of the Ten Perfections that Buddha performed: standing firm, balanced under all vicissitudes of life, exercising perfect *Upekkhā*, or equanimity.

The Buddha encouraged human beings to cultivate these four sublime virtues daily.

Below the twenty *Brahmā* abodes lie the Six Heavens.

The Deva *Abode, or Six Heavens for* Devatas

Keeping precepts and avoiding evil, doers of meritorious deeds obtain rebirth in one of the Six Heavens. These abodes are situated in the Desire Realm, dominated by lust. Birth in these heavens is by direct transformation into the form of *Devas* (gods; literally "shining one," because of the shine or brilliance of the body): *Deva* for male, and *Devi* for female.

Their appearance – youthful, extremely handsome/beautiful – remains the same until they die (i.e., there is no apparent aging throughout their life as there is with human beings). As one progresses to higher abodes, he finds *Devatas* with bodies that are clearer, more refined and more beautiful compared to those living in the lower abodes. This is due to the differences in the extent and quality of the meritorious deeds each individual has accumulated in his or her past existences.

The *Devas'* life span is much longer than the life span of human beings and lasts for 500 celestial years. (One celestial day equals 50 human years.) The life span of the *Deva* increases the higher up the heavens one rises: the higher the heaven, the longer the life span.

Beings in the Desire Realm (these *Devas*), despite their long life span, often die unsatisfied. When it comes to the end of their life, they feel life has been far too short and they that had no time to enjoy. When death approaches, their brilliance fades, certain body smells issue, and they become worried and restless. Usually their death is due to the exhaustion of their merit, or the ripening of heavy, evil *Kamma*. But, sometimes it can be due to over-enjoyment of sensual pleasures and forgetting to eat. Most die unsatisfied and having no reserve of good deeds or good *Kamma*; they die to be reborn in a lower plane of existence.

When a Buddha appears in the world, heavenly beings, on hearing the *Dhamma*, become afraid, for they realize that their life is not eternal and they must also die one day.

Many *Devatas* or *Devas* visit the Buddha, the teacher of gods and men, to ask questions and to receive His teachings. The usual time of these visits is at a certain period before dawn.

Some continue to live in their lofty, lovely celestial abodes in great pleasure and die without hearing the *Dhamma*. But those who hear the *Dhamma* are gripped by fear. In excitement and terror, they exclaim loudly and clearly, "We thought ourselves to be permanent, but we are really impermanent; to be secure, but we are really insecure; to be eternal, but we are really non-eternal; and we are within the personality-groping (physical and mental processes which are impermanent and without an abiding self)." When such a realization dawns on them, they visit the Buddha and ask for advice and receive His teachings, for He is the only Teacher of men and gods.

Sakka, Lord of *Devas* (How He Came to Be One of a Kind)

When Sakka, Lord of *Devas*, was a human being, he undertook to practice unremittingly seven rules of conduct by reason of which he attained his position and honor.

The Seven Rules of Conduct:

- As long as I live, may I support my mother and father;
- As long as I live, may I respect the elders of my family;
- As long as I live, may I speak kindly and gently;
- As long as I live, may I not speak maliciously;
- As long as I live, may I dwell in my house with my mind free from taint of selfishness, be generous, open-handed, pleased to relinquish (possessions), accessible to entreaties, and enjoy caring and sharing with others;
- As long as I live, may I speak truthfully;

- As long as I live, may I control my anger, and if anger arises in me, may I quickly dispel it.

By practicing these seven rules of conduct, Sakka worked and attained his lofty and respectable position of the Lord of the Heavens of Gods, the *Deva* world. The natural result of doing good deeds (practicing giving) and avoiding evil (upholding precepts) is to obtain rebirth in one of the Six Heavens, a *Deva* abode (a Desire Realm) above the human world.

The Human World

The last to mention is the human world.

Its Unique Position

Its position is unique, well placed in the middle just above the nether worlds of suffering and sorrow and right beneath the celestial worlds. Its inhabitants hold their own destiny and are accessible to anywhere and everywhere.

How to Get There

A birth in the human world is the result of former good acts and the serious avoidance of doing evil deeds. It is a unique plane in many respects, as the Buddha has explained time and again in His teachings.

Absolutely Difficult

The Buddha had repeatedly stated that it is extremely rare to be born a human being. He gave this example:

> "Take the case of a blind turtle in a wide roaring ocean. This particular turtle rises to the surface of the ocean once in every 100 years for a gulp of air. There is also a wooden yoke floating on the wide ocean. What chance has this blind turtle to touch this wooden yoke that keeps floating? It would be extremely difficult for the blind turtle to touch it. It would be a long, long time, if it ever touched it. That is how long and how difficult, if not impossible, it is to obtain this human life again."

Why Unique?

In the human world, one can see *Dukkha* (suffering), understand it clearly and know the urgency to get out of it. Unlike animals, human beings are endowed with all the faculties to understand and shape their own destinies. The chance to work for one's own escape from *Dukkha*, the repeated cycle of birth and death, can only be worked out here in the human world, by a human being, purely by human effort and human means.

That was why the Buddha had to return from the heavens to be reborn a human, to work for His enlightenment. When the time came for His Buddhahood, He left the *Deva* world, *Tusita* Heaven, and took His relinking in His mother's womb to be born in the human world.

A Definite Result

Once a being falls from the heavens, it takes a very long time before he can be born in the heavens again; he would not even get the chance to be born as a human being in the human world. The reason for this is quite clear: being in the Desire Realms, having great enjoyment in sensual pleasures, they often forget to do meritorious deeds and to practice the *Dhamma*.

In the case of human beings clouded by ignorance and lack of morality, there will be no check to the committing of evil deeds. A little spark of goodness and reasoning in them is overwhelmed by greed, ill will, hatred and delusion, and it is exceedingly impossible for them to be reborn a human being.

In the *Anguttara Nikāya*, Buddha stated that, after death, few human and heavenly beings will be reborn into the human or heavenly planes; most will find their place in the planes of suffering. Similarly, few of the beings in the planes of suffering will be reborn into the human and heavenly planes; most will be reborn back into the planes of suffering. This being the case, each one of us has passed through uncountable lives in the cycle of existence, and the tears that have been shed in pain and suffering are more than the waters of the four oceans.

By now, we should realize that we have suffered enough and take the only way of escape from cycles of existence by renouncing all desire for sensual pleasures. The Buddha stated, "No one has ever liberated himself from the cycle of existence while living amidst sensual desires, enjoying sensual desires, without abandoning sensual desires." Even if one is not ready to lead a homeless life by choice, one still needs to consider keeping away from the nether worlds of sorrow, suffering and pain. So, heed His teachings, "Do good, avoid evil, and purify your mind."

Uphold Moral Principles (the lowest Five Precepts at a minimum). The extent of merit to be gained from upholding the Five, the Eight, or the Nine Precepts will correspond to the degree of purity of one's practice. Below are the minimum advantages of upholding precepts:

a. By *Dāna* (giving), it is like conserving or saving your wealth for later use. One would be born wealthy, into a wealthy family. There would never be a cause for financial need.

b. A good reputation is gained on account of one's high moral principles and practice.

c. One is able to stand up in public and command respect and recognition because of his good reputation.

d. At the time of death, there would be no cause for fear, because one knows he lived a life free from all evil, in thought, word and deed.

e. Finally, having upheld high moral principles and lived an evil-free life, a person will positively find a good place of rebirth, probably in one of the Six Heavens above.

The nether worlds are just below the human world and, for fear of the impending, grim consequences, one should take great care not to have a slight slip and dive down into the nether worlds. Always be aware, watch your step, and practice His teachings, *Sīla* and *Samādhi* to gain **Paññā**, or Wisdom!

For...
Man is responsible for his actions, good or bad.
They are his inalienable property.

Man is heir to the consequences of his actions, good or bad.

As...
Good actions are a protection against rebirth in worlds of suffering and misery,

And they mitigate and sometimes cancel the result of evil actions to a certain extent (not serious ones).

Remember...
It is through actions born of greed (*Lobha*),
Actions born of hate (*Dosa*),
Actions born of delusion (*Moha*) that there are appearance of beings of hells, of the animal kingdom, the ghostly realms, or any other miserable from of existence.

So practice morality, *Sīla*, and avoid doing evil, and do meritorious deeds.

oooooo

The Swan

THE JUNIOR CORNER

A Few Stories Retold...
Take pleasure, enjoy!

The Prince and the Swan
(As retold by Jonathan Han, Age 7)

Once upon a time, there was a clever prince. His name was Siddhattha. He was always kind and helpful. He was often found walking by a lake.

One day, he was walking to the lake when he saw a swan. He was very happy. He went to tell the king about the beautiful bird. He went to see it again. Again and again, he would go to see it.

The next day, on his way, he heard a very loud "BANG!" He started to run. When he got to the lake, he saw a very big man. He had a gun in his hand. The Prince looked at the man and looked at the swan on the ground.

The Prince shouted. "Why did you shoot the swan?" He picked up the bird.

But the man tried to grab it. He said, "Give that back!"

The Prince held the bird tightly and ran to the King and told him all about the cruel man.

The King sent the swan to the vet, and the man got arrested for trying to kill the animal.

The moral to this story is:

It is wrong to kill or hurt people and animals.
The man in the story deserved his punishment.
We must be kind to every one and animals.

The Story of Kisagotami
(As retold by Laura Han, Age 12)

There was a young woman called Kisagotami. She married a wealthy merchant so they had enough money to raise a family.

Happiness bloomed when they had their first son, but shortly after his first birthday, he fell ill and died. Kisagotami was broken-hearted.

In her grief and bewilderment, she knocked on the doors of the other villagers asking for medicine for her son so she could resurrect him. Most of the villagers ignored her, and others laughed and joked behind her back.

At last, she met a wise and kind man, who felt sorry for her misfortune. "Go and see the Buddha, Kisagotami," he suggested. "Perhaps he will be able to help you."

So Kisagotami, still holding her dead son in her arms, went to the Buddha.

"Lord Buddha, please help me bring my son back to life," she wept.

The Buddha saw how unhappy she was and replied gently, "I will help you, Kisagotami; but first you must go and get me a mustard seed from a house in the village where no one had died."

So, Kisagotami returned to her village and stopped at the first house she saw. She tapped at the door, and a woman about her age answered her knock.

Kisagotami said, "I must fetch a mustard seed from a house where no one has died."

"You may have a mustard seed with pleasure, but my grandmother passed away here last autumn," replied the woman.

Everywhere she went the answer was the same. Everyone she asked wanted to help, but couldn't. In every house she visited, someone had died. Now she understood.

She took her son and buried him, and then, at the end of the day, she went back to the Buddha.

The Buddha immediately asked her, "Did you get the mustard seed, Kisagotami?"

"No," answered Kisagotami, no longer unhappy. "But I now realize I am not alone in my sorrow. Death must come to everyone sooner or later, and it's a part of life."

Then Kisagotami set out to learn the truth about life.

The moral to this story is:
> Death must come sooner or later to everyone, and one must accept it.
>
> One is born, only to die later.
>
> Try to be good and live happily while one is alive.

Angulimala, the Robber
(As retold by Laura Han, Age 12)

There was once a terrible robber named Angulimala. His fearsome name means "finger necklace." Angulimala not only robbed people, but he also killed them, and kept their fingers on a cord around his neck to keep count. He had made a promise to kill 1,000 people, and he meant to do just that. Killing people made him feel proud and powerful.

No one could catch him. His strength and speed made him almost invincible. He was so cunning, he could fool a fox; and so fast, he could outrun the fastest horse. If the king sent his soldiers to get him, he just killed all of them and added their fingers to his gruesome necklace. No one dared to go out at night in case he would be somewhere waiting.

One day, the Buddha heard some people talking about Angulimala and how he killed people. Without adding anything to the conversation, the Buddha left them and went to find Angulimala.

"Don't go that way," warned a passerby. "Angulimala is probably hiding in the bushes and waiting for you."

Still the Buddha walked on. Soon He was the only person out.

From his den, Angulimala sneered, "What a fool! He probably thinks He can kill me!"

With confidence, the wicked robber began to chase the Buddha down the road with his sword brandishing in the air. But a strange thing happened. However fast Angulimala ran, he could not catch the Buddha. The Buddha was always out of reach. Stranger still, the Buddha was just normally walking along and didn't use any effort to avoid him.

Angulimala got angrier and angrier, and was soon out of breath. But he ran on until he could run no farther.

At last, he had to say, "Stop!" He panted, "Stop, or I'll kill you!"

The Buddha replied, "I've stopped." Calmly He kept walking. "It is you who is moving and I who am still."

"You are mad," shouted the robber. "I have stopped and you are moving."

This went on for some time, until the robber had to give up.

The Buddha then explained to the robber. Although his legs were still moving, his mind was calm and still. But Angulimala's mind was racing with anger and hatred, even though his body had stopped.

What the Buddha said made Angulimala think. The Buddha's wise words touched the tiny patch of GOODNESS left in Angulimala's black heart. He suddenly realized his wickedness. He threw his sword into a ditch, buried the necklace of fingers, and asked the Buddha to forgive him.

The Buddha, the great teacher, taught him how to be good, to avoid evil and to control his mind. This must be done by means of meditating, keeping awareness of one's mind. The great robber, Angulimala, took the lesson given by the Buddha seriously and became a good man and great monk.

The moral to this story is that:

Anger gets you nowhere, but calm people get the most out of life.

We must control our anger, and hate no one.

There is also goodness in everyone's heart.

Vessantara
(As retold by Christopher Han, Age 14)

This is the story of a previous life of the *Bodhisatta* who was to be born as Prince Siddhattha to become Gotama Buddha in a later life.

There was once a King called Sandumaha. He ruled the kingdom of Jayatura, in India. The *Bodhisatta* was born as his son, Prince Vessantara. He grew up to be a very clever and kind man. The King gave him many important duties that were always carried out to perfection. The Prince was not only trusted by the King, but was also trusted, loved, and respected by all his people.

In previous lives, the *Bodhisatta* had decided to become a Buddha. During those lives, he had developed his mind and other qualities needed to achieve his goal. He tried to be perfect in every way.

The Prince's fame soon spread beyond the kingdom, as he was generous and charitable. He helped the people and set out to fight against hunger, thirst, poverty, sickness and want. The people loved him.

Soon kings in neighboring countries became jealous of him. One king sent some of his men to ask for the royal elephant, which the Prince used to ride. As instructed by their king, the men came dressed as holy men and asked for the elephant. As always, the Prince would never refuse a request for help, so he gave the elephant away.

This elephant happened to be a very special and invaluable elephant. When the Ministers found out what the Prince had done, they were very furious. They complained to the King and asked for the Prince to be sent to the forest. They demanded that he must be punished for his act. The King had to agree with his Ministers and decided to send the Prince to live in the forest. When the King's decision was made known to the Prince, the Prince was surprised, but accepted it.

His family insisted on going with him when he broke the news. Before leaving, the Prince gave away everything to the people and, accompanied by his wife, the Princess, and their two children, went to live in a small hut in the forest.

They lived contentedly and happily, enjoying only the fruits and vegetables the Princess Mantridevi collected daily from the forest. They soon got used to the new and total change in their way of life.

One day, as the Princess was on her regular round collecting fruits, an old and evil man called Jujaka, came up to the Prince and said, "I have heard that you never refuse a request. I wish for your two children to attend to my wife." The Prince was heartbroken, but because he had developed the practice of non-attachment, he could grant the man's request. He also loved his children and wanted to make sure they would be taken care of by his father. So just as the man took the children away, he asked him to visit his father, the King Sandumaha, who would pay money and get the children back. The Prince was certain that his father would do just that.

When the Princess Mantridevi returned, she fainted on hearing about the charity, the giving away of the children by the Prince. The Prince had to revive her by sprinkling water on her face. She missed her children and wept continuously for many days.

The King of the Deities, Sakka, understood that the Prince was only a life away from becoming a Buddha and decided to test him. He came to the Prince in the form of a holy man and said, "I wish you to give me your wife as a gift." The Prince and Princess were speechless; however, out of kindness in his heart, the Prince did not refuse. Sakka then said, "Only those whose hearts are purified can understand your actions. Because of your generosity and non-attachment, you have given away your nearest and dearest ones." Smiling, he continued, saying, "I am Sakka, the Chief of the Deities. I give you back your good wife. It was only to test how firm you are in practicing the perfections you have vowed to maintain."

After a pause, the Chief of the Deities surprised them again by saying, "Do not be sad about the children; the King has got them back and they will soon be here." After saying that, Sakka disappeared and returned to his home in heaven.

No sooner had the Chief of Deities disappeared than the King and the children were seen standing at the entrance of the hut. The King and his Ministers forgave the Prince, for now they came to know why the Prince had acted in such a way. They asked for his forgiveness and asked him to return to the palace.

This story demonstrates several Buddhist virtues:

Generosity, charity, and the ideology of non-attachment, which would help end the rounds of rebirths.

If we want to succeed in life, we must be single-minded and, with great determination, work hard and long.

Why the Hare Is on the Moon
(As retold by Kaythy Win, Age 11)

A landowner in Savatthi provided provisions for the Buddha and the Sanghas for a whole week. He gave choice and dainty foods, seated them luxuriously, and entertained them. On the seventh day, he provided provisions for them for their journey. On the seventh day, the Buddha thanked the man and told a story for why it was good to provide food and shelter. Here is a narrative of the story:

Once, when the *Brahmadatta* was king in Benares, the *Bodhisatta* (the Buddha-to-be) was a hare. The Hare and his three wise friends lived in a forest in Benares. On one side of the forest, there was a mountain; on another side was a river; and on the third side was a village. They all lived together, and each hunted for food in their grounds. The Hare was wise, and preached the Four Truths to His three friends (namely that alms must be given, moral law must be respected, and religious days must be observed).

In the course of time, the *Bodhisatta* observed the sky and, by looking at the moon, He realized that the next day was a fast day. He told His three friends that the next day was a fast day, to observe the moral precepts, and to feed any beggars with food from their own tables. With that, the animals went back, each to his home.

Early the next morning, the Otter went hunting on the bank of the Ganges. A fisherman had caught seven red fish and buried them while he went downstream to go fishing. The Otter smelt the fish and unearthed them. Three times he called out, "Whose fish is this?" When no one replied, he took the fish and went to his dwelling and decided to eat the fish at a fitting time. He lay down and thought how virtuous he was!

The Jackal, too, went hunting for food. He came across a Field Watcher's hut. He found two spits, a lizard and two pots of milk-curd. Three times he called out, "Whose food is this?" When no one replied, the Jackal carried the food off to his abode and stored to eat at a later time. He also lay down and thought how virtuous he was!

The Monkey went out and collected a bunch of mangoes to eat at a later time. When he got home, he lay down and thought how virtuous he was!

The Hare was sitting in some Kuca grass, and suddenly the thought came into His mind that He could not give grass to a beggar. He contemplated the thought for a while and decided, "I cannot give grass, and I have no rice or fruits or other foods, so what shall I give?" He sat and thought for a minute. Then a thought struck him: "I shall make a great sacrifice and let the beggar eat me," He said to Himself.

At that very moment Sakka, the King of the Angels, came down to test the honorable Hare at this splendid display of virtue. Sakka transformed himself into a Brahmin and came to the Otter's abode and stood there. When he was asked why he was standing there, he replied, "Wise Sir, if I could get some food, after keeping the fast, I would perform my priestly duties." The Otter replied, "Very well, I will give you some food." And as they conversed, he repeated the first verse:

Seven red fish I safely brought from the
Ganges flood.
O, Brahmin, eat thy fill, I pray, and stay
within this wood.

The Brahmin said, "Let be till tomorrow. I will see to it by and by."

Next, he visited the Jackal, and when asked by him why he was standing there, he made the same answer. The Jackal, too, readily promised him some food, and in talking, he repeated the second stanza:

Two spits to roast flesh, I did wrongfully
steal:
Such as I have I give to thee: O, Brahmin,
eat, I pray.
If thou should deign within this wood a
while with us to stay.

The Brahmin said, "Let be till tomorrow. I will see to it by and by."

Next, he visited the Monkey, and when asked by him why he was standing there, he made the same answer. The Monkey readily promised him some food, and while talking he repeated the third stanza:

An icy stream, a mango ripe, and pleasant
greenwood shade,
'Tis thine to enjoy, if thou canst dwell content in this forest glade.

The Brahmin said, "Let be till tomorrow. I will see to it by and by."

Finally, he visited the astute Hare, and when asked by him why he was standing there, he gave the same answer. The *Bodhisatta*, on hearing this, was very pleased and said, "Brahmin, you are in luck for coming to me for food; I grant you a bonus that I have never previously granted, but you shall break no moral laws. Go and kindle a fire, and, when it is burning, call me, and I shall leap into the fire and will be roasted, so you can eat my flesh and complete your priestly duties." And thus addressing him, the hare uttered the fourth stanza:

Nor sesame, nor beans, nor rice have I as food to give,
But roast with fire my flesh I yield, if thou with us would live.

By his miraculous power, Sakka conjured a heap of burning coals and came and told the *Bodhisatta*. The *Bodhisatta* rose from the Kuca grass and came to the fire. Before He leapt, He shook Himself three times, as if to get rid of any insects to let them escape death. Then He leapt into the fire, like a royal swan, alighting on a cluster of lotuses. But the flames failed to heat even a pore of the hair on the body of the *Bodhisatta*, and it was as if He had entered a region of frost. He then spoke to Sakka and said, "Brahmin, the fire you have kindled does not even heat my pores; this fire is icy cold! What is the meaning of this?"

"Wise Sir," Sakka said, "I am no Brahmin, but Sakka. I have come down to earth to test your virtue."

Then the *Bodhisatta* said. "If any inhabitant in the world asked me for food today, I would just as readily have given my life." And with this, the *Bodhisatta* uttered a cry of exultation that sounded like a lion's roar.

Then Sakka said to the *Bodhisatta*, "O, astute Hare, let your virtue be known throughout a whole

Why the Hare is on the Moon

aeon." And he extracted the essence from the mountain, using his divine power, and daubed a picture of the Hare on the orb of the moon. After that, Sakka deposited the Hare on a bed of *Kuca* grass and returned to heaven.

The Hare and his friends lived harmoniously together until they passed away according to their deeds.

The Buddha revealed the Truths and the Birth: "At that time, Ānanda was the Otter, Moggallāna was the Jackal, Sāriputta was the Monkey, and I was the Hare."

The moral to this story is that:
>   Generosity always pays, however big or small. The thought always counts.
>   If animals can keep the moral precepts, we as human must do the same without fail.
>   Be good, kind and generous.

Khantivadi-Jataka
The Perfection of Forbearance
(As retold by WTA, Age 16)

Once upon a time, King Kalabu reigned at Benares. At that time, the *Bodhisatta* was born as Kundaka Kumara, who was a member of Brahmin family. On the death of His parents, He inherited all their possessions and, after careful thought, distributed it among the people who had given alms. He then entered the Himalaya country and led an ascetic life, wandering from place to place looking for alms.

One of the places at which He took up His abode was the royal park in Benares. He went around the city for alms and came upon the house of the commander-in-chief, who was so pleased to see Him that he gave Him the food that was prepared for him. Afterwards, with his consent, the Brahmin got the commander to take Him back to His abode in the park.

One day, King Kalabu entered the park, drunk and accompanied by a troop of dancers. A couch on a royal seat of stone was spread, and the King laid his head on the lap of the favorite of the harem, while the nautch girls provided the musical entertainment. The King soon fell asleep. On seeing the King asleep, the women providing the music discarded the instruments and wandered around the garden.

The *Bodhisatta* was currently seated in this garden, and the wandering women came upon Him and said, "Come hither, ladies, and let us sit down and hear somewhat from the priest, until the King awakes." So, they saluted Him and said, "Tell us something worth hearing." The *Bodhisatta* began to preach the doctrine to them.

Meanwhile, the Royal Favorite, with a movement of her body, woke the King, who, on not seeing the nautch girls, asked where they had gone. She replied that they were sitting in attendance of an ascetic. On hearing this, the King was so angry that he grabbed his sword and went off in haste, vowing to give the false ascetic a lesson.

When the women saw the enraged king, they went to pacify him, but this was of no effect. In great anger, the King went and stood by the *Bodhisatta* and shouted, "What doctrine do you preach, Monk?"

"The doctrine of forbearance, Your Majesty," He replied.

"What is this 'forbearance'?" demanded the King.

"To not being angry when men abuse you and strike you and revile you," replied the Ascetic.

"I will see now the reality of your forbearance," cried the King, and summoned his executioner, who came and saluted the King asking, "What is your pleasure, Sire?" The King ordered him to take the rogue ascetic and, with his lash of thorns, give Him 2,000 stripes. This was done and the Bodhisatta skin was cut through to the flesh.

The King again asked, "What doctrine do you preach, Monk?"

He replied, "The doctrine of forbearance, Your Highness; though you fancy that it is skin deep, it is fixed deep within my heart."

The King, after hearing this reply, ordered the executioner to cut off the *Bodhisatta's* hands and feet, and this was done.

Again the King asked, "What doctrine do you preach, Monk?"

Again He replied, "The doctrine of forbearance, Your Highness. But it is not in my hands and feet; it is fixed within my heart."

The King then ordered that His nose and ears be cut off, and the executioner did so. The Bodhisatta was now covered in blood.

Again the King asked for His doctrine, and the Ascetic replied, "Think not that my patience is seated in the tips of my nose and my ears: my forbearance is seated within my heart."

The King said, "Lie down, false Monk, and thence exalt your forbearance." And so saying struck the *Bodhisatta* above the heart with his foot and left him.

When the King had departed, the commander-in-chief wiped off the blood from the body of the *Bodhisatta* and bandaged Him. He then gently placed Him on a seat, saluted Him, and sitting on one side said, "If, Reverend Sir, You would be angry with one who has sinned against You, be angry with the King, but with no one else." After making this request, he repeated the first stanza:

Whosoever cut off Thy nose and ear, and
lopped off foot and hand,
With him be wrath, Heroic Soul, but spare,
we pray, this land.

The *Bodhisatta*, on hearing this stanza, uttered a second stanza:

Long live the King, whose cruel hand my
body thus has marred,
Pure souls like mine such deeds as these
with anger ne'er regard.

Just as the King was about to leave the garden,
the earth split open in two, and flames issuing forth from
Avici seized upon the King, pulling him into the great
Hell of Avici.

The *Bodhisatta* died on the same day, and the
King's servants and citizens came with perfume and
incense and performed the *Bodhisatta* obsequies.

There are Ten Perfections that *Bodhisattas* fulfil
throughout their many existences:

1. Generosity
2. Morality
3. Renunciation
4. Wisdom
5. Energy
6. Patience
7. Truthfulness
8. Determination
9. Loving-Kindness
10. Equanimity

This story is an example of one of the perfections: determination. He had set His heart to carry out
the Ten Perfections in order to obtain Buddhahood.

The Lord Buddha himself related this account so that everyone would know how hard He had worked to gain enlightenment.

The moral of the story is:
Whatever evil actions one inflicts on another person, the result of that action will immediately return to the doer.

The Divine Messengers

Let us learn something about the "The Divine Messengers." (Refer to the *Anguttara Nikāya*, 111,35.)

One day, the Buddha said, "There are three divine messengers, O, Monks. What three?" Then He set out to answer His own question. This was what He said:

"There is a person whose conduct is immoral in deeds, words and thoughts. Being of such immoral conduct, he, on death, is reborn in states of woe, in a realm of misery, in the lower worlds, in a hell. There, the warders of hell seize him by both arms and take him to Yama, the Lord (of Death), saying, 'This man, O, Majesty, had no respect for father and mother, nor for recluses and priests, nor did he honor the elders of the family. May your majesty inflict due punishment on him!'

"Then King Yama questions that man, examines and addresses him concerning the first divine messenger: 'Did you not see, my good man, the first messenger appearing among man?'

"The man replies, 'No, Lord, I did not see him.'

"Then King Yama says to him, 'But, my good man, did you not see among people a woman or a man, aged eighty, ninety or a hundred years, frail bent like a roof gable, crooked, leaning on a stick, shakily going along, ailing, his youth vigor gone, with broken teeth, with gray and scanty hair, or none, wrinkled, with blotched limbs?'

"And the man answers, 'I have seen it, Lord.'

"Then King Yama says to him, 'My good man, did it never occur to you, who are intelligent and old enough, 'I too am subject to old age and cannot escape it. Let me now do noble deeds by body, speech and thought'?'

"'No, Lord, I could not do it. I was negligent,' says the man meekly.

"Then King Yama says, 'Through negligence, my good man, you have failed to do noble deeds by body, speech and thought. Well, you will be treated in the manner as befits your negligence. The evil action was not done either by your mother or father, or your brothers or your sisters or friends and companions, or relatives, *Devas*, recluses. But you alone have done that evil deed, and you will have to experience the fruit thereof.'

"Just as King Yama has questioned, examined, and addressed the man thus concerning the first divine messenger, he again questions, examines, and addresses the man about the second, saying, 'Did you not see, my good man, the second divine messenger appearing among men?'

"'No, Lord, I did not see him,' replies the man.

"'But, my good man, have you not seen among people a woman or man who was sick and in pain, seriously ill, lying in his filth, who had to be lifted up by some and put to bed by others?' asks King Yama.

"'Yes, Lord, this I have seen,' is the man's answer.

"'Then, my good man, did it never occur to you, who are intelligent and old enough, 'I too am subject to sickness and cannot escape it. Let me do noble deeds by body, speech, and mind'?' inquires the King again.

"'No, Lord, I could not do it. I was negligent,' admits the man, quite truthfully.

"'Through negligence, my good man, you have failed to do noble deeds by body, speech, and mind. Well, as befits your negligence will you be treated. That evil action of yours was not done by mother or father, brothers, sisters, friends, companions, or by relatives, *Devas*, recluses or Brahmins. But you alone have done that evil deed, and you will have to experience the fruit thereof,' is the King's firm reply.

"For the third time, King Yama questions, examines and addresses the man thus concerning the third divine messenger, saying, 'Did you not see, my good man, the third divine messenger appearing among men?'

"The man mumbles, 'No, Lord, I did not see him.'

"'But, my good man, have you not seen among people a woman or man who had died a day ago, or two or three days ago, the corpse being swollen, discolored and festering?'

"'Yes, Lord, this I have seen,' replies the man.

"'Then, my good man, did it never occur to you, who are intelligent and old enough, 'I too am subject to death and cannot escape it. Let me now do noble deeds by body, speech and mind'?'

"'No, Lord, I could not do it. I was negligent,' answers the man honestly.

"'Through negligence, my good man, you have failed to do noble deeds by body, speech and mind. Well, as befits your negligence will you be treated. That evil action of yours was not done by mother or father, brothers, sisters, friends or companions, or by relatives, *Devas*, recluses or Brahmins. But you alone have done that evil deed, and you will have to experience the fruit thereof.'

"Then, having questioned, examined and addressed the man concerning the third divine messenger, King Yama becomes silent.

"Whereupon, the warders of hell [inflicted many kinds of torment on the man] on account of which he suffers grievous, severe, sharp and bitter pain. Yet he does not die until that evil deed of his has been worked out.

"This happens to any person whose conduct has been immoral in thoughts, words and deeds, during his life on earth. All evil actions bring evil, and frightening results."

Thus, we must respect the aged, and the elders. One must be kind, considerate and helpful to them, knowing that we will be like them later. Have consideration and respect for others, too; never be proud and selfish. "Pride always goes before a fall."

Feel sorry for the ill and the suffering: be generous with donations towards funds for the sick and the needy. Charity is a good deed performed.

And always remember that all are born certain to die one day: no one can escape death. When one remembers that all are the same in this respect, one will not be proud and selfish. There are two things guaranteed when one is born; they are CHANGE and DEATH. Everyone has to undergo change and finally meet death.

However, the Thirty-Eight Manifestations explained by the Lord Buddha would help anyone wishing to live a happy and successful life. We need to live by these little principles, or "rules" (if one might call these "rules" for the sake of convenience).

How To Be Happy and Successful in Life

You know that the Lord Buddha was the teacher of men and *Devatas* and *Brahmās*, the sublime beings.

The *Devatas* live in the six planes above the human plane. They live much, much longer than anyone living on the human plane does. But they, too, must die, and need to be good to be reborn in a good plane, and to avoid getting into the suffering planes like the animal world, ghosts, and into other forms resulting from greed and hatred, and hell where they meet the Divine Messengers and King Yama.

From the Mingala Sutta

Early one morning, before dawn, a certain *Devata* visited the Lord Buddha at the Zaydawin Monastery. He respectfully addressed the Buddha and asked His advice on how one should live so that one can be happy and successful in life. This was what the Buddha said: "O, *Devata*, listen carefully, I shall speak," and He gave these instructions:

"The first and the most import advice:
Stay away from fools and bad people.
Always associate with the good and the wise.
Always look up to and respect people who
are worthy of respect and worthy of honour."

It is important with whom you make friends or go about together. As a rule, "birds of a feather flock together," which means people of the same character go together. No one wants to be called a bad person when he is not, but if one keeps bad people as friends, he would certainly be taken for a bad person. Moreover, when one associates with a bad person, he or she will most certainly copy those bad ways and habits and become a bad person. He may also take up bad and harmful habits, like taking drugs and intoxicants that will be harmful and dangerous. So, we should be careful when choosing friends.

> "The next important advice is on where one should live. It should be the most suitable place in all respects. (That will be good for your social and moral wellbeing.)
> One should live in the right manner and in restraint.
> Perform meritorious deeds and have control over one's action in thoughts, words and deeds."

One should learn to consider carefully where to reside, and not think only of material gains. Think about safety and happiness. "Safety first and play the game." Life is far too short and precious, and wise decisions should be made as regards where one should live. Also, knowing that good deeds will bring good results now and in the next life or on rebirth, one must be good, avoid evil in thoughts, words and action.

> "Try to have good habits, be noble and practice morality. (Uphold the five moral principles.)
> Take care to speak kindly, with consideration for others.
> Waste no time, but try to get a good education, general knowledge and be worldly

wise. Acquire any suitable handicraft, arts and crafts; make good use of your time."

"Time and tide waits for no one." You may have heard a wise person say, "An idle mind is the devil's workshop." We must make good use of our valuable time.

"Take care of your parents and support them in return for what they have done for you.

"Be loving and kind and support your family as you have the duty and responsibility.

"As regards earning a living, it must be a right way, honest and harmless, causing no pain or sufferings to others, including animals.

"Be charitable. Uphold the good moral rules. Help relatives. ("Charity begins at home.")

"At times, observe higher moral principles (the Eight Precepts or Nine Precepts) and donate wells and reservoirs, as supplying of water is considered a kind of special meritorious deed, because water is essential for life. No one can live without water.

"Keep away from evil thoughts and speech.

"Avoid taking intoxicants and drugs.

"Always remember the meritorious deeds you have performed and try to do more."

Evil thoughts are thoughts of greed, envy, hatred and ill will; evil speech means speech that would cause anger, bitterness and unhappiness to others. Always remember words spoken without consideration can cause a great deal of harm. There is a saying: "Wounds caused by words are hard to heal." Be very cautious with the use of words; don't make anyone unhappy. Don't make enemies. Be considerate and understanding.

"Respect those you ought to respect. Don't be proud, but always be humble.

"Be content with what you have and with what you can earn.

"Remember others' kindness and never fail to knowledge them.

"Listen to the teachings of the Buddha from time to time."

By being content, one will be happy. There is a common saying, "Contentment means happiness and happiness means all." Be always grateful to others for their kind words and help given to you at any time.

"Be tolerant or forbearing. When someone respectable and wise reprimands you, accept it. Respect and obey your parents, as they are the persons who have taken the responsibility to guide you through life. Pay homage to Monks and discuss the *Dhamma* with them.

"Understand about the Four Noble Truths and practice meditation. Try to be noble and practice diligently to keep those noble habits that have already been made.

"Lastly, be cool, collected and calm. Life, as you know, is suffering or *Dukkha*. One should not be unnecessarily worried and afraid. There are ups and downs in life. One can be rich or poor, happy or sad, praised or blamed, have many attendants or followers or none; do not let such situations make you unhappy."

Without keeping to these rules, no blessings can be enjoyed. Anyone who keeps these rules or manifestations in mind and lives by them will find happiness and success in this very life.

For what we are now is the result of the good or bad *Kamma* or actions we have done in our last life or existence. To make sure that we can have a good rebirth, we must do good deeds and avoid doing evil ones now.

The Summary

1. Do not associate with fools and bad or evil people. Associate with the wise. Honor those worthy of honor and respect.

2. Live in a suitable place. Always perform noble actions and set yourself on the right course.

3. Have good habits, be noble and practice morality. Take care to speak kindly, with consideration for others.

4. Get a good education, general knowledge and be wise. Have a right livelihood. (Have nothing to do with trading in people, animals, poison, drugs and armaments, which brings sufferings to others and is therefore sinful.) Be well and highly trained. Be pleasant in manner and speech.

5. Seriously support parents and fulfil duties to family.

6. Be charitable.

7. Be good in thoughts, words and deeds, avoid taking intoxicants and drugs. Keeping the five moral principles is a must. (Moral principles are: to not harm or kill living beings; to not steal; to not harm yourself and others sexually; to not lie; and to not take intoxicants and drugs that will harm your mind and body.)

8. Be content and show respect and gratitude.

9. Be patient, obedient and discuss the Buddha's Teaching.

10. Be noble, understand the Four Noble Truths and practice diligently.

11. Be cool and calm, whatever happens. (Cool head and steady nerves.)

Our Actions

We must be careful of our actions in words and deeds that are the result of what and how we think. Therefore, we need to take care of our mind (thoughts). Only when our thoughts of others are kind, gentle, loving and unselfish will our actions and speech be free from evil.

Every action has a result. Good actions bring good results, and bad actions bring bad results. This is known as "The Law of Action, or *Kamma*". We must not do anything evil or cruel, which we might regret later.

It is very important to be afraid to do evil deeds and also to feel ashamed to act in the manner that would bring shame to yourself and your family.

Everyone is the owner of his or her deeds. No matter where one is reborn, those deeds will bring their results, good or bad. Remember: "Only good actions will always bring good results!"

What Is Suffering, or Dukkha?

This is what the Great Teacher, the Buddha said: "What is suffering or pain? Birth is painful, old age is painful, sickness is painful. Death is painful; sorrow, lamentation, dejection, feeling depressed or sad are all painful. Again, to be separated from loved ones is painful, because one would be unhappy. To lose what is near and dear to you is painful, and most of all, not getting what one wants is really painful." All these give us no satisfaction but make us unhappy, so they are called suffering, or *Dukkha*.

We cannot avoid these happenings in life. When one is reborn after death, one has to go through these events in life once again. This goes on and on until we try to stop it. In order to stop such pain and suffering that continues to repeat, one needs to live in the right way. The Buddha has found the "Right Way of Living," or the Right Path. He has experienced the good results Himself and has been kind enough to show others the way.

To live happily now and, at the same time, to cease all suffering in the future, the Right Way of Living must be followed. The Right Way is to follow the Eightfold Path:

1. Right Understanding (of suffering, the cause of it, how to stop it by following the Path)
2. Right Thought
3. Right Speech
4. Right Action
5. Right Work
6. Right Effort
7. Right Mindfulness
8. Right Concentration or Meditation

Conclusion

These stories that have been retold by children, (seven years of age and older) show that every child can be taught to understand what is right and wrong. They can be taught to lead the right way of living — upholding moral principles, respecting elders, having consideration for others, caring, sharing — and be well behaved.

However, it is the responsibility of the parents to instill these basic moral principles and good habits in them while in their tender years. It is only during these years, when their innocent minds are like pieces of wet clay, can we mold them into any desired shapes and forms. Children, like little seedlings, need to be patiently, persistently and constantly nurtured in the right and wholesome manner.

With careful and right training, children will grow up to be responsible citizens, and because of their right attitude to life, they will not be a burden to society. Instead, they will certainly be the pride and joy of their parents.

Further, it is an indisputable fact that when children from homes of such responsible parents attend schools, they can be easily disciplined. This alone is of great advantage to both students and teachers. The need for class control is at a minimum - irrespective of class size - and teaching will be effective. Teachers or tutors of well-behaved and well-disciplined children will certainly enjoy taking responsibility in helping with the all-round development of children, for that is what educating means. All three - parents, teachers and pupils - must do their best if this aim and object is to be realized.

Children should be taught to have great fear of doing evil and to be absolutely ashamed to do what is not right and proper. Instilled in young minds, this sense of fear and dread will certainly help children grow up to be respectable, reliable and worthy citizens of the world.

oooooo

A LOOK INTO THE
ABHIDHAMMA PIṬAKA

"Mind" and "body" are two little words often spoken of most casually. Just stop and think! How much do we know about them?

Buddha was the first and foremost teacher to explain about the mind, and the psycho-physic nature of man, or mind and body dualism.

Buddha was born in 623 BCE, went in search of truth at the age of twenty-nine, and attained enlightenment after six years, at the age of thirty-five in the year 588 BCE. He taught us about the importance of the mind and how it works. (Refer to His teachings in *Abhidhamma Piṭaka*, or "Basket of Ultimate Things," which deals with epistemological, metaphysical and psychological matters.)

In the teachings of the Lord Buddha, "mind" and "body" are referred to as *Nāma* and *Rūpa*. What is the body, or *Rūpa*? What is the mind, or *Nāma*? How does the mind work? When such questions are asked, we start to think and realize we may know about them in the general sense of the term, but not specifically or exclusively. Thus began the history of psychology in 588 BCE when the Lord Buddha began His Teaching, the *Dhamma*.

When someone states, "The entire universe is an embodiment or revelation of *Dhamma*, the laws of nature which modern sciences have discovered are revelations of *Dhamma*, for *Dhamma* is the law within the universe which makes matter act in the ways studied in Physics, Chemistry, Zoology, Botany and Astronomy," it must be accepted that Buddha's Teaching, the *Dhamma*, is all about Truths, the Universal Truths, that exist. Because of His omniscient Knowledge, He was able to see and explain all the universal truths to the world. His doctrines are an actuality that can be tested and verified. To fully understand, appreciate and practice His teachings, one should understand the *Abhidhamma Piṭaka*.

The Buddha did not teach us all He knew. He taught us only the facts that were relevant and necessary for one to live a noble and right way of life, worthy of a human being, and to enable one to work for one's own salvation without relying on anyone. For this was what the Lord Buddha accomplished for Himself.

He was potentially aware of whatever He wished or needed to know. He knew precisely which religious and philosophical doctrines that were or might be propounded were (a) true, and (b) conducive to enlightenment. He borrowed nothing, as such, from previous systems - because He did not need to - but He gave His approval to whatever conformed to these criteria. There is, therefore, no justification for the statement that Buddhism is a natural outgrowth of Hinduism.

The Eternal Truths, or *Dhamma*, exist. The knowledge of these Truths does not and cannot change with time, or whether Buddhas arise or not. It is a Buddha that reveals them to the deluded world. The Buddha was not indebted to anyone. As He Himself said, these truths were unheard of before. (Refer to His first discourse, the *Dhammacakka Sutta*.)

It has occasionally been argued that if the Buddha was really all-enlightened, He must have been able to foresee modern scientific discoveries. In fact, He probably could have done so, but that was not His task. It is evident He taught only that which was relevant and necessary, because He declared, "*Bhikkhus*, what I have taught you amounts to the leaves I have in My hands compared to all the leaves in the forest." (This indicates only a very small segment of His extensive and complete wealth of knowledge of the world, the universe and beyond.) He did not wish to confuse any one, but taught only what was required to be taught.

I feel this little statement must be mentioned, for it admits the superiority of His teachings in the knowledge of modern science: "There is, however, one modern science which the Buddha not only anticipated, but also far surpassed, and that is Psychology." This declares the superiority of the Buddha's psychological insights to the findings of the West, which can be readily verified. (Some examples can be found in Anthology of Nyanaponika Thera, Abhidhamma Studies, Buddhist Publication Society, 1965.)

In order to fully understand His teachings, we need to go a little deeper into His scriptures. The object of writing about "mind and body dualism" is to get to the most important part of His teachings, which is rightly called *Abhidhamma*.

What is *Abhidhamma*?

Abhidhamma is a Pāḷi term which I need to explain further. *Abhi* means "subtle" or "ultimate." *Dhamma* means "truth" or "doctrine." Thus *Abhidhamma* means "subtle or ultimate truth or doctrine." This explanation is simple and straightforward. I shall not confuse you by bringing in the Sanskrit form.

Abhidhamma is also known as *Abhidhamma Piṭaka*, and it is an important part of the Buddha's doctrine. The whole doctrine comprises three baskets: the Basket of Discipline (*Vinaya Piṭaka*), the Basket of Discourses, (*Sutta Piṭaka*) and the Basket of Ultimate Things (*Abhidhamma Piṭaka*). The *Abhidhamma Piṭaka* is His doctrine on four ultimate things: Mind (*Citta*), Psychic-factors (*Cetasika*), Matter (*Rūpa*) and *Nibbāna*. It is the most interesting and important doctrine to a profound thinker. As can be expected, in the *Abhidhamma* everything is analyzed and explained in philosophical terms true in the absolute sense.

Understanding the Abhidhamma

In the *Abhidhamma*, all doctrines are systematically elucidated from a philosophical, psychological and physiological standpoint. It is essential to have knowledge of the *Abhidhamma Piṭaka* to fully understand the Buddha's doctrine. It is extremely subtle in its analysis, and technical in treatment, and very difficult to understand without the guidance of an able teacher. The *Abhidhamma* is a philosophy, since it deals with the most general causes and principles of things. It is also an ethical system, because it enables one to realize the ultimate goal, *Nibbāna*.

The Mind *(Nāma)*

Man is the combination of mind and matter (body), or *Nāma* and *Rūpa*. (Read, "What Is the Body Made of?" in the chapter, "Did You Know?")

Many philosophers and psychologists have explained "mind" in various ways. According to the *Abhidhamma*, mind is the power to think and to know. It is comprised of the aggregates of feeling, perception, mental properties and concomitants and consciousness;

these four form the mind. The mind is powerful and can be compared with the colossal energy inherent in electricity. Just as electric power can be used for different purposes - good, bad, or indifferent - we can also use our mind for good, bad and indifferent purposes.

Mind is considered to be like pure, transparent water that can be mixed with anything. When mixed with mud, it becomes thick and defiled. Thus, the supreme, incomparable energy of the mind - by nature clear, bright and transparent - becomes dirty, defiled and poisonous by ill use. The abuse of our powerful mind can bring disastrous effects, even more so than can physical power. We must, therefore, develop it and train it well for good purposes.

The Working of the Mind

Mind = a stream of consciousness that can be expressed as "thoughts." It has a kind of mental energy.

How the Consciousness Receives Objects from Without and Within

While in the state of profound sleep, the mind is blank or vacant (in the state of *Bhavaṅga*). It is in a passive state in which our minds do not respond to objects. Being conscious (although asleep), one might compare it with the current of a river = the flow of

Bhavaṅga. When objects enter the mind, *Bhavaṅga* is interrupted; it vibrates and passes away. This goes on and on. At the arising and passing away of the next consciousness state, the flow is checked and arrested. Then, a state of consciousness that averts towards the object arises and passes away. Following immediately, if the object is visual, visual consciousness arises and passes away, knowing no more about the object.

This sense of operation is succeeded by a **moment of reception** of the object so seen. Next comes the investigating faculty, or **momentary examination** of the object so received. After that comes the stage of **representative cognition,** termed "**the determining consciousness,**" on which depends the subsequent, psychologically important stage of **active consciousness.** It is at this stage, the important stage, that one does good or bad action, *Kamma.*

The Process of Cognition About the Outside World

This process takes place through the five sense doors - eye, ear, nose, tongue and touch - and is called "the course of cognition through the five doors."

There is another door, the sixth, the Mind Door, through which we recognize ideas in memory or imagination, when the object is not presented but represented.

This is known as "cognition through the mind door." Through this door, the information of the inner world, the mental world is received.

An Illustration of the Process of Cognition Through the Five Sense Doors

Take, for example, a traveler sleeping under a tree after a long morning walk. We find him fast asleep for sometime. A fruit falls to the ground and rolls close to him. He is suddenly aroused from his deep sleep, wakes up and tries to find what has caused him such a fright. Surprised, he sees a fruit nearby. He then notices it to be a mango and picks it up. He smells it and, seeing that it is quite ripe and just right to eat, eats it.

1. We compare the traveler's state of being in deep sleep with the **passive state of mind**, *Bhavaṅga*, when it is running its own course, **undisturbed**.

2. **Being aroused** from deep sleep is like the disturbance of *Bhavaṅga*.

3. Waking up is like being **arrested**.

4. Trying to find out what happened is a **hazy** state of mind; he tries to find out whether the stimulus came through the eye, ear, nose, tongue or touch. This is called "**averting**," turning toward the five sense doors.

5. Seeing the fruit is the **arising of the particular sense** involved - in this case, the eye conscious-

ness. It is the pure function of seeing, free from any reflection over the object.

6. Picking up the fruit is the mind receiving stimulation from an independent object existing in the outside world. This is called "**receiving consciousness.**"

7. Smelling and examining the mango fruit is the mind reflecting on the object and trying to understand it in light of previous experience. This is "**investigating consciousness.**"

8. Ascertaining that the mango is quite ripe and good is the mind giving the object a definite place in its field of knowledge, known as "**determining consciousness.**"

9. Finally, eating the mango is the mind tending to adjust the object according to its own suitability. This then is called "**active consciousness,**" because the traveler is fully conscious and determines his own attitude towards the object.

In the course of cognition through the mind door, the object of cognition is not a stimulus from the outside world but an image arising from within, which presents itself with an already ascertained character. Here, the same function of the mind is called "consciousness turning towards impressions at the mind door."

The above explains the function of the mind, each thought moment distinguishable from its previous and succeeding thought moments by the function it performs. It is the **active conscious moment** that is very important, since it is at this point in time that we determine our future by whether the kind of action done - mental, verbal or physical - is influenced by greed, hatred and ignorance, or by generosity, goodwill and insight (resulting in the performance of good or bad, evil actions, i.e., good or bad *Kamma*).

Knowing the nature of our mental makeup and the purity and strength of it, we must be able to harness it for good use and purpose. Our mind needs development and this can only be done with understanding, reasoning, wisdom and drastic training. Just as one sifts the dross from gold, we must practice patiently and persistently to purify our mind to perfection, to a stage as pure as gold, refined gold.

Summary

- Man is composed of mind and matter, *Nāma* and *Rūpa* (mind and body).
- Mind is a stream of consciousness that can be expressed by the word "thought." Thought, however, is not of itself a physiological function; it is a kind of mental energy.
- Thoughts and radiation of current of thoughts are mental elements of the mental world that

correspond to the four material elements of the physical world.

- An individual is essentially the manifestation of his thought forces.
- The forces of thoughts, the current of our thoughts - although subject to change - are never lost.

Developing the Mind, or Mental Development

Why do we need to develop our mind? For the simple reason to be dignified human beings. This might sound childish and pathetic, but stop, see and think: look at what is going on in this morality- and rationality-barren, but rich material world! There must certainly be all-out agreement on the need to seriously train and develop the mind. One must accept that our mind is more intricate than an elaborate painting and needs training and development for the good purpose for which it is intended.

According to Buddhist philosophy there are three **classes of thoughts,** namely:

1. The consciousness of the plane of sense desire,
2. The higher grade of consciousness, and
3. The highest, or "supramundane" grade of consciousness.

The first, **consciousness of the plane of sense desire**, i.e., worldly desire, is mainly of two kinds: good and bad. It has three good roots - unselfishness, goodwill, and insight. Any word and deed done with good thought is called good *Kamma*. Being of philanthropic nature (*Aloba*), compassionate and loving nature (*Adosa*), and sharp and intelligent nature of clear understanding (*Amoha*), these actions produce good effects. Any word and deed done with good thought is called good *Kamma*.

The three bad roots are greed, hatred or ill will, and ignorance (*Lobha, Dosa* and *Moha*). Actions done with such thoughts - such as killing, stealing, lying, sexual misconduct, taking intoxicants and drugs, etc. - are bad action, or bad *Kamma*.

There are also three stages of development:

1. *Sīla* (**morality**) - to be developed by Right Speech, Right Action and Right Livelihood. (Morality makes a man gentle in his words and deeds.)

2. *Samādhi* (**concentration**)- to be developed by Right Effort, Right Mindfulness and Right Concentration. (Concentration makes him calm, serene and steady.)

3. *Paññā* (**wisdom**) - to be developed by Right View or Right Understanding, and Right Thought. (*Paññā* enables him to overcome all defilements completely.)

As previously stated, mind is pure and transparent. Like water, it can be easily contaminated and made impure. A pure mind is defiled by thoughts of greed, anger, and ignorance.

There are also **three stages of defilements** (ten *Kilesa*, or impurities) starting with *Lobha* (greed), *Dosa* (ill will and hatred), and *Moha* (delusion). Take a tree - the tree of *Kilesa* - as an example:

- The first stage when these defilement start to grow would be called the **root** stage, or *Anusaya*. Here the evil tendencies are lying latent. They do not become manifest up to the level of our thoughts, feelings, and emotions. When provoked, they come into action. For instance, when one is provoked, anger will readily come up, like poison rushing up through the trunk from the roots and out onto the branches. We can be easily excited to anger. This proves that we have certain tendencies, like anger, hatred, etc. When they are not provoked, we behave morally well for that moment of time, but when provoked, we act accordingly.
- The second stage is *Pariyuṭṭhāna*. Here defilements are being stored up in the **trunk** of the tree, where they exist in the realm of thoughts and feelings. One might be silent and good for

that moment in time, as there is nothing yet happening to provoke those evil thoughts.

- In the third stage, *Vītikkama*, the **branches** of the tree, defilements spread out, spring out, dash about, fierce and uncontrollable, in word and deed. This is the result seen when something has provoked the thoughts and feelings.

How Might We Act to Combat the Three Stages of Defilement?

The **third stage of defilement**, the branches (like branches seen at the time when provoked, considered the top part of the defilements) can be overcome by the first stage of development, *Sīla*, or morality. At this visible stage, the top branches are cut away by *Sīla*, and moral principles are maintained for the moment. We have succeeded for the time being. (A temporary control or suppression of defilements by *Sīla* is called *Tadangapahana* in Pāli.) When *Sīla*, morality (Right Action, Right Speech and Right Livelihood) is exercised, we are good, free from selfishness, ill will, jealousy, hatred, etc. Our thoughts, words and deeds must not only be good and harmless to others, but they should be helpful and of service, too. Morality will help control our words and deeds. But one should not be satisfied gaining temporary control; one must work further to control the second and the third stages of defilements.

The Tree of Greed, Hatred and Delusion

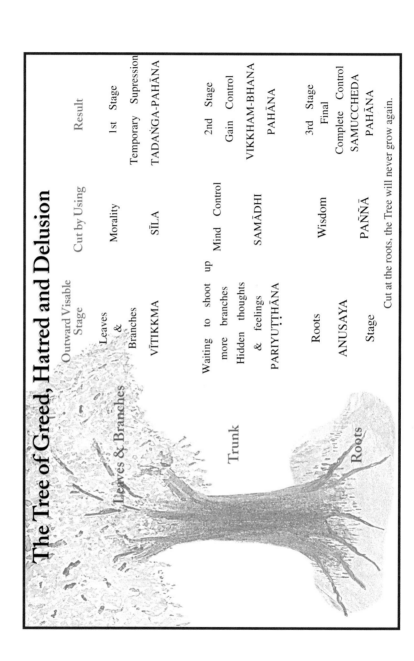

Outward Visable Stage	Cut by Using	Result
Leaves & Branches VĪTIKKMA	Morality SĪLA	1st Stage Temporary Supression TADAṄGA-PAHĀNA
Waiting to shoot up more branches Hidden thoughts & feelings PARIYUTTḤĀNA	Mind Control SAMĀDHI	2nd Stage Gain Control VIKKHAM-BHANA PAHĀNA
Roots ANUSAYA Stage	Wisdom PAÑÑĀ	3rd Stage Final Complete Control SAMUCCHEDA PAHĀNA

Cut at the roots, the Tree will never grow again.

The second stage of development, *Samādhi* (Right Effort, Right Mindfulness and Right Concentration), would be needed to dispel the second stage of defilement. This means mind control and mental culture. By practicing *Samādhi*, good and steady progress has been made, but this by no means represents the complete eradication of defilement.

The first stage of defilement, the root, can only be dispelled by the strongest and the most effective means of development of the mind, i.e., by means of one's insight, wisdom or *Paññā* (the third stage of development). It is by uprooting a tree that we can expect to get rid of it completely and absolutely, confident that it will never grow again. When the tree of *Kilesa* has been uprooted, one can be absolutely sure the defilements are completely eradicated.

Thus, in practice, we need to develop all the three stages of mind development - *Sīla* (Morality), *Samādhi* (Concentration), and *Paññā* (Wisdom or Insight) - to dispel defilements completely and do away with the initial stage of growth from the root. While practicing Concentration, it is easier for one to live rightly and understand rightly, and concentrate rightly. The practice of concentration and awareness exercised during mediation should be carried out daily throughout one's life.

The Mind

What is it whereby the world is led?
What is it whereby 'tis being dragged?
And what is it in whose sole sway
One and all have come to stay?

By mind is it that the world is led.
By mind is it that the world is dragged.
And mind is it in whose sole sway
One and all have come to stay.

SagathaVagga (1.7.2.)

This shows how powerful the mind can be. When it is evil, there can be no boundaries and limitations, resulting in "The Mother of All Evils!" The mind needs control so that no evil deeds will be committed; it must be purified and developed for the good use for which it is intended.

- This assertion of the primacy of mind (*Citta*) is a distinctive feature in the teachings of the Buddha.
- "Mind is the forerunner of all phenomena. Mind is their chief; they are mind made...."
- This shows how powerful the mind is. We must train, develop and purify it and make good use of it.

The Body (*Rūpa*)

"Man is a combination of mind and body, and matter forms the body."

Body is the manifestation of **four fundamental units, or elements of matter**, and their derived qualities:

1. The **element of extension**. Without it objects cannot occupy space. The two qualities of softness and hardness are the two phases of this element. It can be found in earth, water, fire and air, but it preponderates in earth and is therefore called the **element of earth**, *Pathavī*.

2. The **element of cohesion**. It coheres the scattered atoms of matter and forms into mass, bulk or lump. Although it is also present in the three other fundamental principles of earth, fire and air, it preponderates in water and is therefore called the **element of water**, *Āpo*)

3. The **element of heat**. This element matures in all objects of matter. It preponderates in fire and is therefore called the **element of heat** (fire), *Tejo*. It includes cold, since heat and cold are two phases of this element.

4. The **element of motion**, *Vāyo*, is the power of supporting or resisting. All movements and vibrations are due to this element of motion.

The four elements are inseparable and interrelated, and all forms of matter are primarily composed of them. They are also invariably combined with the **four derivatives,** namely, color, odor, taste and nutritive essence. The four elements and the four derivatives are inseparable and interrelated.

Thus, according to Buddhism, matter consists of forces and qualities that are in constant flux, or change, and are therefore impermanent.

Realities

Taking out of the five sense doors only one aspect of the mind that works through the eyes as an example, this is what happens. When we see an object, we do not see its real or intrinsic nature; we see only its appearance, form, as it appears through our sense door. All our thoughts or concepts are based on sense impressions and are, therefore, indirect, second to truth, and not free from personal prejudice. In actual fact, then, we have no direct knowledge of what really exists in the world of physics, although the objects in the outside world of physics are real - though not as an observer sees it.

An object coming into the view of an ordinary man would be seen only in light of his own limited knowledge, in the light of his own imagination. He does not realize the aggregates that have made up the view represented by the object. He then attaches qualities that are either attractive or repulsive, desirable or undesirable. He often imputes qualities to people, but these qualities in point of fact are created out of his own imagination, because he sees only the image of the person concerned. He thereby makes mistakes, for he does not go beyond appearance.

According to the Buddhist philosophy, "I" consists of five aggregates. The combination of these five aggregates in varying degrees constitutes the appearance of that to which we attribute different names. It is right knowledge that makes us discern the ultimate nature of things from superficial appearance, the real from the unreal, and truth from imagination.

When we talk about attractive and unattractive qualities, do they truly exist? According to Buddhist philosophy, there is nothing definite, because what is agreeable or desirable to one may be disagreeable or undesirable to another. Qualities are usually thought to be good or bad as one imagines according to one's taste, habitual outlook and predispositions.

So long as we base our knowledge on sense impressions, imaginations, appearances, we cannot hope to arrive at the truth, i.e., at the ultimate nature of things. We need to train our mind to see the reality, the true nature of things.

As mentioned in the *Abhidhamma* philosophy, there are two kinds of realities:

- **Relative reality** is conventional truth in which things are dealt with in an ordinary sense.

Example: a cup is called a cup, a plate a plate; this is true in the ordinary conventional sense.

- **Ultimate reality** is abstract truth that exists as the irreducible, immutable, fundamental qualities of phenomena. In an ultimate sense, no cups or plates actually exist, only the essential elements that comprise their manifestation.

Therefore, every material object is a combination of these elements in one proportion or another. But as soon as the same matter is changed into different forms, the composite things are held to be mere conceptions presented to the mind by the particular appearance. Thus, we have forms and names.

According to the Buddha's Teaching, or to Buddhist philosophy, these physical objects are made up of four elements, matters or aggregates: the element of extension, the element of cohesion, the element of heat, and the element of motion. Therefore, what we see is only the appearance, the image of the object that appears in the retina of the eye. We imagine that what we see is real, but it is in our own imagination of appearance. Ignorance of this nature leads to delusion in which imagination plays a great part, and which gives rise to craving for and attachment to what does not exist. "Craving is the cause of suffering, or *Dukkha*": this is the second truth of the Four Noble Truths that Buddha taught.

Accordingly, Buddha's Teaching stated that matter consists of forces and qualities that are in a state of constant flux or change: "the law of change." Therefore, being subject to change, everything is not permanent. The Buddhist philosophical term for an individual is *Santati*, i.e., a flux or continuity. It includes both mental and physical elements. Mind, which is the most important part of a man, is a complex compound of fleeting mental states, namely feeling, perception, mental concomitants and consciousness. All states arising in consciousness are non-material. But these states constantly change - not remaining for two consecutive moments the same - and are therefore not permanent. Thus, the Buddha refers to "a being," or "an individual," or what we refer to as the so-called "I" as being constituted by mental and material forces (*Nāma-rūpa*) that are in constant change.

In other words, the bare fact of life is *Dukkha*, or suffering. Why? Because all physical and mental unpleasantness is suffering. Experiencing birth, old age, sickness, death, having to associate with unloved ones and unpleasant conditions, and being separated from loved ones all constitute sufferings, or *Dukkha*. A striking example of *Dukkha* is not getting what one wants, because man by nature is greedy and ambitious. Sorrow, lamentation, pain, grief are sufferings of greater degree. It is the nature of the universe that things constantly change. A happy feeling, a pleasant happy condition of life, etc., does not last long. Especially where greed is concerned. One might earn a huge fortune and may be happy for sometime, but later he will desire to have more. Or, should he lose it, he will certainly be very unhappy. Then, how long does his happiness last? The result is unhappiness, which is mental suffering (*Citta Dukkha*). Though not physical, it is still suffering, or *Dukkha*. Suffering is universal and everyone experiences *Dukkha*: this is the first of the Four Noble Truths the Buddha explained.

What attachment should one have to one's body? For, actually the body is...

The body's like a lump of froth,
Feeling is like a water-bubble.
As a mirage is perception,
As a plantain tree are activities.
A magical illusion consciousness;
So the Kinsman of the *Adicca* did illustrate.

In whatever way it is observed
And properly examined,
Empty it is and unsubstantial,
To him, who sees it wisely?

This body at the outset,
Was taught by Him of wisdom wide,
When abandoned of three things
It cast aside, rejected.

Life, warmth and consciousness,
When body is bereft of these,
Then thrown away,
Lies insentient - only mere food for others.

Such is the fate of it,
A childish illusion,
A murderer, it is called,
No essence here is found.

Thus should the aggregates be looked upon
By a *Bhikkhu* of strong energy,
Constantly, both day and night,
Clearly aware and forever mindful!

Let him leave behind all fetters,
Make a refuge for himself and,
As though his head were all afire,
Act aspiring for the deathless state.

Khandha Vagga XX, 11.95

So-called man is composed of mind and matter. According to Buddhism, the aggregates of feeling, perception, mental properties (concomitants) and consciousness, these four form the mind, and matter forms the body. Therefore, man is a combination of mind and matter.

Summary

- In reality, on careful examination, an individual is just a composition of mind and matter.
- One should go beyond the surface, beyond the appearance.
- One discovers that what one calls "soul," the ego personality "I" is nothing but a mere composition of mind and matter, the body.
- When analyzing mind and body (*Nāma* and *Rūpa*), one discovers the composition of the four forces and the kinds of elements and qualities. These forces are only qualities.
- Therefore, mind and body are subject to change. Anything that is subject to change is impermanent and really undesirable.
- What is transient, i.e., impermanent, is therefore subject to suffering. And where change and sorrow prevail, there can be no permanent ego = no soul. The three characteristics of life are *Anicca* (impermanence), *Dukkha* (suffering), and *Anatta* (soul-less-ness).

Philosophy of Change

It is crystal clear from His teachings that all conditioned things are in a state of flux or change and, thus, impermanent. The ever-changing nature of both mind and matter proves the insubstantiality of life and the instability of existence.

The Natural Law of Cause and Effect governs every process in the Universe. The cause always becomes the effect, and the effect becomes the cause. So birth is followed by death and death, on the other hand, is followed by birth - birth and death being the two phases of the same life process. This cycle of life of birth and death is called *Saṁsāra*.

The Buddha has explained: "Death is a temporary ending of temporary phenomena. It is not a complete annihilation of the being, although the organic life has ceased; the *Kamma* force, which hitherto actuated it, is not destroyed."

When the present form perishes, another form takes its place according to the bad or good volitional impulse at the moment of death. This *Kammic* force remains entirely undisturbed by the disintegration of the physical body and the passing away of the present consciousness condition: the coming into being of a fresh one is another birth. Rebirth takes place immediately.

How Rebirth Takes Place

When one rebirth consciousness arises, it cannot work by itself and needs a body. The material qualities of the body that are produced by *Kamma*, or life force, continue to bring about birth through germ plasma or other life conditions. Thus, another existence begins. A child is born. The only guarantee it has is "change and death."

Many Views on the Nature of Existence and Reality

Some believe that there is an individual entity called a human being, a man, a woman, etc., that this is reality. This implies the existence of self, the principle of an ego or a soul. Some hold the definite view that this individual entity or ego-entity goes on to the next existence, and to succeeding existences, forever. Others hold that this individual entity or ego-entity disappears or is annihilated when the present existence comes to an end. There are about 62 views on the nature of existence. All these views are considered mistaken according to the Buddha's teaching.

The Right View of a Buddhist

A human being, a man or a woman, or any other sentient being is not an individual entity, but merely a term for a complex of mental and physical phenomena.

- This complex of mental and physical phenomena is always in flux, always changing, and always arising and disappearing.

- A sentient being is a continuum of little births and little deaths every moment.
- This process, this continuum is extended to the next existence when death occurs in this life.
- Rebirth occurs immediately, and a new existence begins.
- There is no interruption of this process, and no transfer or transmigration of any individual entity or ego or self or soul.
- Death being a momentary incident, rebirth takes place immediately.
- Thus, the cycle of life deaths and rebirths go on and on, round and round, just as a wheel turns round and round.

The Doctrine of the Wheel of Life, "Paṭicca Samuppāda"

Most probably, a number of questions will enter one's thoughts now. Where do we come from? Why are we here? Why are we here in this world as human beings? Where are we going next, after death?

It was not until the Buddha realized this doctrine of *Paṭicca Samuppāda*, the Wheel of Life, or the continuous process of cause and effect, that He was able to find the answers to those questions for us. Please see the Wheel of Life on page 332.

Getting Back to the Time When He Realized This Doctrine of Law of Causation

Immediately after His Enlightenment, the Buddha continued His stay at the foot of the *Bodhi* tree on the bank of the River Nerajana in the province of Uruvelā. He spent the whole week sitting in a cross-legged posture, enjoying the Bliss of Emancipation, or *Vimutti Sukha*. (This famous paean of joy is explained in the *Dhammapada*, vv. 153 & 154). With His mind so composed, clear, perceptive, straight, free from defilement, Buddha reflected on the recollection of earlier births He had already perceived. This was the start. He continued His recollection of His previous births in all their detail and special relationships, and finally perceived the meaning of this theory of "Dependent Origination" (*Paṭicca Samuppāda*).

Next, He began to concentrate on the deaths and births of beings, the cause of the cycle of birth and death, the cause of suffering, and the final path leading to the cessation of suffering. He mused on the cessation of these very things once their causes have been removed. He reflected on both death and arising and the cessation of all things conditioned and interdependent, in the present, in the past and in the future.

He sat deep in concentration and, suddenly, in the first watch of that night, He found Himself reflecting on "The Dependent Origination" (*Paṭicca Samuppāda*), i.e., the answer to all the above questions. He was thoroughly satisfied. Having perceived the meaning of this theory, the Buddha uttered forth this verse of joy: "When Truths thus become manifest to the strenuous and meditative *Brahmana*, then all His doubts vanish away since He has realized the cessation of causes."

Then, in the last watch of the night, the Buddha fully contemplated on the cause and effect of things both in their direct order and in their reverse order. At the end of His contemplation, He uttered another verse of joy: "When Truths thus become manifest to the strenuous and meditative *Brahmana*, then he dispels the forces of *Māra*, and remains like the sun which illuminates the sky."

The Doctrine of the Wheel of Life, *"Paṭicca Samuppāda"*

> On ignorance depends *Kamma* (*Saṅkhāra*);
> On *Kamma* depends consciousness;
> On consciousness depend name and form (*Nāma-rūpa*);
> On name and form (*Nāma-rūpa*) depend six organs of senses;
> On six organs of senses depends contact;
> On contact depends sensation;
> On sensation depends desire or craving;
> On desire depends attachment;

On attachment depends existence;

On existence depends birth;

On birth depend old age and death, sorrow,
lamentation, misery, grief and despair.

Thus this entire aggregation of misery arises.

But ...

On the cessation of ignorance ceases *Kamma*
(moral and immoral conditions
and activities);

On the cessation of *Kamma* ceases consciousness;

On the cessation of consciousness cease name
and form;

On the cessation of name and form cease six
organs of senses;

On the cessation of six organs of senses
ceases contact;

On the cessation of contact ceases sensation;

On the cessation of sensation ceases desire
or craving;

On the cessation of desire or craving ceases
attachment;

On the cessation of attachment ceases existence;

On the cessation of existence ceases birth;

On the cessation of birth cease old age and
death, sorrow, lamentation, misery, grief,
and despair.

This doctrine, *Paṭicca Samuppāda* - "dependent arising," "dependent origination," "conditioned genesis," or "co-production," as it is translated in many and varied terms - is the central and profound teaching of the Buddha. It is the key to understanding His teachings. **Broadly speaking, it is a doctrine of the conditionality of all the phenomena of existence - physical, mental, and moral. It shows how everything in the universe arises and passes away depending upon a variety of conditioning factors, factors which themselves depend, in turn, upon other factors. Nothing can exist independently, unrelated to and unaffected by the other phenomena in its environment.**

This principal shows specifically the origin of suffering and its cessation by the removal of its causative and supportive conditions. For this purpose, Twelve Factors are spread over the periods of time - past, present, and future lives - falling into groups as being active or causative, and passive or resultant. The first two Factors, Ignorance and *Saṅkhāra*, or volitional activities (moral and immoral conditions and activities, or *Kamma*, just to make things easier to understand) give rise to their resultants in this life: Consciousness, Mind-and-Body, the Six-Fold Sense Field, Contact and Feeling (Factors 3, 4, 5, 6 and 7). Craving, Grasping, and Becoming (Factors 8, 9 and 10) are the present causative factors with resultants in a future life, represented by Birth, Aging-and-Death, etc. (Factors 11 and 12).

Only with the understanding of this theory can one understand the real nature of cause and effect, the cause of suffering, and how suffering arises. The cause of suffering, or *Dukkha*, is craving, or *Tanhā* (the second of the Four Noble Truths). By understanding the Four Noble Truths (the foundations of Buddha's teachings) and actually taking The Eightfold Path seriously, one can hope to end this cycle of rebirths and deaths. By meditation, one can understand, without doubt, the rising and passing away as a human being.

The Buddha's advice is to get rid of our ignorance, to get rid of our masks of delusion and illusion, so as not to be attached and entangled in the whirlpool of life, worldly life. Work for a spiritual life and be absorbed in reality, and gain the supreme bliss of *Nibbāna* (from the Sanskrit word, *Nirvāna* meaning "extinction of thirst (craving) or defilements").

Paṭicca Samuppāda *and the Four Noble Truths*

In the *Mahānidāna Sutta*, the exposition on the Four Noble Truths, the cause and effect principle of *Paṭicca Samuppāda* is presented in brief by the dictum that the sum total of *Dukkha* (suffering) identified with *Nāma-rūpa* (mind and body) is entirely due to craving, *Tanhā*, and that, if craving were absent, the sum total of *Dukkha* identified with *Nāma-rūpa* would not arise at all.

Therefore, just as it is said correctly that whatever doctrine expounded by the Buddha is within the scope of the doctrine of the Four Noble Truths, it can also be said that any doctrine expounded by the Lord Buddha is within the scope of the doctrine of *Paṭicca Samuppāda.*

Paṭicca Samuppāda *and* Vipassanā Bhāvanā *(Insight Meditation)*

Vipassanā Bhāvanā is contemplation or meditation to gain insight into the true nature of mental and physical phenomena (*Nāma* and *Rūpa*). One needs to believe that a human being is just a complex of mental and physical phenomena (*Nāma* and *Rūpa*) and that these phenomena arise only because of certain causes. Without these causes, these phenomena will not arise, will not occur. This insight as to the true causes of mental and physical phenomena can be gained through the knowledge of the doctrine of Dependent Origination or *Paṭicca Samuppāda.*

In *concluding Vipassanā Bhāvanā, the fo*llowing points will be understood:
- How consciousness and mental and physical phenomena, or mind and body (*Viññāṇa* and *Nāma-rūpa*), are mutually conditioned or mutually caused.
- Why this mutually conditioned interaction of *Viññāṇa* and *Nāma-rūpa* is taken to be individual entities, called human beings, *Devas, Brahmās.*

- How one can discard the belief of soul, self or ego (*Atta*).
- Finally, the realization of the true nature of life in light of the three characteristics, *Anicca*, *Dukkha* and *Anatta* (impermanence, suffering and soul-less-ness, or non-self).

It is with this understanding that all kinds of cravings (craving for sensual pleasures, craving for becoming, craving for annihilation) will cease. When these three kinds of cravings (*Tanhās*), the root cause of sufferings (*Dukkha*) cease, the aim and objective of insight meditation is realized, and the bliss of *Nibbāna* is experienced, even in this very life, when wisdom, or *Paññā*, is gained.

Growth of Wisdom, Paññā

There are four things that are conducive to the growth of wisdom, or *Paññā*.

- Associating with noble-minded persons.
- Hearing the good *Dhamma*.
- Reflecting on the *Dhamma*.
- Leading life in accordance with the *Dhamma*.

Easy reference to the terms in the Wheel of Life:

Ignorance	means	*Avijjā*
Volitional actions, good or bad	means	*Saṅkhāra*

Consciousness	means	*Viññāṇa*
Mind and body	means	*Nāma-Rūpa*
Six-sense sphere	means	*Saḷāyatana*
Contact	means	*Phassa*
Feeling	means	*Vedanā*
Craving	means	*Tanhā*
Attachment	means	*Upādanā*
Becoming	means	*Bhava*
Reborn	means	*Jāti*
Old age and death	mean	*Jarā* and *Maraṇa*

Death is followed by all the rest: sorrow, lamentation, misery, grief and despair.

Death and Rebirth as a Buddhist Sees Them

At death, the *Kammic* force remains undisturbed by the disintegration of the physical body, and with the passing away of the present consciousness conditions, the coming into being of a fresh one is another birth. This means that the continuity of the flux at death is unbroken in point of time, and there is no breach in the stream of consciousness and there is no room for any intermediate stage between this life and the next, or between any two lives. Rebirth takes place immediately. (Death being a momentary incident, rebirth is immediate.)

Example of a transmitter and a receiving set: The transmitting of the life-force from one existence to another may be compared to a transmitter sending out a message to a receiving set that responds to the particular wave length, thousands of miles away. The *Kammic* force or force of life, like radio waves, has no obstacles, solid walls or distance that will prevent it from reaching the appropriate receiving end. In this way, the restless *Kammic* force or force of life continues to bring about birth through appropriate germ-plasmas or other life-conditions.

In light of this understanding:

- Every birth is conditioned by a past good or bad *Kamma* (actions, moral and immoral volition).
- Moral-immoral volition, *Kamma*, predominates at the moment of death.
- Our forms are only the outward manifestations of invisible *Kammic* force.
- Invisible *Kammic* force carries with it all our characteristics, which usually lie latent, but may rise to the surface at unexpected moments.
- The death of a person is merely the temporary end of a temporary phenomenon.
- The present perishes and another takes its place in accordance with the thought that is most powerful at the moment of death.
- When a person is about to die, no renewed physical function recurs as from the seventeenth thought moment reckoned backwards from the point of death.

- The material qualities of the body that are produced by *Kamma*, temperature, mind, and nutri-
  ent from food arise no more. (This is the critical
  moment comparable to the flickering of a lamp
  just before it extinguishes.)
- Rebirth takes place immediately.

A Buddhist regards death as a momentary incident between one life and the next, and takes its
approach calmly. His only concern is that his future
should be such that the conditions of that life may provide him with better opportunities for perfecting himself. He believes in the doctrine of *Kamma*, uses his
power to modify the quality of life force that continues
in the next birth. He knows that his future environment
will depend entirely on what he does, upon how he
behaves in this and in his previous lives. A Buddhist
believes in the doctrine of *Kamma* and the result of
moral and immoral volition. He will always try to do
good deeds, avoid evil, purify his mind, uphold his moral
principles (*Sīla*), develop *Samādhi*, and meditate to gain
Paññā, wisdom.

oooooo

TAKING THE "PATH" WITH UNDERSTANDING, ENTHUSIASM AND DILIGENCE

It is hoped that this easy approach to the understanding of His Teaching would now be at a satisfactory stage for anyone who gets as far as this chapter of the book!

Understanding in Depth

The Four Noble Truths and *Paṭicca Samuppāda* are founded on the bedrock of facts. They can be tested and verified by personal experience because these facts, these Truths exist. It was the Buddha who discovered them by His own intuitive knowledge and then revealed them to the deluded world.

In addition to the Four Noble Truths, the quintessence of Buddhism, *Kamma* and rebirth, form two interrelated, fundamental tenets or principles of His teachings. The Buddha explained and formulated them in the completeness in which we have them today.

The answers to these many questions - From where do we come? Why are we here in this human world? Where are we going? Why are there rounds of rebirth? Do we have choices? - are to be found in the theory of *Paṭicca Samuppāda*, for it explains how things work (the Wheel of Life, the continuous process of cause and effect, and the nature of things in the universe).

Manifold Destinies of Men in the World

Looking around we find inequalities and manifold destinies of men in the world: some are always sick and infirm, while others are healthy and strong; some handsome, while others ugly; some born millionaires, many paupers; one is a genius while another an idiot; and so on.

"What is the cause of the inequalities that exist in the world?" What would the answer be? Certainly it cannot be due to blind chance. Science is all against the theory of chance. In this world of science, all works in accordance with the law of cause and effect.

One of the three divergent views that prevailed at the time of the Buddha was that whatsoever a person experienced - happiness or pain or neutral feeling - all that is due to the creation of a supreme deity. Commenting on this fatalistic view, the Buddha said, "So, then, owing to the creation of a supreme deity, men will become murderers, thieves, liars, slanderers, unchaste, abusive babblers, covetous, malicious and perverse in view. Thus, for those who fall back on the creation of a god as the essential reason, there is neither the desire to do nor the necessity to do this deed or abstain from that deed."

Referring to the naked ascetics who practiced self-mortification, the Buddha went on to say: "*Bhikkhus, if beings experience pain and unhappiness as the result of God's creation, then certainly these naked ascetics must have been created by a wicked God, since they are at present experiencing such terrible pain.*" (*Devadaha Sutta*, No. 101; *Majjhima Nikāya*, 11.)

According to Buddhism, the inequalities and manifold destinies of men in the world are due, to some extent, to heredity and environment and, to a greater extent, to a host of causes (*Kamma*) that are not only present but also proximate or in the remote past. That is why the Lord Buddha stated, "Man himself is responsible for his own happiness and misery. He is the master of his own destiny, child of his past and parent of his future."

What is *Kamma*, the Law of Cause and Effect?

Kamma, from the Sanskrit word *Karma*, is a *Pāli* word and means "actions" - verbal, mental or physical.

In its ultimate sense, *Kamma* means moral and immoral volition (*Kusala Akusala Cetanā*). It embraces both past and present action. The past influences the present, but does not dominate it, for *Kamma* is the past as well as the present. The past and the present influence the future; the past is the background against which life goes on from moment to moment, the future is yet to be.

It is to be noted that *Kamma* is a law in itself that operates in its own field without the intervention of any external, independent ruling agency. This law of *Kamma* explains the problem of suffering, the mystery of fate and predestination of other religions, infant prodigies, and above all, the inequality of mankind.

Rebirth is the corollary of *Kamma*. It is *Kamma* that conditions the rebirth. Past *Kamma* conditions the present birth, and present *Kamma*, in combination with past *Kamma*, conditions the future. But the present moment exists, and the responsibility of using the present moment for good or for ill lies with each individual. Every action produces an effect, and it is the cause first, the effect afterwards. We, therefore, speak of *Kamma* as the Law of Cause and Effect. There is no end to the result of actions, no end to *Kamma*, so we should be very careful about our actions so their effect will be good. It is, therefore, necessary for us to do good and avoid evil.

The Buddha said, "Mental volition, O, *Bhikkhus*, is what I call action (*Kamma*). Having volition, one acts by body, speech and thought." (*Anguttara Nikāya*, 111)

The Knowledge of the Decease and Rebirth of Beings

Soon after gaining His enlightenment, the Buddha sat under the *Bodhi* tree. He saw beings as they were about to die or find a new rebirth - the low and the high, the beautiful and the ugly, the privileged and the unprivileged - and He saw that whatever happens to them happens in accordance with their deeds. He was able to explain the Law of Cause and Effect, the Law of *Kamma*.

Thus, with this understanding of the Law of *Kamma*, a man should conduct his daily activities with awareness of the fact that, whatever happens - pleasant or unpleasant - he must take it calmly and act reasonably and rationally, for life, after all, is *Dukkha*. He must rely on himself and be guided by moral principles and the Law of Righteousness and, with the understanding of *Kamma*, try to lead a noble life and make the most of the opportunity of being born a human. Time and again, the Buddha had repeated that a life as a human is almost impossible to obtain, and that a man has the faculty to better the condition of the present life and engineer for the kind of a future life he will have, if he so desires. (For further reading on "*Kamma* and Classification of *Kamma*," see *The Teaching of the Buddha*, my first book.)

The Law of Cosmic Order
(Buddha's Teaching and Science)

This is another law the Lord Buddha explained together with the Law of *Kamma*. Buddha has said that *Kamma* is the chief cause of the inequalities in the world. Buddhism does not teach fatalism or the doctrine of predestination, for it does not hold the view that everything is due to past actions. The Law of Cause and Effect, *Kamma*, is only one of 24 causes described in Buddhist philosophy. Both *Kamma* and Cosmic Order *Niyāmas* are laws in themselves and operate in the Universe. Thus, the need to understand the Law of Cosmic Order.

Utu Niyāmas: Caloric or Physical Inorganic Order, the fixed process that determines the four successions of evolution, continuance, dissolution and avoidance of the Universe. The succession of the seasons and the bringing forth by plant life of flowers and fruits are all explained in this *Niyāmas*.

Bija Niyāmas: Germinal or Physical Organic Order determining that the sprouts, shoots, trunks branches, twigs, leaves, flowers and fruits which spring from the germ or seed are always of their particular species, type or family (e.g., rice produced from rice seed, sugar taste from sugarcane or honey, etc.). The scientific theory of cells and genes and physical similarity of twins may be ascribed to this order.

Kamma Niyāmas: Order of Act and Result (e.g., desirable and undesirable acts produce corresponding good and bad results). As surely as water seeks its own level, so does *Kamma*, given opportunity, produce its inevitable result, not only in the form of a reward or punishment, but also as an innate sequence. This deed and effect is as natural and necessary as the way of the moon and stars.

Dhamma Niyāmas: Order of the Norm (e.g., the natural phenomena occurring at the advent of a Bodhisatta in his last birth). Gravitation and other similar laws of nature, the reason for being good, and so forth may be included in this group.

Citta Niyāmas: Order of the Mind, or Psychic Law, i.e., the process of consciousness, arising and perishing of consciousness, power of mind, etc. Telepathy, telesthesia, retro-cognition, premonition, clairvoyance, clairaudience, thought reading, all psychic phenomena (*Abhidhammavatāra*).

These five Orders embrace everything in the world, and every phenomenon - mental or physical - could be explained by these laws. Being laws in themselves, they require no lawgiver, and *Kamma*, as such, is one of them.

Taking Care of Kamma

The essential nature of action (*Kamma*) of man is mental, and it is the mind one has to take care of so that no bad *Kamma* will be committed. Just as an action performed again and again becomes a habit, it is the same with the mind: when a given thought arises in one's mind a number of times, there is a definite tendency for that thought to recur. Depending on the kind of thought, verbal and physical actions are accordingly produced.

When a man thinks a good thought, speaks good words, does a good deed, the effect upon him is to increase the tendencies to goodness present in him, making him a better person. On the contrary, if he does a bad deed in thought, in speech or action, he strengthens in himself his bad tendencies, making himself a bad person. Naturally, such bad people will become worse, as they will gravitate to the company of men of the same worse character. On the other hand, a man of a character that is continually growing better will naturally tend to the companionship of the good.

According to Buddhist philosophy, everything mental or physical arises in accordance with laws and conditions. Still, man has a certain amount of free will, and there is almost every possibility to mould his life or to modify his actions. Even a vicious person can by his own free will and effort become the most virtuous person. One may at any moment change for the better or for the worse. It is entirely up to every individual to make his or her choice.

With knowledge of the law of *Kamma*, we must be careful of our thoughts, words and deeds. Make it a habit to have good and wholesome thoughts and practice *Sīla*, morality (Right Speech, Right Action and Right Livelihood = Numbers 3, 4 and 5 of the Eightfold Path). Practice these good *Kamma* so that they will become habitual *Kamma*.

Habitual *Kamma* means actions one does constantly, all the time. It is, therefore, very important that such actions be good and benevolent ones. In the absence of the Death-Proximate *Kamma*, these good habitual *Kamma* will be remembered at that crucial moment of death. It is necessary for everyone to have timely thoughts of his good *Kamma* done during his present life, so that he or she can have a good place of rebirth.

Good *Kamma* (to practice):

- **Generosity** (*Dāna*) yields wealth.
- **Morality** (*Sīla*) causes one to be born in noble families in states of happiness.
- **Meditation** (*Bhāvāna*) gives birth in planes of form and formless planes and helps gain higher knowledge and emancipation.

- **Reverence** (*Apacāyana*) is the cause of noble parentage.
- **Service** (*Veyyāvacca*) is the cause of large retinue.
- **Transference of merit** (*Pattidāna*) causes one to be able to give in abundance in future rebirth.
- **Rejoicing in others' merit** (*Pattānumodanā*) is productive of joy wherever one is born.
- **Hearing the doctrine** (*Dhammasavana*) is conducive to wisdom.
- **Expounding the doctrine** (*Dhammadesanā*) is conducive to wisdom.
- **Forming the correct view** (*Diṭṭhijukamma*) is essential for the growth of wisdom.

Bad *Kamma* (to avoid):

Immoral *Kamma* is rooted in greed (*Lobha*), anger (*Dosa*), and delusion (*Moha*).

- **Killing**: Destruction of any living being, including animals of all kinds. Conditions necessary to commit this offence are: a being, consciousness that it is a being, intention of killing, effort and consequent death.
  The evil effects of killing: short life, sickliness, constant grief caused by separation from loved ones, and constant fear of impending danger.

- **Stealing**: To commit the offence: it must be the property of others, consciousness that it is so, intention of stealing, effort and consequent removal.

  The evil effects of stealing: experiencing poverty, wretchedness, unfulfilled desires, and always having a dependent livelihood.

- **Sexual misconduct**: One has the intention to enjoy the forbidden object, effort, and possession of that object.

  The evil effects are having many enemies, getting undesirable wives, birth as a woman or as a eunuch.

- **Lying**: To commit this offence four conditions are necessary: telling untruth, the intention to deceive, effort made, and communicating that falsehood.

  The evil effects are being tormented by abusive speech, being subject to incredibility.

- **Slandering**: This offence is made when one's intention is to separate people, causing disharmony, effort and communication to result in the division of persons.

  The result of such an offence: one suffers in return the dissolution of friendship without any sufficient cause.

- **Use of harsh language**: With angry thoughts, using abusive words, displaying anger and spite or jealousy.

The result: being deserted by others, being blamed regardless of no apparent fault, and being endowed with a harsh, unpleasant voice.

- **Engaging in frivolous talk** may not seem to be serious, but it is not a decent act. It is far from being a noble one, because it will certainly hurt others' feelings and make them unhappy for your own gratification of pleasure. Two conditions are necessary: the inclination toward frivolous talk, and its narration.

  The effects of having engaged in frivolous talk: disorderliness of bodily organs, especially vocal organs, causing unacceptable speech.

- **Covetousness:** To commit this offence, one must have a strong desire for someone else's property in thought and say, "Would that or this property were mine!"

  The effect: having one's wishes never ever fulfilled.

- **Ill will:** Intention of doing harm to another being. Result: one will be ugly, have a detestable nature, and be unhealthy, sickly in the next existence and even after.

- **False view** (*Micchādiṭṭhi*) means viewing an object in a perverted manner. This gives rise to the misunderstanding of the real nature of an object and of facts.

The effects: having attachment to unworthy things and ideas, lack of wisdom, dull wit, and suffering prolonged illness.

The Benefit of Understanding the Law of Kamma

Understanding *Kamma*, one will have patience and take the adversities of life calmly and intelligently. He or she will readily accept the fact that the present is the result of past *Kamma* and learn to behave well and perform meritorious deed so as to gain a better future rebirth, be wiser and not create more suffering, *Dukkha*. He will have self-assurance and self-confidence, knowing that there is nothing to fear in this wide world, except his misdeeds or bad *Kamma*. Thus, he will only rely on himself and exercise self-control, refraining from doing evil deeds for his own sake as well as for the sake of others. By doing so, he will build up his will power and strength to modify his present life and work hard to benefit from a better future.

Whether *Kamma* is wholesome or unwholesome depends on the state of mind at the moment of action. Thus, we must take care that our thoughts be free of greed, anger and ill will to avoid creating unwholesome *Kamma*. With the understanding of the doctrine of *Paṭicca Samuppāda* (the doctrine of the conditionality of all the phenomena of existence - physical, mental and moral), one should seriously refrain from committing unwholesome *Kamma*.

In conclusion, we must bear in mind what the Buddha has said: "Purity and impurity belong to oneself, no one can purify another."

Summary

The Buddha stressed the psychological importance of *Kamma*. He said, "O, *Bhikkhus*, it is volition (*Cetanā*) that I call *Kamma*. Having willed, one acts through body, speech, and mind."

- Thus the understanding of moral causation urges a thoughtful person to refrain from unwholesome deeds and to do good deeds.
- One who acknowledges moral causation knows well that it is his own actions that make his life miserable or otherwise.
- They know that the direct cause of the differences and inequalities of birth in this life are due to their good and unwholesome actions of past existences. They will do their best to perform good deeds in the present life.
- With this understanding, they will strive to promote moral and spiritual progress, paving the way towards the realization of the Four Noble Truths.

How One Should Take "The Path"

With Complete Understanding of the Law of Kamma *and the Doctrine of* Paṭicca Samuppāda, *and with Enthusiasm*

First Step - Practice Sīla and Samādhi

First of all, the groundwork of morality, or *Sīla* has to be laid. This means that Right Speech, Right Action, and Right Livelihood have to be practiced. A man of morality always observes the elementary Five Precepts. He might go a step further and observe the Eight Precepts, or even the Ten Precepts.

Next, he practices *Samādhi*, the culture or development of the mind, the second stage on the path (Right Endeavor or Right Effort, Right Mindfulness, and Right Concentration). One needs to work diligently now, for concentration represents a higher mental culture that is more powerful than morality, *Sīla*.

- By Right Effort or Endeavor, one must make all out effort to avoid evil and unwholesome thought from arising in the mind; try to maintain good or wholesome thoughts that have risen; and maintain those thoughts that have already arisen.

- By Right Mindfulness, one must be mindful of the body, mind, and object of the mind. The need here is to be conscious of our movements and acts, both physical and mental. When the power of attention enhances, the point where no phenomena that arises in one's mind is missed. One is able to check one's feelings and minimize selfish moral values. This practice of mindfulness or memory, when fully developed, will result in attaining the knowledge of remembering former births. However, this should not be our sole aim, for we must work for the final goal, to attain *Nibbāna*.

- Right Concentration means to employ one's thought on something, a single object. It means narrowing your thought, focusing your thoughts, for thoughts could be scattered. Concentration can be done on one thing at a time. Meditation means thinking deeply and quietly and this can be practiced only after concentration.

- Finally, the development of *Paññā*, or wisdom (Right View or Right Understanding, and Right Thought) is gained by meditation.

Second Step - Practice Mettā Bhāvanā

Another important practice required before meditation is the *Mettā Bhāvanā*, the meditation on love or friendliness directed towards all living beings. It should be developed whatever other meditation practices one employs and in conjunction with them. The development of *Mettā*, or Loving-kindness, as well as the development of faith by contemplating the virtues of the "Triple Gem," is essential in the spiritual life inasmuch as it gives an outlet to the emotions, directing them away from purely worldly values.

What is *Mettā*, Easily Understood as Loving-kindness?

Mettā is not an emotional, sensual, sentimental, self-satisfying love, but an active benevolence. It is a kind of love which, when actively administered, promotes the welfare and happiness of mankind and provides the basis for social progress. With deep and genuine *Mettā*, one will have sympathy for all mankind, regardless of color, creed or race. The world is always in great need of *Mettā*; it is now in greater need than ever before.

In the *Dīgha Nikāya*, the Lord Buddha said, "Almost every virtue such as unselfishness, loving sympathy, loving-kindness is included in *Mettā*. With heartfelt *Mettā*, one can accomplish anything - the most difficult of all, succeeding in attempting to break away all barriers that separate beings from one another." This is the model held up by the Buddha to the world. This is the ideal of what man should be to man. Buddha compared

Mettā to that of the love a mother has for her child, sincere, pure and boundless. It has no limit and is termed *Appamana* in Pāḷi. *Mettā*, loving-kindness is one of the Ten Perfections that Buddha practiced in countless numbers of existences right up to the time of His *Parinibbāna*.

Meditating on *Mettā* is to be started within our own selves. First of all, wish, "May I be free from harm, selfish tendencies, ill will and hatred." No enemy can harm one as much as one's own thoughts of craving, thoughts of hatred, thoughts of jealousy, and so on. So, meditate *Mettā* on oneself first. Then, sincerely wish, "May all sentient beings be free from danger; may they be free from oppression; may they be happy and healthy, etc." Mean what you say, and feel that you are wishing them all the best. Imagining your loving-kindness has been sent out, feel the warmth of your loving-kindness going out to them.

Through meditation on *Mettā*, one's heart softens. It is a kind of mental cultivation, refining one's own nature. It is only when one is right with oneself that one can begin to be right with others.

Next, find a quiet, secluded spot, sit crosslegged, with body erect and mind alert, eyes closed, and begin to meditate. Start purifying your mind by avoiding the Five Mental Hindrances - sensual desire, ill will, sloth and torpor, restlessness and worry, and doubt.

The Third Step - Mental Cultivation for Development of Concentration (Samādhi)

This, again, consists of two steps - purifying the mind from all defilements and corruption, and having it focused on a point. A determined effort must be made to narrow down the spectrum of thoughts in the wavering, discursive mind.

Rapt attention (Right Mindfulness or Attentiveness) must then be focused on a single object of meditation until the mind is perfectly still. In such a state, the mind becomes pure, tranquil, powerful, and clear, as it is free from the Five Mental Hindrances. The practice of mental cultivation that ultimately results in one-pointedness of the mind is known as tranquil meditation, or *Samādhi Bhāvanā*.

There are many methods of meditation by which to bring about one-pointedness of mind. The Lord Buddha, knowing the diversity of character and mental make-up of each individual and the different temperaments and inclinations of those who approached Him, would guide them appropriately. A little table is given on page 277 to give a fair idea to anyone interested.

Fourth Step - Practical Methods of Mental Cultivation for Development of Insight Knowledge (Paññā, or Wisdom)

As a progressive step in the practice of meditation, after achieving concentration (*Samādhi*) - when the concentrated mind becomes purified, firm and imperturbable - the yogi (person meditating) can direct his or her mind to insight knowledge (*Vipassanā Ñāṇa*). Any one who has gained this insight is able to discern, fully understand the three salient characteristics of the phenomenal world, i.e., impermanence (*Anicca*), suffering (*Dukkha*) and non-self (*Anatta*).

As one advances steadily in his practice, his mind becomes more and more purified, firm and imperturbable, then he is able to focus his mind on the knowledge of the destruction of the taints (*Asavakkhaya Ñāṇa*). Now, he understands *Dukkha*, the cause of *Dukkha*, the cessation of *Dukkha* and the path leading to the cessation of *Dukkha*. He also understands the moral taint (*Asavas*) as they truly are, the cause of them, the cessation of them and the path leading to the cessation of them. He has liberated himself and knows that rebirth is no more for him and that he has gained *Magga* (Path Insight) and *Phala* (fruition).

Meditation

One important aim of the Buddha's teaching is the extinction of suffering (*Dukkha*) and one's release from conditioned existence (*Saṁsāra*) which one could obtain through meditation (for insight, *Paññā* or wisdom).

By means of His power (*Ñāna*), through a Buddha's eyes, the Buddha saw the different characters and mental make-ups of all those who came for His guidance. He gave each one a method of meditation to suit his or her temperament and level of intelligence (acting very much like a physician treating a patient according to the kind of illness he is suffering from). That is why we find numerous methods of meditation recorded in the *Piṭaka Sutta*, or Basket of Discourses.

The *Piṭaka Sutta* is divided into 26 books, with more than 84,000 discourses preached by the Buddha and, in some cases, His chief disciples. However, each and every method was intended to bring about one-pointedness of mind. He meted out different methods to different persons, suited to their special character needs.

Meditations should be appropriate to the character and temperament of those who undertake them. The six types of characteristic behavior are classified as : greed, hate, delusion, faith, intelligence, and discursiveness. Accordingly, there are six kinds of persons: some dominated by greed, others by hate or delusion, while others by faith, intelligence or discursiveness.

Please refer to the tables on the following three pages.

oooooo

This arrangement refers to those exercises that directly counteract some given faults, or that are particularly beneficial to some given type. Four kinds of concentrations should be developed further:

- The contemplation of the repulsiveness of decaying corpses will help to forsake greed.
- The cultivation of friendliness will help to forsake ill will.
- The practice of mindful respiration will help to cut off discursive thoughts.
- The attention to impermanence will help to uproot the pride that says, "I am."

Furthermore, there are seven subjects of meditation given in *Rāhula Sutta*. They are friendliness, compassion, sympathetic joy and even-mindedness, meditation of the corrupt nature of the body and on the fleeting nature of things, and finally, mindfulness that comes from ordered breathing.

To understand the truth, the Four Noble Truths, we take a path, "The Eightfold Path," in which the eight paths that constitute it are interdependent and interre-

Table I

Mental states found in the various types are as follows:

Greed Type	Hate Type	Delusion Type
Deceit	Anger	Sloth
Craftiness	Grudges	Torpor
Conceit	Belittling the worth of others	Excitedness
Temptations	Imperiousness	Worry
Ostentatiousness	Envy	Perplexity
Discontentedness	Meanness	Obstinacy
Love of finery		Tenacity
Fickleness		

Table II

Ruled by Faith	Ruled by Intelligence	Ruled by Discursiveness
Liberal generosity	Gentleness	Excessive talkativeness
Desire to see holy men	Capacity for friendship with wise men	Fondness for society
Desire to hear the *Dhamma*	Moderation in eating	Dislike for wholesome practices

This table continues on the next page

Table II, continued

Great cheerfulness	Mindful and fully conscious of all his doings	Unsettled in all his doings
Straightforwardness	Inclined to the practice of alert vigilance	By night, he broods over what to do next day
Guilelessness	Agitation by things which should agitate	By day, he carries out last night's plan
A serene confidence in things that deserve confidence	Wise effort resulting from this agitation	Aimless rushing about

Table III

The suitability of the 40 Subjects of Meditation for these six types can be seen from the following table:

Greed type (11)	Ruled by Faith (6)	Hate type (8)	Ruled by Intelligence (4)
Ten repulsive things (i.e. nature of corpses decomposing)	Recollection of the Buddha the *Dhamma*	Friendliness Compassion Sympathetic joy	Recollection of death Recollection of peace Analysis of body into

Recollection of own body, changing, impermanence

the *Sanghas*
Morality
Liberality
Devas

Even-mindedness
Blue device
Yellow device
Red device
White device

the four elements
Perception of disgusting aspects of food.

Delusion Type (1)
Mindful respiration
A large *Kasina* object is preferable

Ruled by Discursiveness (1)
Mindful respiration
A small *Kasina*-object is preferable

All Types (10)
Earth device
Water device
Fire device
Air device
Light device
Enclosed-space device
The four formless trances

Table IV

lated and, at the highest level, function simultaneously. At the beginning of practice (taking the Path), each path needs to be infused with some degree of right understanding. This has to be done if we are to practice seriously, sincerely and diligently the teaching of the Buddha: "To refrain from all evil; to do what is good; to cleanse one's mind."

Taking care of the mind is essential. It is by no means an easy task. When one experiences problems or unpleasant feelings, it is due to one's own mind: one sees or hears and makes his or her judgment, positive or negative, according to one's own disposition. This depends on one's state of mind, which is changeable. This is because our mind is defiled. The Buddha said that: we are responsible for our own happiness and sorrow; we create our own heaven and hell; our judgments and feelings are dependent on our own ego, or personality and the ignorance that is latent in the mind. It is, therefore, an absolute necessity to purify the mind (first establishing *Sīla*, or morality).

To go on to higher morality, one has to practice *Samādhi* and *Paññā*, which will lead to the attainment of the highest wisdom or enlightenment. Higher morality (*Adhisīla*) is required here. This is because unwholesome actions and speech are performed only when the mind is overwhelmed by greed, anger or delusion. *Kamma*, mental volition, becomes wholesome and unwholesome according to the state of mind. Once again we are talking about the mind. Without practicing *Samādhi* and *Paññā*, one is unable to achieve higher morality, which will help to uproot latent mental aberrations or defilements that brings negative forces to the mind, conditioning the accumulation of unwholesome mental actions. It is only through the practice of *Vipassanā* meditation that unwholesome mental dispositions are eradicated and the complete understanding of the Four Noble Truths will be gained.

- Elementary steps:
    Take refuge in the Triple Gem.
    Observe the Five, or Eight, or
    Ten Precepts.
    Observe *Mettā Bhāvanā* (give out
    Mettā, loving-kindness).
- Next, develop *Samādhi*, mind development: concentrate the mind at will on one object (exercising right effort, right mindfulness and right concentration).
- With insight meditation, with one-pointedness of mind, one is able to get the correct view of life, seeing nothing but the three characteristics of impermanence (*Anicca*), suffering (*Dukkha*) and soul-less-ness (*Anatta*) wherever he glances.
- Now, having the correct view of life, one stands in equilibrium in the midst of worldly things, finds genuine happiness, and sees that every

form of pleasure is only a prelude to pain. He knows that whatever is impermanent is painful and, thus, that where change and sorrow prevail, there cannot be permanent happiness.

- Advancing further, a spiritual man then takes the one of the above three characteristics that appeals to him most and intently keeps on developing insight in that particular direction until he realizes *Nibbāna* for the first time in his life. At this point, he gains the first *Ariyan* stage and is called a *Sotāpanna*, one who enters the stream that leads to *Nibbāna*. He escapes the states of woe and is assured final enlightenment.

He has gained: More than any earthly power,
More than the joys of heaven,
More than rule o'er the
entire world
Is the entrance to the Stream.

In the first stage of attainment, a *Sotāpanna* has destroyed the first three of the ten fetters: self-illusion (*Sakkāya Diṭṭhi*), doubts (*Vicikicchā*), and indulgence in rites, rituals and ceremonies (*Sīlabbataparāmāsa*). Since he has not destroyed the will to live, he will be reborn as a human being seven times at most if he does not quickly reach a further attainment.

- In the second *Ariyan* stage, one becomes a *Sakadāgāmī* or Once-Returner. Having been encouraged by his results, a *Sotāpanna*, a spiritual man, develops deeper insight. He weakens two more fetters - sense desire (*Kāmarāga*) and ill will (*Paṭigha*) - to become a *Sakadāgāmī*. He is also called a Once-Returner because he will be reborn on earth only once more if he does not attain *Arahat*ship.

- In the third *Ariyan* stage, one becomes an *Anāgāmi*, a Never-Returner. Working further, the man reaches the third stage and destroys the two fetters that he has weakened. He has no more desire for worldly pleasures and, after his death, will not return to be reborn on earth. He will be reborn in the Pure Abode (*Suddhāvāsa*), a place that is exclusively for *Anāgāmis*, and from whence he will become an *Arahat*.

- In the final attainment stage - where one becomes an *Arahat* - encouraged by his great success, an earnest spiritual man endeavors further, makes his final advance, and destroys the remaining five fetters: desire for life in the Realm of Form (*Rūparāga*), desire for life in the Formless Realm (*Arūparāga*), conceit (*Māna*), distraction (*Uddhacca*) and ignorance (*Avijjā*). He has attained the fourth supramundane stage and is called an *Arahat*, one whose heart is free from *Arahat* sensual passion, free from the passion for existence, and free from ignorance.

An *Arahat* stands on heights higher than celestial beings, realizing the unutterable bliss of *Nibbāna*. Being free from ignorance (*Avijjā*), he arises no more, passes away no more, for there is nothing in him to cause re-arising. Because he arises no more, he will not grow old. Growing old no more, he will not die again; dying no more, he will not tremble; and trembling no more, he will not desire.

The essence and purpose of a holy life does not lie in acquiring alms, honor or fame, or in gaining morality, concentration or wisdom, but in the unshakable deliverance of the heart, and the attainment of *Nirvāna*.

What is Nirvāna?

Nirvāna is a Sanskrit word. *Ni* is a negative particle, and *Vana* means "lusting" or "craving." It is called *Nibbāna* in Pāli, meaning departure from lust or craving. The Buddha said that the world is in flames kindled by greed, hatred and ignorance; also by the fire of birth, old age, death, pain, lamentation, sorrow, grief and despair. *Nibbāna* means the blowing out of the flames of personal desires.

Nirvāna or *Nibbāna* is neither a mere nothingness nor a state of annihilation. Exactly what it is no words can express. It is a positive, unconditioned state;

thus, it is boundless, to be sought after, happy, because it is free from all suffering, free from birth, death, and a host of things that come with being reborn. Neither is *Nibbāna* situated in any place, nor is it a sort of heaven where a transcendental ego resides. It is a state that is dependent upon our own selves.

In the Buddhist scriptures, there are many positive definitions of *Nibbāna*, such as: meaning the highest refuge; safety; unique; absolute purity; supramundane; security; emancipation; peace; and many others. *Nibbāna* is, therefore, not a negative concept. It is the cessation of craving, the blowing out of man's selfish desires that ends all causes for committing unwholesome *Kamma*, resulting in freedom from all sufferings, freedom from all bonds.

How would one attain *Nibbāna*? It is only by having knowledge of the Four Noble Truths and following the Eightfold Path, which includes the practicing of *Sīla* (morality) and *Samādhi* (mind development or concentration) to gain *Paññā* (wisdom).

A Profound Tribute To Ven. Mahasi Sayādaw (a Long-Experienced Teacher)

I sincerely feel I should not end this chapter without mentioning the great *Sayādaw*, the great, learned Mahāsi Sayādaw, who lead the Sixth Buddhist

Council in Rangoon. The method of meditation he taught is widely practiced and needs mentioning.

According to his method, the meditator or *Yogi* - after performing the elementary groundwork (taking *Sīla*, observing *Mettā Bhāvanā* and other acts of purification of the mind) - will sit in a quiet secluded place with the right posture for meditation.

He should begin by noting the element of air (*Vāyo Dhātu*), the characteristics of which are stiffness, pressure, and motion and which become evident in the region of the abdomen. As the abdomen rises, the yogi will note "rising." As it falls, he will note "falling." One begins with noting just these two motions, rising and falling. But this does not comprise all that is to be done.

While noting the rising and falling of the abdomen, if thinking arises, note that, too, as "thinking, thinking," and then return to noting the rising and falling. If something painful occurs in any part of the body, note that, too. When it subsides, or when it has been noted for some time, return to noting the rising and falling. If there is bending, stretching, or moving of the limbs, the meditator must note it: if bending, note "bending, bending"; if stretching, note "stretching, stretching." Whatever bodily movement occurs, one should note it in the precise moment of its occurrence, and then return to the rising and falling of the abdomen.

The meditator acts precisely in the same manner when he sees, hears anything clearly: note "seeing" or "hearing" for a moment, and then return to the process of noting the rising and falling of the abdomen. One keeps strict awareness of all changes that take place.

Even when going to bed, one notes "wanting to sleep" and all actions - changing, approaching the bed, lying down, body touching the bed, pillow, movements of hands and legs, and every little movement. All feelings and all bodily reactions that give rise to feelings, all kinds of consciousness that appear, any kinds of thoughts must be noted. However sleepy one may be, meditation goes on. If there is nothing to be aware of, one must go back to concentrating on the falling of the abdomen, till one falls asleep.

When one gets up and becomes aware of being awake, one has to start being conscious of all thoughts and actions one is wanting to perform and is performing. With practice, the meditator will become aware of every process and will be able to note each attentively; his mind becomes evidently calm and concentrated. This is the beginning of the development of insight, which distinguishes mind from matter or objects.

In the beginning, it will not be possible to be mindful of everything. Do not be disappointed if you cannot concentrate properly. After you have built up *Samādhi* (mental development), it will become easy to concentrate on many more things and every little thought and movement you experience.

Many have benefited through this guidance and teaching. We owe a depth of gratitude to the Great Learned Mahāsi Sayādaw. Although he passed away over two decades ago, he is profoundly respected and missed.

Today, there are many well-qualified teachers of insight meditation with an increasing number of centers established in every part of the world. Meditation tends to self-discipline, self-control, purification and enlightenment. There is everything to gain by meditation: tranquility and peace of mind at the present moment in time, at the very least. Remember one of the six attributes of the *Dhamma* is *Akālika*. It means that the results of the *Dhamma* are not delayed and the benefit can be enjoyed immediately. More and more people are beginning to understand and enjoy the good results gained by practicing meditation. (Refers to the four *Maggas*, or paths that are followed immediately by their respective *Phalas*, or fruitions.)

One should take the Path, with complete understanding, enthusiasm and diligence.

Benefits Gained

The highest benefit gained by observing *Sīla* throughout one's life is rebirth as a human or a *Deva*.

The highest benefit gained by observing *Samādhi* is rebirth as a Brahma.

However, as humans, *Devas*, and *Brahmās* are *Puthujjanas* (those who have not achieved *Maggas*), they have the following defilements: (a) a belief in *Atta*, and (b) doubt about the Four Noble Truths. Thus there appear to be these weaknesses:

a) Their faith in the Triple Gem will not be firm.
b) Their rebirths will be endless.
c) As the observance of *Sīla* will never be firm, the abandonment of it is also possible.
d) The perpetual following of evil *Kammas* - if they chance to manifest close to the last few moments of their life - can cause these *Puthujjana* persons to be reborn in one or the other of the four nether worlds.

Hold fast to *Sīla*, develop *Samādhi* and work hard to gain *Paññā* by taking the Path and seriously practicing *Vipassanā Bhāvanā*.

Hierarchy of *Ariyas* (Noble Ones)
(Refer to Brahmajala Sutta)

First stage: *Sotāpanna* - One who has achieved the first *Magga*, the *Sotāpatti Magga*. The *Sotāpanna* is no longer a worldling (*Puthujjana*). He has become an *Ariya*, a noble one. At this stage, he has initially uprooted three fetters: self-illusion (*Sakkāya Dhiṭṭhi*), doubts (*Vicikichā*), and adherence to wrong rites and ceremonies (*Sīlabbataparāmāsa*).

- His faith in the Triple Gem is firm.
- Under no circumstances would he violate the Five Precepts.
- His *Akusala Kammas* - which could cause him to gain rebirth in one of the four nether worlds - have become *Ahosi* (abortive) *Kammas*. A *Sotāpanna* will, therefore, never we reborn in one or the other of the nether worlds or regions.
- His rebirth will not be endless. He cannot go beyond the seventh rebirth. He is known as "stream-enterer" and is destined for enlightenment.

Second stage: *Sakadāgāmi*. The *Sakadāgāmi* is named after the *Sakadāgāmi Magga*, which he has gained. Although he has not totally uprooted another five *Anusayas*, he has taken away proclivities or tendencies to them. He cannot go beyond the second rebirth and, therefore, is known as a "once-returner."

Third stage: *Anāgāmi*. The *Anāgāmi* is named after the *Anāgāmi Magga*, which he has gained. He has uprooted two more *Anusayas*: *Kāmarāgānusaya* (attachment to sensual pleasures) and *Paṭighānusaya* (anger, worry and fear). An *Anāgāmi* cannot go beyond one more rebirth.

Fourth and Final Stage: *Arahat.* The Arahat is named after the *Arahatta Magga*, the final *Magga* gained. He has uprooted *Mānanusaya* (pride, conceit), *Bhavarāgānusaya* (attachment to rebirths), and *Avijjānusaya* (non-comprehension of the Four *Ariya* Truths). There will be no rebirths following his death.

Fifth: *Mahāsāvaka.* *Mahā* means "great"; *Sāvaka* means "disciple of the Buddha." The *Mahāsāvaka* is an *Arahat* with special attainments such as *Abhiññā* (supernormal powers) and *Paṭisambhidā* (mastery of analytic insight). There will be no rebirth after his death.

Sixth: *Aggasāvaka.* Agga means "exalted"; *Sāvaka* means "disciple of the Buddha." The two chief disciples are called *Aggasāvakas*. The first *Aggasāvaka* is second to the Buddha in wisdom. The second *Aggasāvaka* is second only to the Buddha in *Abhiññā.* There will be no rebirth upon his death.

Seventh - Paccekabuddha. Like the Buddha, the *Paccekabuddha* achieves the four *Maggas* by himself. However, unlike the Buddha, a *Paccekabuddha* does not achieve *Sabbaññuta Ñāṇa*, which would enable him to know all there is to know. There will be no rebirth following his death.

Eighth: the highest - Buddha. A Buddha achieves the four *Maggas* by himself. Simultaneously with the achievement of the *Arahatta Phala*, he achieves *Sabbaññuta Ñāṇa* (after self-training for perfection for a period of four *Asankhyeyya* and 100,000 worlds). Obviously, there is no rebirth following his death. The death of a Buddha is called *Parinibbāna*.

Depending on one's desire and will, self-perfection can be worked for and gained. Nothing is impossible.

Names of the Buddhas

The twenty-ninth - and future - Buddha is called *Ashin Maitreya*. At present, he resides in the Tushita heavens, one of the six realms of *Devas*, awaiting to take his last rebirth when the time is ripe. (Read "*Maitreya*, the Future Buddha", Chapter Two of the Buddhist Scriptures, as translated by E. Conze.)

In most *Theravāda* countries, it is the custom for Buddhists to hold elaborate festivals to honor 28 Buddhas. In the Chronicle of the Buddhas (the *Buddhavamsa*), mention is made of only 24 Buddhas having arisen before Gotama Buddha.

Following are the names of the 28 Buddhas:

The Buddha	City	Parents
1. Tanhankara	Pupphavati	King Sunanda & Queen Sunada

2.	Medhankara	Yaghara	King Sudeva & Queen Yasodhara
3.	Saranankara	Vipula	King Sumangala & Queen Yasodhara
4.	Dipankara	Rammavati	King Sudeva & Queen Sumedha
5.	Kondnna	Rammavati	King Sunanda & Queen Sujata
6.	Managala	Uttara	King Uttara & Queen Uttra
7.	Sumana	Mekhata	King Sudatta & Queen Sirima
8.	Revata	Sudannavati	King Vipula & Queen Vipula
9.	Sobhita	Sudhamma	King Sudhamma & Queen Sudhamma
10.	Anomadassi	Candavati	King Yasavanta & Queen Yasodhara
11.	Paduma	Campaka	King Asama & Queen Asama
12.	Nārada	Dhānnavati	King Sudeva & Queen Anoma
13.	Padumuttara	Hamsavati	King Ananda & Queen Sujata
14.	Sumedha	Sudassana	King Sudatta & Queen Sudatta
15.	Sujata	Sumangala	King Uggata & Queen Pabhavati

16. Piyadassi	Sudhanna	King Sudatta & Queen Sucanda
17. Atthadassi	Sobhana	King Sagara & Queen Sudassana
18. Dhammadassi	Sarana	King Sarana & Queen Susanda
19. Siddhattha	Vebhara	Kind Udena & Queen Jayasena
20. Tissa	Khema	King Janasandha & Queen Paduma
21. Phussa	Kasi	King Jayasena & Queen Sirima
22. Vipassi	Bandhumati	King Bandhuma & Queen Bandhumati
23. Sikhi	Arunavati	King Arunava & Queen Pabhavati
24. Vessabhu	Anupama	King Suppatita & Queen Yasavati
25. Kakusandha	Khema	Aggidatta & Brahmani Visakha
26. Konagamana	Sobhavati	Yannadatta & Brahmani Uttara
27. Kassapa	Baranasi	Brahmadatta & Dhanavati
28. Gotama	Kapilavatthu	King Suddhodana & Queen Mahā Māyā

oooooo

A Corner for Lovers of Poems and Sayings

The *Dhammapada*

The *Dhammapada* was arranged and classified in its present form at the first Council and is part of the Buddhist scriptures. It consists of about 420 verses, arranged in 26 chapters, and each verse is accompanied by a story about the persons and circumstances related to the saying. These are just a few of His words from the *Dhammapada*.

General matters

All conditions have mind as their originator; mind is their chief, and they are mind made. If one speaks with a wicked mind, unhappiness follows him, even as the wheel follows the hoof of the draught-ox. (V. 1)

Similarly, if speaks or acts with a pure mind, happiness follows him like a shadow that never leaves. (V. 2)

In those who harbor such thoughts as "He abused me," "He struck me," "He overcame me," and "He robbed me," hatred never ceases. (V. 3)

In those who do not harbor such thoughts, hatred will cease. (V. 4)

Hatred never ceases by hatred in this world. Through kindness alone they cease. This is an ancient law.   (V. 5)

Foolishness

A fool who thinks he is a fool is for that reason a wise man: the fool who thinks that he is wise is called a fool indeed.   (V. 63)

Wisdom

As a solid rock is not shaken by the wind, even so the wise are not shaken by either praise or blame.
(V. 81)

Self-conquest is, indeed, far better than the conquest of all folk.   (V.104)

Personal Matters

All tremble at punishment. Life is dear to all. Comparing others with oneself, one should neither kill nor cause to kill.   (V. 130)

The Self

One is the guardian of oneself; what other guardian could there be? With oneself fully controlled, one obtains a protector who is hard to obtain.   (V. 160)

By oneself is evil done, by oneself is one defiled. Oneself purifies one. Purity and impurity depend on oneself. No one can purify another. (V. 165)

Happiness

Victory breeds hatred; the defeated live in pain. The peaceful ones live happily, giving up victory and defeat.

(V. 201)

Anger

One should give up anger; one should abandon pride.

(V. 221)

Conquer anger by kindness; conquer evil by good; conquer the stingy by giving; conquer the liar by truth.

(V. 223)

Handicap

Whosoever in this world destroys life, tells lies, takes what is not given, misuses the senses and is addicted to intoxicating drinks, such a one interferes with their own progress in this world. (V. 246 and 247)

Miscellaneous

If by giving up a slight happiness one may achieve a large one, let the wise person give up the lesser happiness in consideration for the greater happiness.   (V. 290)

He who wishes his own happiness by causing pain to others is not released from hatred, being himself entangled in the tangles of hatred.   (V. 291)

The Wise Man

He that does no evil through body, speech or mind, who is restrained in these three respects, him I call a wise man.   (V. 391)

Karma (Kamma)

If it's suffering you fear, if it's suffering you dislike, do no evil deeds at all - for all to see or secretly.
(*Sanskrit Dhammapada*)

On Morality[1]

If it's suffering you fear, if it's suffering you dislike,
Just do no evil deeds at all - for all to see or secretly.

Even a flight in the air cannot free you from suffering,
after the deed that is evil has once been committed.

Not in the sky or ocean's middle,
Nor if you were to hide on cracks in mountains,
Can there be found on this wide earth a corner
Where *Kamma* does not catch up with the culprit.

But if you see the evil others do, and if you feel you
    disapprove,
Be careful not to do likewise, for people's deeds remain
    with them.

Those who cheat in business deals, those who act
    against the *Dhamma*,
Those who swindle, those who trick - not only harm
    their fellowmen,
They hurl themselves into a gorge, for people's deeds
    remain with them.

Whatever deeds a man may do, be they delightful, be
    they bad,
They make a heritage for him; deeds do not vanish-
    without trace.

The fool, while sinning, thinks and hopes, "This never
    will catch up with me."
Wait till you're in the other world, and there the fate of
    sinners learn!

The prudent man will lead a moral life
When he considers it has four rewards:
A sense virtue gives him peace,
His body is not over-taxed,
At night he sleeps a happy sleep,
And when he wakes, he wakes with joy.

The man of wisdom who did good,
The man of morals, who give gifts,
In this world and the next one too,
They will advance to prosperity and happiness.

Knowledge

Those who know not suffering,
Nor how suffering comes to be,
Nor yet how all such suffering
To a final end is brought,

They who do not know the Path
Leading to its calming down,
Cannot find the heart's release,
Cannot be by wisdom freed.
With no chance to made an end,
To birth and aging they're condemned.

Those who do know suffering,
And how suffering come to be,
Know too how all such suffering
To a final end is brought,

They who know the Path indeed
Leading to its calming down,
They can find the heart's release,
They can be by wisdom freed.
They know how to make an end,
To birth and aging to more bound.

(LVI, 22)

A Golden Rule

See all; hear all;
Say not a word at all.

For speech is silver,
Silence is golden.
**And Forbearance brings peace,
That everyone seeks.**

There is no use arguing.
It only upsets oneself.
For the truth will always prevail.
In the end; without fail.

Forbearance is not easy to uphold.
Still... it is a noble task.
Try...you must ...
It will stand you in good stead.
You will be happier for that.

Try it out once.
How marvelous it works.
Stick to this golden rule.
Don't forget, you'll never regret:
For it's proven to be true.

Tyrants are always tyrants.
Despots are always despots.
The Leopard never changes his spots.
Meet them ... you will...
There are too many around.

When you do....
Just adorn your Armour, 'Forbearance'.
And remember this golden rule.
You'll safe yourself in this way.
Find, not a ruffled hair nor bruised skin;
Harmony maintained, smile and walk away.

April 17th 1999   /s/

Greed

Greed is like a raging fire
Of sensual pleasure,
For wealth, position, etc.

continued on next page

Burning ferociously
It crackles aloud.
"I want, I want.
I can't do without.
Have it, I must....
By any means ... fair or foul.
ANYHOW!"

A desire so deeply profound,
Nothing deters,
Nothing quenches,
Till that sought for is found.

Greed, like a thick fog...
Heavy with discontent and desire,
With Selfishness, Jealousy and Rivalry,
Coming together, Parting never:
Intensifying the blackouts,
Forever and forever,
Till one is called to retire.

"How should one get out of it?"
If one should ask,
Just say ... "Think, fumble for a switch,
'The SWITCH OF WISDOM,'
For that alone can do it."

September 9, 1997 /s/

Craving

Craving ...Craving ...
What a sweet little word!
Looks cute: But acts like a brute.
Drives one endlessly, with no effort to restrain,
A vicious cycle; its always maintained.

Craving, a driving force, innate in everyone.
What to go for...good or evil?
How far to go...eternity?
Is absolutely the choice of each and everyone.

However cute, it looks:
Never take it on board.......
Or, you'll be hooked.
Restlessly, working under its influence,
Would certainly be like-
A possible encounter with 'Hurricane Mitch.'
You'll be carried through...
In total devastation, you'll stand.
One should understand.

Instead, ...take Contentment as your mate.
A safe Life's Voyage, you'll make.
All things in place, at ease and leisure.
What a great pleasure!
Besides, 'Contentment means Happiness.'
A universal desire of all beings.
Be wise...Make the right choice!

With Contentment and Awareness....in hand.
Walk down the 'Sublime Path'
"The Noble Eightfold Path"
This vicious cycle breaks at the end stage
To your great advantage.

View this with the Eyes of Wisdom....
Trudge patiently.... right to the end.
It's by no means an easy task.
You'll get there if you say, 'I must'
There 'An Eternal Bliss' is waiting;
Yours... for the taking.

November 1998 /s/

Writing Is Fun

I write not for a name or fame,
But just to explain,
What I see, think and feel,
To share the same,
With those who like to join in my game.

No two people think or feel alike,
Just as a coin has two sides.
Won't it be interesting to see the other side?
So, why don't you spare a moment,
To join in and savour this moment.

Writing is fun, you'll later learn,
For to have an idle mind,
Most people will surely find,
It's waste of one's precious time.

Life is not long for you to fool around,
But, look around, you must,
Give a smile, a kind word, once in a while.
Unburden the load of others.
Extend a helping hand whenever you can,
Try, make this world a happy place.
Make your time worthwhile.

Sharing and Caring, like boomerangs,
When sincerely thrown, return back to you.
Come now...share my thoughts and feelings,
For that's what I intend to do.

June 9, 1998 /s/

Wake up! Wake up!

Wake up, Wake up,
From a sleep of ignorance,
Or from hibernation in the realms of evilness.
Wake up, you must!

Now! —- to the need, an urgent need,
For purity of words and deeds.
The mind can be noble and sublime,
Or with all kinds of unimaginable evil entwined.
The mind, the place where all originates,
Noble, ignoble; good and bad,
Everything that could make anyone sad.

Seek no one divine,
To purify your mind.
Either to please the gods or to please yourself?
Effort, all must make
To live up to one's dignity and grace.

Each one is responsible to make this place,
The world — a happy and safe place.
Do not shun! Do not shirk!
The responsibility that alone is yours
Seriously, you must take.

Make haste!
Avoid doing all evils (words, thoughts and deeds)
Do good and travel along the Noble Path.
Purity of mind is all that is asked.

Wake up! Wake up!
To this urgent call
"Do good, avoid doing evil, and purify your mind"
Make the world a safe and happy place for all!

September 11th 2001   /s/

oooooo

Footnotes

1   These verses have been compiled under the heading "Morality" with no mention of verse numbers for each individual verse; the purpose = for the convenience and enjoyment of the reader.

CONCLUSION

The Essence of His Teachings

The essence of Buddha's teaching is the practice of a moral life, for a man must live happily and also win the goal of purity and nobility by himself. His weakness and unwholesome acts arise within his own mind: he, alone, is responsible for his misdeeds and errors. Therefore, he needs to understand about himself, the nature of things surrounding him, and the universal truth of cause and effect, the Law of *Kamma*.

To sum up the Buddha's advice:

> To refrain from all evil,
> To do what is good,
> To purify the mind.

To understand every doctrine taught by the Buddha, one needs to understand the Law of Cause and Effect, *Kamma*. It is only with the understanding and belief in *Kamma* that a man will conduct his thoughts and actions in a wholesome manner. He is, therefore, required to know:

• *Causes for the origin of* Kamma

There are three causes for the origin of *Kamma*: greed, hate and delusion.

From these three bad roots come our bodily action (*Kāya Kamma*), verbal action (*Vacī Kamma*), and mental action (*Mano Kamma*).

Our actions must be born of non-greed, non-hate and non-delusion if we wish to have a good rebirth in a happy form of existence: celestial beings, humans, and other forms belonging to a happy form of existence.

- *The need for extinction of* Kamma

The Buddha declared:

> "Monks, actions (*Kamma*) willed, performed and accumulated will not become extinct as long as their results have not been experienced, be it in this life, in the next life or in future lives. And as long as these results of actions willed, performed and accumulated have not been experienced, there will be no end to suffering.

> "Taking of life, I declare to be threefold: as caused by greed, caused by hate, caused by delusion.

> "So also are the taking of what is not given, sexual misconduct, lying, tale bearing, harsh speech, vain talk, covetousness, and ill will.

> "Wrong views, too, I declare to be threefold: as caused by greed, caused by hatred and caused by delusion.

"Hence, greed is the producer of *Kammic* con-catenation (the forming of a sequence or combination); hate is the *Kammic* concatena-tion; delusion the *Kammic* concatenation."

"Only by the destruction of greed, hate and delu-sion, is there destruction of *Kammic* concatenation."

The *Kammic* concatenation above mentioned - when engaged, practiced, and done - sums up to "taint-ed failure in living." In each unwholesome act, the *Kamma* committed is either threefold in bodily acts (*Kāya Kamma*), fourfold in verbal acts (*Vacī Kamma*), or threefold in mental acts (*Mano Kamma*).

To illustrate: Someone has ill will in his heart. He has depraved (morally bad) thoughts, such as, "Let these beings be slain! Let them be killed! May they per-ish and cease to exist!" He has unwholesome volition - though only in thought first - but this has resulted in his committing *Mano Kamma*. In the next step - being a very cruel man, burning with hatred, consumed by great hatred - he then slays, or kills, or murders. This commit-ting of unwholesome volition - threefold in bodily acts, the result of hatred and ill will - is an example of *Kāya Kamma*. Having no compassion, the man is cruel. He has blood-stained hands. He is evil. *Vacī Kamma* is fourfold in verbal acts when unpleasant remarks are made or harsh and cruel words are said because of greed, hatred, ill will or delusion.

A man is expected to have compassion, loving-kindness (*Mettā*) not only for his fellow beings, but also for animals. He is expected to be kind in thought, word, and deed.

When such unwholesome volition - *Kāya Kamma, Vacī Kamma,* and *Mano Kamma* - is committed, the result will be appropriate. Just as a perfect throw of dice, when thrown upwards, will come to rest firmly wherever it falls, beings will be reborn in states of woe due to those tainted failures in living caused by unwholesome volition. The result of their *Kamma* will be experienced in this life, in the next life or in future lives; there is no getting away with them.

However, in the case of success in living, having been caused by wholesome volition, the threefold bodily acts, fourfold verbal acts and threefold mental acts produce happiness, result in happiness. It is due to that very success in living that beings after death are reborn to a happy destiny, in a heavenly world. Just as a perfect throw of dice, when thrown upwards, will come to rest firmly wherever it falls, beings will be reborn to a happy destiny, in a heavenly world, due to success in living caused by wholesome volition, good *Kamma*.

- *How to have success in living*

  - Avoid doing unwholesome volition, *Kamma* (bodily, verbal, and mental actions).
  - Uproot greed, hatred, ill will, delusion. (*Lobha, Dosa,* and *Moha*)
  - Practice *Brahmā-vihara*, which will ensure a happy and peaceful life.
  - Uphold *Sīla* (morality), develop *Samādhi* (which means mental development) and try to gain *Paññā* (wisdom or knowledge) by practicing insight meditation.

  Practicing *Brahmā-vihara* means to practice meditation on *Mettā* (loving-kindness), *Karunā* (compassion), *Muditā* (sympathetic joy), and *Upekkhā* (discerning rightly).

Mettā (Loving-kindness)

To put it clearly and make it easily understood, loving-kindness means love sincere and true to the nature of the love that a mother has for her child. There is no selfish or sentimental nature of any kind. This is the kind of love each and every one of us should have for everyone, without discrimination, expecting nothing in return. The sense of caring and sharing goes with loving-kindness. It is a virtuous thought to cultivate all the time.

This will keep one's thoughts away from greed, hatred, and ill will.

This is what the Buddha has to say about loving-kindness:

> "For seven years I cultivated thoughts of loving-kindness. Having cultivated a heart full of loving-kindness for seven years, I did not return to this world for seven cyclic aeons (cosmic time) of world-destructions and world-origination. Whenever the world was destroyed, I entered (by way of rebirth) the realm of the Radiant Gods: and when the world unfolded again, I was reborn in the *Brahmā* abode. And thirty-six times I was the *Sakka*, ruler of gods, and many times, I was a worldly ruling king, a just and righteous one. It is a deed of merit, and I have enjoyed desirable, pleasant and agreeable results from performing this meritorious deed."

(This shows how long and arduously one must train for perfection to attain Buddhahood.)

Some translate *Mettā* as "universal love" and "good will," but it means more than good will.

This would be how one should meditate on loving-kindness:

May all living beings be healthy and happy!
May they be free from harm and oppression!
May they have all their wishes fulfilled!
May they be free from greed, hate, and ill will!
May they be able to lead a peaceful and
successful life!

This embraces all living beings. It is a sincere wish for the welfare and happiness for all creatures great and small, seen or unseen; dwelling afar or near; born or awaiting to be born.

Send out your loving-kindness. It is an unlimited self-giving compassion flowing freely toward all creatures that live, an ideal compassion resulting in one's own spiritual progress and refinement.

Karuṇā (Compassion)

To have compassion, a feeling of pity that makes one desire to help and be merciful is required. It has no base in selfishness and attachment.

"May all living beings without exception be free from all kinds of suffering!" Wishing thus, one practices the thought of compassion. The result: one heart responds to the willingness to help when others are seen to be subject to suffering.

Volunteers offer their services out of *Karunā* or compassion. They do so with an altruistic motive, seeking nothing in return, not even gratitude. Some take it to be a social obligation, as it is a meritorious deed performed.

Muditā (Sympathetic Joy)

Muditā is translated as pure, sympathetic joy, boundless and unconditional.

This special happiness or joy is to be practiced when others are successful and happy. It is natural to feel happy when someone near and dear succeeds, but not so when others do. This pure joy must be felt when others succeed in the same manner as it would be felt when your own kith and kin succeed. One must learn not to be selfish.

The practice of *Muditā*, sympathetic joy, is effective in destroying feelings of resentment and jealousy. Man, by nature, is ambitious and greedy, and he will find it difficult to practice *Muditā*. However, one should practice this for one's own happiness.

Upekkhā (Right Discernment)

Upekkhā (equanimity) is the most difficult and also one of the most essential sublime states. Literally, it means discerning rightly, viewing justly without partiality. It is an experience gained after the attainment of meditative absorption.

One must learn to take the vicissitudes of life in such a way that he or she would not feel the pressure. The belief in the law of *Kamma* could help in developing *Upekkhā*; inequalities in life depend on *Kamma* done in one's previous life. By practicing *Brahmā-vihara*, one can live in peace and harmony with everyone.

As the Great Benefactor of Mankind, Buddha on "Truth," the *Dhamma*, and Teaching

At the request of the *Brahmā* and out of His boundless *Mettā* and *Karunā* (great loving-kindness and compassion for the deluded world), Lord Buddha taught the *Dhamma*, the Sublime Truth. His doctrine is "The Doctrine of Actuality" that can be tested and verified by any one at any time.

Although, as gained from His enlightenment, Buddha was the possessor, the sole possessor of Omniscient Knowledge, He taught only what was relevant and required for the right and dignified way of living and the way to get out of the cycle of rebirths and deaths (*Saṁsāra*). He is the teacher of men and gods (human beings, the celestial beings, and the sublime beings, the *Brahmās*).

Omniscient Knowledge means knowing everything, having unlimited knowledge. Unlike other spiritual teachers of His time, Lord Buddha boldly declared, "Hear My Teaching, but don't take it as a gospel truth, something a sage says; don't take it for granted as something that has been handed down from generation to generation. Test it, verify the truth. Only when you feel it is for your own welfare and happiness, and also for that of others, take it and try to live by it."

There are no grounds on which to believe that the Buddha converted this person or that, or members of other sects. It was those persons who converted themselves on hearing the *Dhamma*, the Doctrine of Actuality. When those who converted themselves ask permission to be accepted as His disciples, He would ask them to think over their sudden change of heart and ask permission of their teacher. This is because the Buddha taught only out of compassion and not for fame or gain. His Order of Monks was set up to serve as messengers of Truth.

As Regards Practice, the Setting of Example

The Compassionate Teacher set good examples. He practiced as He preached. With great compassion and loving-kindness, this is what He did:

- He showed compassion and set an obligatory act for all *Sanghas* to nurse and help the sick. He did it Himself, and said, "Those who succor the sick, succor me."

- He condemned the sacrificing of animals and stopped the practice of slaughtering. Because of His teaching and practice of kindness and compassion for animals, we have societies for the prevention of cruelty to animals.

- He was the first to recognize human rights by condemning slavery and abolishing the caste system prevailing in India during His time.

- He championed women's liberation, by giving them respect, equal opportunity and authority in society.

- He was a great pioneer of the pacifist movement. He took the time and trouble to act as mediator between two parties disputing over the right to use of the waterway. His influence and advice prevented a war that would have resulted in great bloodshed and lost of lives.

His Teaching, the *Dhamma*, as a Religion

"Buddhism is unique mainly because of rationality, practicability, efficacy and universality. It is the noblest of all unifying influences and the only lever that can uplift the world to deliverance from suffering." "If by religion is meant a system of deliverance from the ills of life, then

Buddhism is the religion of all religions." (Remarks by Karl Marx, the great philosopher and social reformist.)

Science

In this respect, one can go on writing endlessly, as every day new findings by scientists have brought to light the revelation of the *Dhamma* in relation to science. We need no further proofs. We can confidently say straight away, "Yes, it is true," for this is what the great scientist Albert Enstein has remarked, "Science is a methodology and Buddhism is a spiritual methodology analogous to that of physical science."

Furthermore, Albert Einstein, the greatest scientist of the twentieth century also stated, "The religion of the future will be a cosmic religion. It should transcend a personal God and avoid dogmas and theology. Covering both the natural and the spiritual, it should be based on a religious sense arising from experience of all things, natural and spiritual and a meaningful unity. Buddhism answers this description. If there is any religion that would cope with modern scientific needs, it would be Buddhism."

In view of the above remarks made by the great philosopher Karl Marx and the great scientist Albert Einstein, there is no wonder more and more people are coming to realize "the acceptance of any pure 'belief system' to be superfluous."

His Teaching and World Peace

Do we seriously desire peace and happiness in the world? Yes, we do. We have had many international conferences of spiritual leaders. What results have we seen? None. Why?

The real spirit of fellowship that can be promoted through religion is lacking in the world today. Religion is an education of the heart with the view to refining and elevating us in the scale of human beings. Generally speaking, the practice of a moral life is the very core and essence of religion, for it is action and not speculation, practice and not theory, that counts in life. There must be the will to do, followed by actual doing. A mere declaration of belief in a faith, reading out the holy book, show of piety, and all the outward displays of goodness, etc. are things that have not helped and will not help in any way to bring peace and happiness to any one person, not to mention the world. The goodness must come from the mind of each individual.

What can the International World Congress of Faith do? We need to understand the fundamental spiritual realities of life. No spiritual leader can do wonders. Each and every one of the world's citizens must take his or her responsibility to live and behave in the right manner that will bring peace and happiness not only to himself or herself, but also to his family, society and the world.

We need a powerful spiritual influence, helping all men to make the world a safe and happy place. This can be given by anyone, irrespective of whatever faith or religion he may profess to hold, if only he will put his good faith into practice and live the right way of life. This right way of living - "Do good, avoid doing evil, and purify the mind" - has been practiced with success and taught by the Buddha.

The world has just seen and experienced the product of an evil mind. An evil mind, the place of "a devil's workshop," has brought an unimaginable extent of destruction, the loss of lives of thousands of innocent people, and unfathomable sufferings to the world. We would not wish to have such an experience again. No one in his right sense of mind would. What can be done? Who can police the world? Is there a remedy to this illness, if one might call it a malady? One may go on searching and searching to the end of time to find a CURE for it and still find nothing. The search will be long, endless and definitely futile if we do not know the cause.

But now we know the cause, because the Buddha has revealed it to us. He has not only revealed the cause, but has also prescribed a cure. He Himself has proven its efficacy and amazing result. This cure is not out of our reach; as a matter of fact, it is not far to find. It is to be found in everyone's own heart. It is as simple and straightforward as that.

What, then, ought to be done now? Take immediate action. Act without a moment's delay. Action: It is up to each and every world citizen to take upon oneself the responsibility "to avoid doing evil and try to purify one's mind." Only then can we have the weapon we need, or the medicine we seek in despair to combat this illness and save ourselves from such an entire world-devastating situation.

We have lived and still are living in despair and hopes. How long can this go on? Action, sensible action is needed now. Just as the Buddha has said, the remedy is in the heart and mind of everyone. "No one can purify another person's mind." It is up to each and every world citizen to "do good, avoid doing all evil and purify the mind."

Until and unless everyone can control his mind and avoid doing evil, we cannot expect to see even a slight ray of hope for peace and happiness in the world. If we truly wish to have something, we must work for it in earnest. Work, we must: by understanding and observing the fundamental spiritual realities of life that The Great Compassionate Teacher has taught us, and by acting accordingly. For there are no other conceivable means or ways by which we can achieve our desired goal. *It is only with the understanding and observing of the fundamental moral and spiritual realities of life and acting accordingly that we can hope to achieve our desired goal — PEACE and HAPPINESS.*

oooooo

FACTS AT A GLANCE

The Teachings of the Buddha

Dhamma means:

a) The TRUTHS, the law which exists in everyone's heart and mind.
It is the principle of righteousness existing not only in man, but also in the universe.

b) All the universe is a revelation of *Dhamma*.

c) The Buddha has proven that each man has the power to liberate his own self.

Understand the **Four Noble Truths**, or the Four Great Truths:

1. The noble truth of suffering, or *Dukkha*.

2. The cause or origin of *Dukkha* is craving, or *Tanhā*, selfish desires.

3. Cessation of suffering comes by the annihilation of selfish desires, all kinds of cravings, or *Tanhā*.

4. To realize the Third Truth one has to develop the Noble Eightfold Path / the Middle Way / the *Majjhima Paṭṭipadā* / the PATH leading to the cessation of suffering.

Threefold *Dukkha*

1. Ordinary suffering   *Dukkha Dukkha*
2. Suffering experienced
   by change   *Viparināma Dukkha*
3. Suffering experienced
   by conditional state   *Saṅkhāra Dukkha*

Dukkha could easily be understood as suffering or sorrow. All life - to one who sees deeply - is suffering.

Tanhā means finding delight in sense pleasures, craving for existence or becoming, or craving for non-existence or self-annihilation = the root cause of *Dukkha,* or suffering.

- Complete cessation of craving = giving it up, being released from it, detached from it.
- One takes the Path, the Noble Eightfold Path, to the cessation of suffering.

The Five Aggregates

1. *Rūpakkhandha*
2. *Vedanākkhandha*
3. *Saññakkhandha*
4. *Saṃkharakkhandha*
5. *Viññānakkhandha*

all combined give *Nāma-Rūpa,* which forms "I" or a being or an individual

These Five Aggregates are constantly changing and are therefore impermanent. The nature of impermanence is *Anicca*.
By understanding what *Dukkha* (suffering) means, really means, one will grasp the meaning of the nature of absence of self = *Anatta* or soul-less-ness.

Beings made up of five aggregates of physical and mental phenomena have these three characteristics *Anicca, Dukkha* and *Anatta* (impermanence, suffering and being without self or entity).

> Oneself is one's own refuge,
> What other refuge can there be?
> Purity and impurity depend on oneself,
> No one can purify another.

Advised by all Buddhas: To cease from all evil,
To do what is good,
To cleanse one's mind.

The Path of Purification   The taking of the
Noble Eightfold Path

The Paññā *Group: Wisdom*

RIGHT VIEW OR
UNDERSTANDING   *Sammā Dhiṭṭhi:*
(knowing things as they really are)

a) *Kammassakatā Sammā Diṭṭhi*: right view of wholesome and unwholesome *Kamma* and their results that cause rounds of rebirth.

b) *Dasavatthuka Sammā Diṭṭhi*: understanding the ten kinds of subjects.

c) *Catusacca Sammā Diṭṭhi*: understanding of the realities of the Four Truths.

RIGHT THOUGHT   *Sammā Saṅkappa:*

a) *Nekkhama Saṅkappa*: Right thoughts free from greed and sensuous desire. Aiming at an escape from round of rebirths.

b) *Abyāpāda Saṅkappa*: Right thought for the welfare of all living beings.

c) *Avihiṁa Saṅkappa*: Right thought for the non-injury of all living beings.

The Sīla *Group: Morality*

RIGHT SPEECH   *Sammā Vācā:*

Refraining from telling lies, refraining from backbiting.

Refraining from using abusive language, and Refraining from frivolous talk, which is fruitless.

RIGHT ACTION — *Sammā Kammanta*:
Refraining from killing and injuring the living.
Refraining from taking property not given (stealing).
Refraining from taking intoxicants and from having sexual misconduct.

RIGHT LIVELIHOOD — *Sammā Ajīva*:
The right kind of living that does not cause harm to anyone in anyway; no slaughtering of animals, trading in human beings, selling of arms, taking of intoxicants, drugs and poison.
Avoiding all kinds of dishonest ways of trading.

The Samādhi *Group:*

RIGHT EFFORT — *Sammā Vāyāma*:
To cultivate and purify the mind.
Avoiding evil thoughts, preventing them from arising.
Developing good and wholesome thoughts and maintaining those that already have arisen.

RIGHT MINDFULNESS — *Sammā Sati*:
Bodily actions - whatever feeling or sensation - pleasant, unpleasant, or neutral.

Thoughts - whatever mental actions and thoughts of general objects - on seeing, hearing, etc.

Having awareness and being conscious of all our movements, both physical and mental, will help us to have the right understanding of life, and monitor our actions (good or bad *Kamma*). It is a good practice we need to have at all time.

RIGHT CONCENTRATION   *Sammā Samādhi*:

As mentioned in the *Maggaṅga-Dīpanī*, there are four kinds

· *Paṭṭhamajjhāna Samādhi*,
· *Dutiyajjhāna Samādhi*,
· *Tatiyajjhāna Samādhi* and
· *Catutthajjhāna Samādhi*.

Concentration is produced by fixing one's attention on one of the objects of *Samatha*, such as *Kasiṇa*.

Kamma

The cause of all our troubles is our actions, which always bring appropriate results. Thus, one must understand the Law of Cause and Effect, the "Law of *Kamma*" (*Karma* in Sanskrit).

Kamma are bodily actions (*Kāya Kamma*), verbal actions (*Vacī Kamma*) and mental actions (*Mano Kamma*) born of greed, hate and delusion.

Kamma willed, performed and accumulated will never become extinct; their results will be experienced in this life, in the next or future lives.

By the destruction of greed, hate and delusion, one can stop *Kammic* concatenation.

Avoid performing unwholesome *Kamma*. Cultivate virtuous thoughts.

Practice and meditate on loving-kindness (*Mettā*), compassion (*Karunā*), pure sympathetic joy (*Muditā*), and equanimity (*Upekkhā*).

Vipassanā Bhāvanā (Insight Meditation)

Vipassanā means "insight, wisdom."
Bhāvanā means "development, meditation."

Thinking: usually generally, no definite subject or purpose. Without purpose your thoughts may lead to danger.

Concentrating: Focusing our thoughts on the object.

Meditating: Thinking exclusively on a chosen object, gaining benefit.

   1. Your intellectual power increases.

2. You keep a clear mental picture of the object.
3. You develop power of knowing or seeing things as they truly are.
4. It is a clear constructive practice of thinking.

However, meditation must be practiced only after concentration. It is a constructive practice of thinking, for our thoughts will become pure and the development of wisdom, *Paññā* will be gained. Mental tranquility and an unusual sense of contentment - happiness and an astonishingly clear consciousness - will also be obtained.

Vipassanā Bhāvanā must be practiced under the tutelage of a good and efficient teacher of meditation. By practicing *Vipassanā Bhāvanā* or Insight Meditation:

- The meditator observes both the physical and mental processes of the Five Aggregates as meditating objects and realizes them to be impermanent, full of suffering and soul-less.
- On realizing the truth at that moment of time - although, temporarily at first - the *Yogi* (meditator) gains the power to abandon craving.
- At the same time, delusion (*Avijjā*) ceases, for his misapprehension of the world and objects as permanent ceases.
- This realization through temporary cessation is known as *Tadanga-nirodha*. This is just the start

of the happiness one gains by practicing *Vipassanā* meditation.

The *Vipassanā* Path is developed every moment through understanding the true nature of *Anicca*, *Dukkha*, and *Anatta*.

Saṁsāra: Wheel of Life, Round of Rebirth, the Cycle of Death and Birth

The Law of Causation of Dependent Arising:

1. Depending on Ignorance gives rise to moral and immoral Conditioning Activities.
2. Depending on Conditioning Activities gives rise to Re-linking Consciousness.
3. Depending on Re-linking Consciousness gives rise to Mind and Matter.
4. Depending on Mind and Matter gives rise to Six-Sense Sphere.
5. Depending on Six-Sense Sphere gives rise to Contact.
6. Depending on Contact gives rise to Feeling.
7. Depending on Feeling gives rise to Craving.
8. Depending on Craving gives rise to Attachment.
9. Depending on Attachment gives rise to Becoming.
10. Depending on Becoming gives rise to Birth.

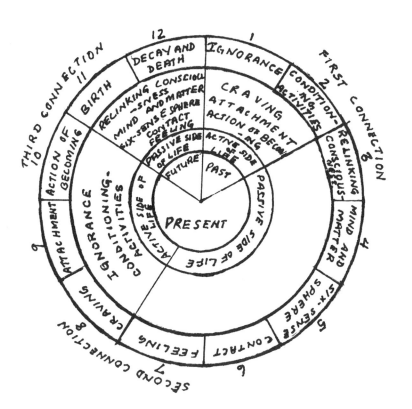

THE WHEEL OF LIFE

11. Depending on Birth gives rise to decay and death.

Death is followed by sorrow, lamentation, pain, grief and despair. Thus does the whole mass of suffering originate.

Accordingly, when the cause ceases, there would be no effect. Get to the root cause and cease the rounds of rebirths.

The Path to *Nibbāna*

One gains the first stage by observing *Sīla*, morality (Nos. 3, 4, and 5 of the Eightfold Path).

One gains the second stage by practicing *Samādhi*, the culture of the mind (Nos. 6, 7, and 8 of the Eightfold Path).

One reaches the third stage by gaining *Paññā*, wisdom (Nos. 1 and 2 of the Eightfold Path).

With one-pointedness of mind, one looks at the world and gets the correct view of life.

One sees *Anicca* (impermanence), *Dukkha* (suffering), and *Anatta* (soul-less-ness) wherever one glances. Whatever is impermanent is painful. Thus, where change and sorrow prevail, there can be no permanent happiness.

In the first *Ariyan* stage, one is called *Sotāpanna* (one who enters the stream that leads to *Nibbāna*). He has destroyed the three fetters self-illusion (*Sakkāya Diṭṭhi*), doubts (*Vicikicchā*), and indulgence in rites, rituals and ceremonies. He will be reborn as a human being seven times at most, if he does not make quick further attainment.

In the second stage, a *Sakadāgāmi* (a once returner) with deeper insight, he weakens two more fetters, sense desire (*Kāmarāga*), and ill will (*Paṭigha*). He is reborn on earth only once more.

In the third stage, as an *Anāgāmi* (never returner), the two weakened fetters are now completely destroyed. After death, he is reborn in the Pure Abodes (*Suddhavasa*) from whence he will become an *Arahat*.

In the last stage, in the final advance, one destroys the remaining fetters, namely, desire for life in the Realm of Form (*Rūparāgā*), desire for life in the Realm of Formlessness (*Arūparāgā*), conceit (*Māna*), distraction (*Uddhacca*), and ignorance (*Avijjā*). The total ten fetters now completely destroyed, he gains the last stage, *Arahat*ship.

Note: *Māna* conceit is the hardest nut to crack!

oooooo

GLOSSARY OF PĀḶI WORDS

A

Adhiṭṭanā	determination
Adosa	non-hate
Aggasāvaka	chief disciple
Ājīva	livelihood
Ākāsa Dhātu	space element
Akusala	unwholesome
Anāgāmi	never returner, non-returner
Ānāpānasati	mindfulness of in and out breathing
Anatta	non-self
Anicca	impermanent
Anusaya	underlying, latent disposition or tendency
Āpo	water
Āpo Dhātu	element of water, the quality of cohesion in material form
Arahat	the perfect one who has eliminated all passions
Arahattā	the quality of being an Arahat
Ariya	noble
Arūpa	formless, the realms of formless Brahmas
Āsava	taint
Atta	soul, self
Attavāda	doctrine of self or soul
Avijjā	ignorance
Avijjāsava	taints of ignorance

B

Bhava	becoming
Bhava-tanhā	attachment of becoming or life
Bhāvanā	development, meditation
Bhavaṅga	life continuum consciousness
Bhikkhu	monk
Bhikkhunis	nun
Bhūmi	ground, place, soil, stage, realm
Bīja	seed
Bodhi	awakening, enlightenment
Bodhisatta	the future Buddha, an aspirant for enlightenment
Brahman	absolute reality, such-ness in Hinduism
Brahmā	a sublime being
Brahma-vihāra	divine abiding
Buddhi	enlightenment
Byādhi	sickness

C

Cāga	generosity
Cakkhu	eye
Cakkhu-viññāṇa	eye consciousness
Cetanā	volition
Cetasika	mental state, concomitant
Chanda	will, zeal
Citta	mind, conciousness
Citta Visuddhi	purity of mind
Cuti	death

D

Dāna	giving, generosity
Deva	celestial beings, "god"
Dhamma	the law or the teaching of the Buddha
Dhamma	state; thing; phenomenon, mental object.
Dhātu	element
Diṭṭhi	view, belief
Diṭṭhi Visuddhi	purity of view
Domanassa	grief
Dosa	hate, ill will, anger
Duggati	unhappy destination, unhappy rebirth
Dukkha	suffering

H

Hadaya	heart
Hadaya Vitthu	heart basis (physical basis of the mind)

I

Indriyasaṃvara Sīla	the morality of restraining the senses
Isipatana	the stags' resort

J

Jarā	old age
Jāti	birth
Jhāna	meditative absorption
Jhānalābhi	one who accomplishes absorption
Jīva	soul

K

Kāma	sensuality
Kāmacchanda	lust or zeal for sense pleasures
Kāmāsava	taints of the sense pleasure
Kāma-loka	sensual plane
Kāma-rāgā	greed for sense pleasures
Kamma	action, deed
Kamma Bhava	becoming, present action
Kamma-niyāma	law of kamma
Kammapatha	course of action
Karma (Skt.)	action, deed, *Kamma*
Karunā	compassion
Kāya	body
Khandha	aggregate, group
Khanika	momentry
Khantī	patience
Khema	security
Kilesa	defilement
Kusala	wholesome

L

Lobha	greed

Loka	the world or universe, life
Lokiya	mundane, worldly
Lokuttara	supra-mundane

M

Magga	path, path in sight
Maggadātā	one who shows the way
Māna	conceit
Māra	evil beings, obstructors
Maraṇa	death, dying
Māyā	illusion, ignorance
Mettā	loving-kindness
Mettā Bhāvanā	developing of loving-kindness
Micchā	wrong
Moha	delusion, ignorance
Muditā	sympathetic joy
Mūla	basic

N

Nāma	mind
Nāma-rūpa	mind and matter
Ñāṇa	knowing, insight, realization
Ñāṇadassana	insight and vision
Nandi	delight
Ñāta	knowing
Nekkhamma Saṅkappa	thoughts free from sensual desire, renunciation

Nibbāna	extinction of greed, hate and delusion
Nicca	permanent
Nirodha	cessation of Dukkha
Niyāma	cosmic law

P

Pacceka	private, by himself
Pahāna	abandonment, eradication
Pahātabba	to be uprooted
Panca	five
Pañcakkhandha	five aggregates
Pañcasila	five basic precepts of morality required by laymen
Paññā	wisdom
Panīta	sublime
Parama Sukha	excellent, happiness
Pāramitā	perfection
Parideva	lamentation
Parinibbāna	complete extinction of aggregates, final liberation
Pariyutthañhāna	obsession
Pathavī	earth
Pathavī Dhātu	the element of earth, the quality of heaviness and lightness in material form
Paticca	having dependent; due to; dependent on

Paṭicca Samuppāda	dependent origination, causal genesis
Paṭimokkha Samvara Sīla	the morality of the vows of monastic order
Paṭipadā	way, practice, path
Phala	fruition
Phassa	contact
Pīti	rapture, joy
Puthujjana	ordinary man, worldly man

R

Rāga	attachment
Rūpa	form, matter
Rūpakkhandha	form or matter aggregate

S

Sabbaññuta	omniscient knowledge
Sacca	truth
Saddhā	confidence, faith, devotion
Sakadāgāmī	once returner (second stage of realization)
Sakkāya Diṭṭhi	the concept of self
Salāyatana	six-fold base
Samādhi	mental development, concentration
Samana	sage, recluse
Samatha	serenity

Samatha	
Bhāvanā	development of concentration
Sammā	right
Sammā	
Ājīva	right livelihood
Sammā Diṭṭhi	right understanding
Sammā	
Kammanta	right action
Sammā	
Saṅkappa	right thought
Sammā	
Samādhi	right concentration
Sammā Sati	right mindfulness
Sammā Vācā	right speech
Sammā	
Vāyāma	right effort
Saṁsāra	wheel of live, round of rebirth
Samudaya	the origin or the cause (of suffering)
Sangha	the order, community
Saṅkhāra	condition, action and reaction
Sāsana	dispensation
Sati	mindfulness
Satta	a being
Sīla	morality
Sīla Visuddhi	purity of morality
Sotāpanna	one who enters the stream of noble path (the first stage of realization)
Suka	happiness
Sutta	discourse given by the Buddha